Sir Donald Wolfit C.B.E.

Sir Donald Wolfit C.B.E.

*His life and work in the
unfashionable theatre*

RONALD HARWOOD

Amber Lane Press

Originally published in 1971

This edition published in 1983 by
Amber Lane Press Ltd
9 Middle Way
Oxford OX2 7LH

Copyright © Ronald Harwood 1971, 1983

ISBN 0 906399 43 2

Printed in Great Britain by
The Pitman Press, Bath

Contents

Contents

FOR

ROSALIND

and for

Charles and Matthew Graham
Gabrielle and Christian Woolfitt
Lucy Amis

In Memoriam

SIR Donald Wolfit's last will and testament contained the following bequest:

> to my good friend Ronald Harwood the sum of *FIFTY POUNDS* with the hope that he will undertake (with the aid of my press books and letters) some form of biography of my work in the theatre with the assistance of my said wife.

He never mentioned his intentions to me during his lifetime, although on the last occasion I saw him, in his hospital bed, three days before his death, I hinted that I had it in mind to write about my first year with him at the King's Theatre, Hammersmith. He showed interest but made no comment. When the will was read I was moved and honoured; but I must confess that both reactions soon wore off when I realised the full implications of the task that confronted me. He left twenty-three press books, two thousand letters, fifty diaries. There were people to be interviewed, a mass of background material to be read, and, of course, ultimately a book to be written. I rebelled on more than one occasion, put off the dread act of beginning (and thus irrevocably committing myself), but without fully realising it, suddenly discovered the first three chapters written. There was no turning back.

In the course of my researches, I met with various reactions. Those who had been close to him, his family, friends and admirers, encouraged me. Those, less enthusiastic about the actor in his lifetime, feigned polite interest. Two of his distinguished contemporaries refused to see me, pleading 'embarrassment'; others, however, as highly esteemed, were generous with their time and gave me warm words of encouragement. But just as I was about to embark on the final part, the most virulent response of all was reported to me: a once well-known West End actor, on hearing that a biography of Wolfit was nearing conclusion, asked, 'Now why would anyone want to write a book about *him*?'

The question represented an attitude towards Wolfit that was widely held by some members of his profession, one of almost total disregard, and to answer it by pleading a clause in his will would, I knew well, be unsatisfactory: hollow, defensive and cowardly. But the question did make me ponder my motives as to why I had fulfilled the hope Wolfit had posthumously expressed. High-sounding phrases blessed my self-examination: duty, loyalty, friendship, setting the record straight, dead men's wishes, etc.; these I painfully dismissed as superficial and facile, but at last reached a conclusion that seemed to approach the truth. The less personal and, therefore, more important purpose of the work will, I must hope, appear in the reading of it, and serve to answer the question in another way; if not, I have failed; but to explain my motives on the least important level I give now a brief résumé of my friendship with Wolfit and, in so doing, record his effect on my life.

In 1951, aged seventeen, I journeyed from South Africa, where I was born, to England, where I hoped to live. After a year at the Royal Academy of Dramatic Art I obtained, through the good offices of Joseph O'Conor, the actor, and R. B. Marriott, the critic of *The Stage*, an introduction to Wolfit who accepted me as a student-member of his company at the King's Theatre, Hammersmith in 1953. With an impudence that now makes me shudder, I bullied and badgered him into taking me on as a full-time professional actor. Cautiously, he promised to consider my request, provided that I inform Sir Kenneth Barnes, the Principal of the R.A.D.A. of my intentions. Sir Kenneth, on hearing my future plans, said that he could not countenance my studying in two places at once; I would have to choose between the Academy and Wolfit; I chose Wolfit. The decision was not difficult; I was unfortunate to catch the dying fall of Sir Kenneth's long reign—he had been appointed to his post by the Academy's founder, Sir Herbert Beerbohm Tree, in 1909—and the teaching methods then employed were outdated, sterile and lifeless; the atmosphere of the most famous academy of acting in the world was very like a genteel finishing school, and no place for anyone with the degree of ambition I possessed.

My departure from the R.A.D.A., I later discovered, endeared me to Wolfit, for he could not believe that anyone should want to give up what he considered those fashionable advantages for the hard, tough grind of his company. He confessed, many years afterwards, that my youthful persistence also impressed him; he had been similarly single-minded in his early days.

The first time he appeared to notice me occurred on stage. Although, at my interview with him, he had said, 'I think we can pull you into the crowd,' I found myself with the role (if one can call it that) of leading on Sir Lewis Casson, as the blind Tiresias in *Oedipus the King*, the opening production. Sir Lewis, to give the effect of gouged eyeballs, had cut in half a table-tennis ball, painted blue and green, and stuck the hemispheres over his eyes, a pin-prick in each to allow him, he hoped, to see. In the event, Tiresias's blindness was very real indeed and, one night, Sir Lewis lost all sense of direction and began to make his exit towards the footlights. I stood rooted to the spot, in a dark down-stage position, watching with horror the actor-knight perilously approaching the orchestra pit. All at once, I became aware of Wolfit in the wings on the opposite side of the stage. He was glaring at me and hissing, 'Get him off! Get him off!' Obeying the order, I seized Sir Lewis by the arm and pulled him off stage. After the performance, Wolfit asked to see me. He was far from pleased. 'We saved tonight a distinguished man of the theatre, an actor-knight, from certain death,' he said gravely. 'For that, I have no doubt, the Theatre as a whole and Dame Sybil Thorndike in particular will always be grateful. If I had not been there, my boy, you would by now be giving evidence to a police inspector, and by tomorrow I should have to bail you out of one of Her Majesty's Prisons. In future, should an emergency arise, act quickly, if at all. *Watch it!*'

Later, during that season, I became his dresser, a position that placed me in his confidence. His first act of friendship came after I witnessed a performance of *King Lear*. Dressed as one of the hundred knights—six in Wolfit's production—I stood in his dressing-room waiting for him to change. I was still hopelessly moved by the last scene and Wolfit, naked, but wearing his beard and wig, looking like an elderly nature-curist, saw my tears and walked solemnly to a portrait of himself as Lear that hung on the wall. He took it down, stuck a piece of paper on the back and inscribed it. I clutched the gift, turned to leave the room when his voice rang out, 'No, my boy, put it back, take it at the end of the season.'

I continued to work for him in a variety of capacities, from 1953–8: actor, understudy, dresser and, aged twenty-three, his business manager. By then, we had become friends outside the theatre, spending much time together. I called him 'sir' until he was knighted when, paradoxically, he asked me to call him Donald. I cannot recall any serious disagreement between us, but I did incur his displeasure on one occasion and the episode, although trivial in itself, reveals a side of Wolfit's nature that is essential to understanding the demands of his friendship.

During the pre-London tour of *The Strong Are Lonely*, at Birmingham, Robert Harris, Ernest Milton, David Oxley and I motored to Stratford-upon-Avon to see a matinée of Laurence Olivier in *Macbeth*. It was, and still is, one of the greatest performances I have ever seen. Memories of it were buzzing in my head when I entered Wolfit's dressing room at the half hour. He detected at once the excitement in me and asked the reason. I told him—I realise now that I went on rather tactlessly about Olivier's performance—and when I had finished he instructed me to clean his make-up tray. He was unusually quiet and remote during the evening and, in a small scene we had together, looked at me not at all. At the end of the performance he said, 'I noticed your concentration was elsewhere this evening. I suggest you do not go to the theatre on matinée days,' and added sonorously, '*throughout the run of this play!*' Wolfit demanded unqualified loyalty from those close to him, for he gave unqualified loyalty in return.

To those who admired Wolfit, defending him in public and in private became a familiar task. I hope that no one reading this book will accuse me of being blind to his faults; I did not love him in spite of those faults, but because they were part of him; his virtues, too, were numerous.

I have never encountered anyone with Wolfit's size of personality, or anyone more unashamedly individual. I am able to remember well the awe in which I first held him, the terror I experienced in his presence both on and off the stage. I remember, too, that he was a good friend and a wonderful companion. I possessed a profound respect for his energy, his determination, his sense of service, but above all, his talent. When I first met him, I was consumed by ambition to be an actor; in seeing Wolfit night after night performing the great roles in his repertoire, by being present when he prepared for a performance or afterwards when he relaxed, I began to realise my own inadequacies: how paltry my talent, how misplaced my ambition, how half-hearted my determination. Not that I consciously measured myself against him; on the contrary, the awakening was rather a gradual, painful process, inward and concealed. It was this awareness of what it meant to be a real actor, the demands such a gift made on the individual, that caused me to reflect, and brought to the fore in me other perceptions, other insights. In 1959 I wrote a play and a novel; I ceased to be an actor; for better for worse I became a writer. I owe much to Wolfit: he was, by far, the most important influence on my early adult life. The decision, then, to write this book was not forced on me by a clause in a will; I had no choice in the matter.

Liss, Hampshire
February 1971

Foreword

WRITING the life of an actor, Laurence Irving warned, 'is a task, seemingly, which by ordinary means is foredoomed to failure'. In the canon of theatrical biography, few books bring to life the vivid reality of their subjects' personality and gifts. However, Laurence Irving himself succeeded absolutely in his magnificent work, *Henry Irving, the Actor and his World*. The significance and importance of the subject, both as an actor and theatrical personality who was a leading social figure of his time, are superbly matched by the scope and style of his biographer; it is a weighty book. At the other extreme, there is an equally brilliant re-creation of an actor's presence in *Mac** by Harold Pinter,† a tribute to Anew McMaster, personal, colourful, pertinent: an actor's book about an actor.

To write of Donald Wolfit, an approach half-way between the two seemed to suggest itself. Wolfit as a theatrical figure never captured the imagination of his contemporaries in the way Irving did; Irving was the undisputed leader of his profession and universally acknowledged (except by Shaw and Henry James) as a great actor; there was nothing undisputed about Wolfit's life or his talent. On the other hand he seemed to be of greater importance than McMaster, if for no other reason than that he reached a larger public, but more profoundly, perhaps, because he represented a tradition of English acting that reached back into some crude, ancient past. Irving and McMaster, as actors, were originals; Wolfit was not.

No actor of his generation was surrounded by more controversy than Wolfit. Every aspect of his life and work was subject to dispute. Some dismissed him contemptuously; others thought of him as a joke; yet others claimed that no one who held the stage in the last fifty years possessed, in such abundance, the qualities befitting a great actor. The argument did not only rage over his talent, but also over his personality: he was hated and loved, disliked and admired, shunned and welcomed. Sometimes he was misunderstood, at other

---

*In *Poems and Prose 1949–1977* (1978, Methuen London Ltd.) Anew McMaster (1894–1962) Irish actor-manager. A famed Hamlet, Macbeth, Coriolanus, Petruchio, Richard III, Shylock and, above all, Othello. Last played in England, at Stratford, in 1938.

†As an actor a member of both Wolfit's and McMaster's companies.

times understood too well. He was large and yet petty, compassionate and cruel, magnanimous and mean. Above all, he was an actor from the crown of his head to the soles of his feet; and he was intensely human.

Taking my cue from him ('a play called *Hamlet* was *about* Hamlet —if not, then Shakespeare would have called it something else') I have attempted to embrace, in the title of this work, the conflicts within him that expressed themselves in every facet of his existence.

Sir Donald Wolfit, C.B.E.: that was how he liked to think of himself, the actor-manager, the Victorian, distinguished, honoured, respected; it was, undoubtedly, the greatest handicap to his career. Wolfit, the manager, served Wolfit, the actor, ill. Yet those ambitions, which took him nearly forty years to achieve, produced in him the very qualities that made him individual and unique, as if he encouraged his personality to attain a stature commensurate with his public image: pompous, grandiose, egocentric. But, between the prefix and the suffix, existed the man: the gentle, sometimes sweet individual, the boy from New Balderton endowed with loyalty, ingenuousness, gaiety and an unquenchable enthusiasm for life and for the theatre.

It was Wolfit's misfortune that his career coincided with the falling into disfavour of the virtuoso performer. The democratising process was an historical and universal one, not peculiar to the theatre. Wolfit, as an actor, was described as everything from 'great' to 'ham'. His detractors enjoyed thinking of him as a barnstormer, roaring and ranting his way through Shakespeare in Wigan or Southend. Certainly, at his worst, he fitted that description; at his best, he generated passion and power that was magnificent and overwhelming. Even his direst critics were unable, at one time or another, to resist his gifts and, as Miss Caryl Brahms observed, 'He was never a favourite of the critics, which makes their praise of him the more impressive.' And to those who will never be convinced of his genius, let Edmund Kean's words stand: 'A man may act better or worse on a particular night, from particular circumstances, but although the execution may not be so brilliant, the conception is the same.' Only the truly great actor can be ridiculous on one night, and sublime on another.

The word 'unfashionable' in the sub-title of this work is not intended as the antonym of 'High Society'. On the contrary, social distinctions do not enter into it; nor does the degree of popularity. Rather, it pertains to the 'acceptability' of personalities to their own times and, because the actor's art is ephemeral, the reputations gained in life live on long after death. Writers are sometimes reclaimed; actors, never.

'The Unfashionable Theatre', for the purposes of this book, is that section of the theatrical profession, actors in particular, who are regarded by their fellow men with a mixture of grudging admiration, disdain, and often amusement. For this, there can be many reasons. An actor, by virtue of his style, personality or behaviour, may appear to have been born out of his time; not necessarily too late; perhaps too soon. It does not mean that he himself is altogether blameless for being labelled an outsider; it may well be that his preference lies in that direction. But ultimately the judgement is made by others and, where the actor is concerned, mainly by three bodies of opinion: first, by the publicly acknowledged leaders of the profession—actors, dramatists, directors, managers; secondly, by journalists—gossip-writers, columnists; thirdly, by the 'intellectuals' or *cognoscenti* among the theatre-going public. All these, in turn, help to mould, in varying degrees, public success, to which they then toady, abandoning their standards of critical judgement. I deliberately exclude critics from the list of opinion-makers, for paradoxically the most influential and knowledgeable of them at any given time have actually championed unfashionable causes though, more often than not, with little effect.

Actors, of course, are not the only members of the unfashionable theatre. William Poel was unfashionable, yet he was responsible for moulding the modern style of Shakespearean speaking and production. Ben Iden Payne was another. He had the fortune to be the director of the first repertory company in England, only for it to be known to posterity as 'Miss Horniman's company'; Gordon Craig was the most unfashionable figure of all.

The 'Unfashionable Theatre' should not be confused with what Norman Marshall, in his very fine book of that name, calls 'The Other Theatre'; this deals in experimental groups, festival theatres, pioneering spirits, some of whom became very fashionable indeed; the Old Vic is an example.

But it is with an actor, in the main, that we are here concerned. There are always valid reasons why one actor is fashionable and another is not. I do not wish to imply conscious competition between the two groups, or to make comparisons as to whether one actor is more gifted than another; that is irrelevant to my theme. But I shall be less than honest if I do not admit that my sympathies lie with the unfashionable actors, for the judgements made upon them often seem so hasty and perverse, founded on shifting standards and tastes, on prejudice and jealousies, on a lack of understanding and knowledge. I must repeat, however, that the judgement is not always unfair; time and again, the unfashionable actors bring isolation upon themselves. The pity is that their contribution to their art is not fully acknowledged, for repeatedly it is these men who make secret inroads into the

drama for others to proclaim publicly. The actor who stands outside the established *côterie* is remembered, if at all, more for his faults
than for his virtues, more for his failures than for his achievements,
more for his private eccentricities than for his public performances.
What causes them immeasurable suffering during their lifetime is that
they so often observe their more fashionable colleagues being forgiven
the sins for which they themselves have been damned.

There appears to be no common factor among the unfashionable,
but in their more fortunate contemporaries they all produce a common reaction: a shudder of discomfort and embarrassment at the
mention of their names.

The list on both sides of the fence is endless, but some examples
may be given from the two camps.

Henry Irving, Johnston Forbes-Robertson, Gerald du Maurier,
John Gielgud, Laurence Olivier, Ralph Richardson and Paul Scofield,
are all fashionable actors. Barry Sullivan, Matheson Lang, Ion
Swinley, Baliol Holloway, Randal Ayrton, Anew McMaster, Wilfred
Lawson, Ernest Milton, are all unfashionable. And to their number is
to be added the subject of this biography, Donald Wolfit.

Part One

DON WOOLFITT

1902–1924

CHAPTER ONE

Of Woofett, Woffitt, Wolfyt, Woulflete, Woolfitt and others

> *. . . . Fie, foh and fum,*
> *I smell the blood of a British man.*
> *—King Lear*

I

THE first mention of the name that lends itself to an almost infinite variety of spellings appears in the baptismal register of Laxton, in the county of Nottinghamshire, 1571–2. On 14 February, Elizabeth, daughter of John Wolfet, was baptised. The second mention is twelve years later and already there is a second spelling: on 21 July 1583, the baptism is recorded of Zacharias, son of William Wolfett. By the beginning of the eighteenth century, however, the family had, with some exceptions, settled on 'Woolfitt' as an acceptable standard. It was not to be changed again for more than two centuries and then by an actor who thought it looked crisper spelt with one 'o' and one 't' and who thought that simplifying it would enable journalists and critics to reprint it without mistakes.

Certainly no member of the family before him achieved any special distinction and the very derivation of the name suggests pastoral tranquillity. It would be pleasing to accept the theory that it is derived from the two Anglo-Saxon words 'Wulf' and 'Geat', for the Geats were a race of legendary heros of whom Beowulf was one, but it is more likely that the Anglo-Saxon words 'woul' and 'flys' are the source: wool and fleece, the simple descriptions of the family's traditional livelihood. The Woolfitts were most of all remarkable for their constancy to their county and to their age-old trades and skills. Nothing in their past hints even remotely at the profession of their most famous son; nothing suggests a reason why, after centuries of peaceful, rural development, they should suddenly give birth to an extraordinary human being: a vital, talented, robust, full-blooded man, an actor whose life was to be as tempestuous as theirs was placid and serene.

They were, for the most part, Nottinghamshire men, deeply wedded to the land. Some reared sheep, others followed kindred trades, such as fellmongering or the tawing of hides, and they lived out their lives in the villages, parishes and farms that flourish round Newark-on-Trent: Claypole, Muskham, Dry Doddington, Bottesford, Bleasby, Rolleston, Fisherton, Norwell, Averham.

The Woolfitts were not all poor humble folk: the marriage registers reveal four husbandmen (farmers) and a yeoman. Some were church-wardens and several were married by licence, which suggests that they were fairly well-to-do; most of them could write and two had votes in the election of 1710. Another, a William Woolfitt, was 'of the bar'.

They did not venture far afield. Laxton was their centre and its records reveal the family's self-containment: when they married it was to cousins, as was usual in those days, or if outside the family, at least to people living in the same parish. One, however, Edward Woolfet, married into the landed gentry: on 30 November 1664, he wedded Elizabeth Roose whose family were the Lords of Laxton Manor, but the Rooses had, by that time, been struck by poverty: it is recorded that Bridget, the mother of Gilbert 'the last Lord of Laxton of the noble race, was reduced to so great poverty, that she gleaned corn amongst other poor people in Laxton Field'.

In a hitherto unpublished memoir on his family written in 1969, a modern William Woolfitt, a cousin of the actor, writes:

> The heavy brows, square jaw and high cheek-bones . . . are reminiscent of pictures of the old Boers of the last century and lend credence to the theory that the family was influenced by inter-marriage with Dutch immigrants who came to England with William of Orange at the beginning of the eighteenth century to inject new blood into the wool trade.

The memoir seeks also to demonstrate that certain inherent charac-teristics reproduce themselves upon the generations with uncanny fidelity: a belief in hard, honest labour and in frugality. The Woolfitts were concerned with the essentials of life and none of their number is ever recorded as being a spendthrift or squandering the family's meagre resources. On the contrary, they produced men with a fervent love of detail in matters financial, which

> . . . no doubt accounts for three generations of Woolfitts adopting a career in banking. . . . The persistent determination for factual, rather than sensational expression often leads to accusations of obstinacy and even pomposity but it is in effect only an in-bred hesitancy to appear flamboyant.

Of Edward Woolfitt who died in 1935, aged ninety-six, the story is told that he gave a rather headstrong pony to a young grandson who, on returning from his first ride, admitted, 'She ran away with me, grandpa, but we came to a steep hill which slowed her down and I was able to get her under control again.' 'That's where you did wrong, boy,' said old Edward. 'You should have kept her galloping up the hill and shown her you were master.'

William's memoir also reveals the skeleton in the family cupboard, although the black sheep in their case was not of Nottinghamshire stock; unsurprisingly, his stamping-ground was London. He is not a direct ancestor, but his appearance and activities are worth mentioning, if only for the fact that they so closely resembled the kind of character that would have been played with such relish by his descendant.

William Harrison Ainsworth in his monumental work *The Tower of London* notes that in the sixteenth century the names of the inquisitory team of the Tower of London were Renard, the Spanish Ambassador, Sorrocold the surgeon, Nightgall the jailor, Mauger the executioner and Wolfytt the 'sworn tormentor' or torturer. He describes Wolfytt as 'a wild and uncouth figure with strong but clumsily formed limbs, coarse repulsive features, lighted up by a savage smile. . . . He was attired in a jerkin and hose of tawny leather. His arms and chest were bare and covered with a thick pile of red hair. His ragged locks and beard, of the same disgusting colour, added to his hideous and revolting appearance. He was armed with a long iron pitch-fork and had a large hammer and a pair of pincers stuck in his girdle.' It is recounted that it was this Wolfytt who was alone upon the scaffold scattering clean straw round the block as Lady Jane Grey was led to her execution. This seems to have annoyed Mauger, the headsman, who wanted the scene to himself for performing the ritual of begging his victim's forgiveness and he ordered Wolfytt to leave 'the stage'; Ainsworth does not tell us whether the latter complied or not but one is sorely tempted to think that he remained and, at the most crucial moment, twirled his pitchfork, perhaps, to distract the crowd's attention.

II

Further north, the less colourful Woolfitts pursued their tranquil, pastoral lives. On 24 April 1862 in Newark-on-Trent, Nottinghamshire, William Pearce Woolfitt was born. He was one of a large family; several had died in infancy and he was the third of four survivors, brought up by his eldest sister who was at least twelve years his senior. He was educated at the Mount School, a Church of England foundation, but because of his family circumstances, had to start work at an early age. He possessed the Woolfitt fidelity in abundance, for at the age of seventeen, he joined a firm of brewers, Messrs Warwick & Richardson, and remained with them all his working life.

He was a solitary man with a passion for orderliness, walking and rowing. He went to church every Sunday and was regarded, rightly, as conventional and dependable. From the age of eighteen until his death, he kept a weekly account book in which he entered every item of expenditure in minute detail. Together with records of his salary and annual increases, he noted down small investments which illustrated a strong belief in hard work and thrift. Frequently he had his boots repaired, for he was a dedicated walker and he paid his subscription to the rowing club as it fell due. Also in the account book was an entry recording the purchase of an engagement ring.

At the rowing club he met a young man, Tomlinson, son of a well-known Newark family whose forefather, James Tomlinson, had set up the first printing press in that town in 1778; two years later he was printing playbills for the Newark Theatre. Woolfitt was introduced to Tomlinson's youngest sister, Emma, an attractive girl with a determined chin and gentle eyes; she was now twenty-four, a young woman whose deeply felt Christian beliefs were expressed, in her teens, by a desire to serve her fellow men; thus, she left Newark to train as a nurse at the Liverpool General Hospital. On one of her visits home the meeting with William Woolfitt took place and their courtship began. They must have been well suited: he, shy and somewhat formal, found himself at ease with Emma whose modesty, sincerity and sense of humour helped him to overcome his natural reserve. He had already turned thirty and had waited a long time to find his ideal partner, six years his junior. He proposed. She accepted, but during their engagement continued to work in Liverpool. She wrote frequently, describing in graphic detail the victims of dockside fights who were nightly brought in for medical attention. To William, far away in sleepy Newark, the descriptions must have seemed as though his loved one was herself in hourly danger. Determined to free her from so rough and violent an environment, he paid a small sum of money to release her from her probation. She returned to Newark and in July 1894 they were married at the parish church of St. Mary Magdalene.

Their marriage brought together markedly dissimilar family backgrounds, for the Tomlinsons were possessed of a wanderlust, a restlessness, in sharp contrast to the placid, settled ways of the Woolfitts.

Emma's father, another James, was a colourful romantic figure.*

---

* The only source of material concerning James Tomlinson is contained in Donald Wolfit's autobiography *First Interval*. Certain passages, regarding his alleged drinking habits, so offended some Canadian aunts that they refused to have the book in the house. Another claim that the family was descended from 'roaring Wesleyan preachers' is also stoutly denied. The present author has been unable to verify all the facts.

At nineteen he emigrated to Australia but returned penniless; three years later he was off on his travels again, this time aboard the S.S. *Culloden* bound for Canada. The master of the ship, the steamship company announced, 'had undertaken twenty voyages in her in comparative safety' and, somewhere in mid-Atlantic, the wild young man met and fell in love with Louisa Rooks of Tiverton, Devon. It was a whirlwind romance and they married not long after the ship reached Canada.

The newlyweds were soon on the move again, visiting her relations in Detroit and then re-crossing the border into Canada. The young husband evidently found it difficult to settle down; at one time he was a postman, at another a printer, thereby reverting to the family trade still carried on back at his native Newark home.

The couple produced seven children; Emma was the youngest and was born in London, Ontario, on 3 February 1868. Two months later her mother going out on to the wooden porch was horrified to see an enormous brown bear peering into the cradle. She seized her husband's gun from the wall and fired close enough to frighten the beast, which lumbered off into the woods. Very soon afterwards, perhaps not surprisingly, the family returned to England. An opening was made for Tomlinson in the family printing firm. Later he drifted towards journalism and became the editor of the local newspaper, *The Newark Advertiser*.

After Emma's marriage to William Woolfitt, James and Louisa Tomlinson took to the seas again and returned to Canada where he became business manager of the *Calgary Herald*. In Alberta the old man dabbled in real estate and eventually lost all his money in the collapse of a trust company in British Columbia. He appears, however, to have felt some remorse for his wild ways; shortly before his death he embraced the Catholic faith and died just before the First World War.

William and Emma settled down to married life in Balderton, a village on the outskirts of Newark. William continued to work hard at the brewery in which he was well established as a clerk.

Into the account book he was now entering the expenses of a doctor, midwife and nurses, for he and Emma had begun a family. They were to have five children, three boys and two girls. Their second son was born at 6 a.m. on 20 April 1902. He was christened Donald.

III

The Woolfitts lived at 8 London Road, New Balderton, a semi-detached villa of the late Victorian period, with a small garden at the front and a larger one at the rear which backed onto a field. Some time in the early 1900s the house was named 'Homeleigh' and it stood near the post marking the boundary of Balderton and Newark.

It was into a small village community that the Woolfitt children were born: Philip in 1896; Eva in 1898; Norah in 1900; Donald in 1902; Albert in 1905.

All the recollections of their family life, whether from Don or the others, paint a picture of contentment. There can be little doubt that it was a happy home with Mrs. Woolfitt much occupied in trying to instil in her brood a respect for learning, obedience and for Christian precepts.

She was a small, energetic woman with a fresh complexion and her children adored her. Don wrote of her 'tremendous courage and fore-sight, and a simple, but profound belief in the power and efficacy of prayer. From her father she inherited a great sense of humour and a gift for reading aloud.'

It was she who perceived early on that Don had in him some extra-ordinary fire, a talent that she admired, was proud of and thus en-couraged. Nevertheless, whatever encouragement she may have given him was quiet and gentle, almost surreptitious, for had she been more overt, it would have brought her into direct conflict with her husband who strongly opposed the theatre as a career.

William Pearce Woolfitt has been described by one of his children as 'a conventional man'. In many ways he embodied those virtues of middle-class Victorian England that were to be so revered until the outbreak of the First World War. He put his faith in the Church of England, Freemasonry and the Conservative Party. His children's views of him were various. 'He had a degree of integrity, it would be difficult to match' wrote his elder daughter Eva, and the younger Nora: '. . . Father was a scrupulously fair man.' His relationship with Don, to him the most difficult and unmanageable of all his children, was to be uneasy and distant. In 1955, in a letter of con-dolence to a friend* who had just lost his father, Don wrote:

> . . . life is never quite the same afterwards. I never had a great affection for my own [father] but he grew in my respect and memory when he had gone.

Certainly the clash between father and son was founded in an age-old conflict: the parent understandably insistent on a safe and steady career for his offspring; the offspring determined in the face of all opposition to pursue a course in life of his own choosing whatever the risks, whatever the costs.

Of the children Don was the only one who profoundly disturbed his father's quietude and composure and it was for this reason that he

*K. Edmunds Gateley.

described him as a man 'of irascible and uncertain temper'. The other children never found him so.

In later life, Don grew to look like him. William had large heavy features and was broad and muscular, no doubt from his passion for rowing. When that became too strenuous, he took up golf and played bowls occasionally but his chief interests were the Newton Lodge No. 1661, of which he was a founder member, and the parish church of St. Mary Magdalene, where he was first sidesman and, afterwards, for years churchwarden. He served the community whenever he could and devoted himself to a great deal of voluntary work, much of it known only to himself and to those he helped. This service to the community was shared by his wife and it expressed in a practical and useful way, without affectation or the wish to appear virtuous, the sincerity of their religious beliefs. For Mrs. Woolfitt, too, devoted what little free time she had to social and charitable pursuits and, in particular, to the welfare of orphaned children in Dr. Barnardo's Homes.

There are two assessments of William Woolfitt from outside the family which seem to support his daughters' view of him. They were contained in letters of sympathy written in 1938 by two Freemasons.

From S. A. Hildage, headmaster of Don's preparatory school, to his former pupil:

The integrity and sincerity your father displayed in everything he undertook was especially noticeable in our order, and it is a matter of some regret to us that you yourself had not the opportunity to see more fully the love and affection which all Freemasons had for him. . . .

. . . your father was one of the most highly respected men in Newark. Could you but hear the universal expression of sympathy and personal loss expressed on all sides I am sure that you would not so much mourn, as rejoice that you are the children of such a noble man. . . .

And in the same vein from J. Gardner, the Newark Borough Surveyor, to Norah:

In my humble opinion you have one great consolation and that is to know that he lived up to the Masonic principles, and by that I mean to convey that his life was as near perfect as it was possible to be for anyone on this earth.

But that nobility and perfection went unnoticed by his son. Don, however, was never a rebel against authority; all his life he reverenced it; he never showed his father anything but filial obedience in all matters except one.

CHAPTER TWO

The Horrible Secret

Oh, 'tis a parlous boy;
Bold, quick, ingenious, forward, capable. . . .
—Richard III

I

THERE is no single moment in Don's childhood which dramatically signals the future. Certainly Don, from his earliest days,
was driven by his talent for acting; that was his motor; that was
his pivot. From his first moments of real awareness, life, as it un-
folded around him, was seen from the point of view of an actor and
assessed with an actor's imagination. If the stimuli to which all the
Woolfitt children were exposed, as a family, had special significance
for him and not for the others, it was, simply, because he himself was
special.

He was nicknamed Don and sometimes Donnie. When he came to
write about his childhood he tried to find a pattern to his early life
that would point a way to his future, and some of the incidents he
recalls are worthy of repetition not only for the events themselves, but
also to illustrate the imagination upon which they acted. These
incidents were remembered not as pointers to the writer's character
or to his development as a personality, but as signposts read, as it
were, after the journey had been completed.

As children we looked upon it as the climax of the day when she
[his mother] consented to read, and more especially so on Sundays,
when from an amazing work called *Sunday Echoes and Weekday
Hours* we would listen to a lurid drama entitled *A Peep Behind The
Scenes*. This was an especial thrill for me, and held a fascination far
stronger than any other story: the travelling showman in his
caravan, the faded actress with the child she is endeavouring to
educate, the tinsel and the glare of the circus ring, the heartbreak
and death from consumption—all the best ingredients for bringing
lumps to the throat and tears to the eye.

He looks for and finds a clue to his prodigious memory:

> Perhaps this Collect learning was the most valuable memory training I received, for from early days I seem to have had little difficulty in memorising lines and speeches, and even now can recite odd paragraphs and rubbish rhymes which were repeated to me once or twice in those days.

Then he is reminded of the influence of the Church which, he writes,

> played a great part in our family life. . . . For most of our lives as children we lived some two miles from the church, and morning and evening services (entailing never less than eight miles' walk) were regularly attended on the Sabbath.

But it was the drama of the services that appealed to him most. He recalls the organist at funerals:

> The most exciting piece of all to me was the Dead March from *Saul*, when he would open full the diapason stop, and the whole church would shake as the water seemed to rush beneath one's feet. Our family pew stood right above this water pipe, and I can remember to this day the beating of my heart as the moment came in the music. I remember also the almost morbid interest I took in the health of elderly and fading aldermen and other ailing members of the congregation, wishing at one time that they would depart from this vale of woe at regular weekly intervals so that every Sunday morning service might be prefaced with this church-shaking piece of music.

In the parish church he received his religious instruction, was confirmed, served at the altar and

> . . . for a time was inclined to make the Church my vocation.

It was doubtful, however, if the inclination lasted very long, although this early influence was to survive through his life, but it was not so much an involvement with formalised worship as a deeply felt awe, an almost mystical attraction to conflicts and matters spiritual.

But what impressed Don most were the people he met, the out-of-the-ordinary characters who crossed his path. The one who made the most impression was an elderly merchant, one Ebenezer Smith, who made violins, 'blended tea and sold coffee, candles and matches'. In his reminiscences of this man, Don reveals, in passing, how impressionable he was as a child, how romantic, but most of all, how detailed an observer he was, even then:

> He [Ebenezer Smith] had a magnificent set of white side-whiskers that shone like silver, a wonderful flow of conversation, and a pretty

daughter who gave piano lessons in the upper chamber and from whom I learned to play.

Don had piano lessons from Miss Smith once a week.

I think these were the times I loved best in the whole of my boyhood. I would cycle into the town half an hour before the lesson was due in the early evening. If the shop was empty I would walk through to the little back room and there be regaled by the whiskered patriarch with lurid stories of crime and punishment mingled with religious dogma and theosophical dissertations. All the time he talked, a fiddle would be in the making. . . .
It was always an interesting twenty minutes I spent in the little back room before he would rise and move to the blower which was fixed to the wall. He would remove the wooden plug from this homely device and blow a long shrill whistle through his teeth. I could hear it squeak at the other end of the pipe two stories higher. Then came a distant thin voice of inquiry from the beautiful music mistress and the answer from Silver Whiskers, 'Master Donald is here for his music lesson, Gladys.' The cap was replaced and I was told to mount the dark twisting stairs to the room with the Georgian windows facing the market square.
As I mounted my head would be buzzing with the complexities of the Christian religion, and with stories of murder and sudden death, of bulls being baited by dogs in the market square (which Silver Whiskers had seen and taken part in as a boy), of dancing bears led on chains to be baited after the bulls were led away, until in my imagination the whole of the great square was full of these bloodcurdling sights and sounds. Notwithstanding all these excitements, I had to force my fingers to the mastery of scales and arpeggios, and to keep my eyes on the music instead of on the beautiful daughter of Silver Whiskers. It is true that in later years when my passion had reached more reasonable proportions, I came reluctantly to the conclusion that perhaps she applied a quantity of rouge, eyebrow and lipstick; but in those days such thoughts never entered my head and I was in the presence of a goddess who could smile and bewitch me and guide my fingers over the keys in an effort to teach me the rudiments of piano playing.

He describes the entertainments available to a young boy in a small county town just before 1914: the occasional concert in the town hall and the home-made variety with his mother at the piano; the vagabond entertainers who held sway in the market square; the sword swallower, the May Fair where he had his 'first glimpse of buskers and barnstormers'. The highlight of the year was, however, the visit of

Lord George Sanger's Circus when the Woolfitt children would be awakened especially early to watch the procession pass their house. These were the exciting events of Don's childhood, as they were for his brothers and sisters. But they were of an overwhelming significance to him above all, for he wrote:

> A conviction was steadily growing in my mind that above all else I wanted to be an actor. . . . The idea of the theatre or music-hall as a profession was, of course, unthought of by my parents, and the voicing of such a longing would have been greeted by them with amazement. To them the theatre was a place of evil. I did not divulge my horrible secret.

This steadily growing conviction was to turn into a passionate aspiration; it would consume his thoughts, his daydreams, every waking hour. The horrible secret was festering like an obsession; sooner or later it would have to be divulged.

II

The child who nursed 'the horrible secret' had a slightly chubby face, a flat nose and a wide, cheeky grin. Adults liked him and, his sister Norah wrote, 'the charm of his smile could win over all our parents' friends as a little chap'. He was mischievous and difficult to discipline and, sometimes, 'when playing or teasing would go too far, not knowing when to stop'. On a visit to Uncle Billy, a dearly loved cousin of his mother's, he had had to take shelter from a heavy shower. When it had passed, the road was alive with tiny frogs. Don filled his pockets and on arrival at Uncle Billy's emptied the frogs out, still hopping, onto the sitting-room carpet. He was surprised that the welcome was not as warm as usual. On another occasion, his sister Eva recalled, he 'decided to put on one of his "acts" to terrorise us, which he did successfully, chasing us up and down the house with a carving knife, resisting every attempt to stop him throwing toys, wooden building blocks into the fire in the kitchen range etc. until Mother returned to put a stop to his Reign of Terror.'

Whatever Don did he did wholeheartedly. There were no half-measures. Again, from Eva: '. . . in those days he was headstrong, determined to go through with any project on which he had set his heart.'

That determination reflected itself in all things. His brother Albert wrote, 'When he had a bicycle at school they called him "Jehu"—for he rideth furiously.'

He played cricket and rugby, although he was not especially good at either; he did, however, win the 220 yards and collapsed upon breasting the tape.

This 'collapse', real or not, is an interesting pointer to Don's hunger for attention. The 220-yards sprint is not all that arduous for a schoolboy; nevertheless Don felt compelled to show publicly the effort and the energy he had spent in winning it. He was not fully satisfied just to have won; his fellows must be made to realise what the victory had cost him physically. In later life, after all his theatrical performances (whether Lear or Touchstone), he would unashamedly display the outward trappings of exhaustion. He liked people to know that he worked for his living.

Don, even in these early prep-school years, was beginning to display clearly-defined character traits: wholehearted enthusiasm for any venture that captured his imagination, sometimes amounting to uncontrolled exuberance; bull-like obstinacy; fiendish single-mindedness; grim determination. To these qualities would be added the one ingredient that was to make them cohere and serve his aspirations.

Just before his tenth birthday, Don was taken to see a performance given by the scholars and staff of Magnus Grammar School of *The Pied Piper of Hamelin*. Sitting there in the darkened auditorium, the little boy admitted to feeling intensely jealous of his brother Philip who was playing one of the townspeople. It was the first full-length entertainment he had ever seen, and it was the first time, unknowingly, that he was experiencing a deeply felt need to act.

This need in its infant stages was expressed by a talent for recitation. His mother taught him poems and rhymes which he spoke on birthdays or at Christmas. One such poem, extracted from a Canadian magazine sent by Grandfather Tomlinson from Calgary, was entitled 'Somebody poisoned my dog', which Don delivered at children's entertainments. Writing many years later of one such performance, Don recalled that he rendered the poem

> with such force apparently that an elderly lady who happened to be present fainted away and told my mother very firmly that such a power and vehemence was not natural in a young boy of my age and should be most definitely discouraged.

The woman who fainted at Don's histrionic prowess showed some affinity to a female spectator of Edmund Kean's Sir Giles Overreach, but even if the Woolfitts had known that, it is doubtful whether it would have made any difference; Don was forbidden to recite the poem ever again.

Nevertheless, he had for the first time tasted the actor's power over his audience and it was a taste greatly to his liking. He began to learn new poems, sing songs, write short plays. The ingredient had been added: his driving qualities were beginning to be properly focused. It only required another impetus for the vision of his future to be sharply defined.

III

His first part of any note was Robin Hood at the age of seven at the Parish Church School but his first venture into actor-management was in the cellar of a schoolfriend's house in Church Walk, Newark. The year was 1912; he was ten. Planks of wood were laid across barrels and admission was by production of a number of cigarette cards (later, if the entertainment was for the benefit of parents, pins were produced). The actors played bold, bad pirates on the good ship 'Yakka Hikki Doola'. Don was impresario and of course played the leading part. The success of the venture encouraged him to continue his efforts and the planning and production of similar home-made entertainments were to consume his leisure hours for the next eight years.

1912 was an auspicious year for him. Just before Christmas, Mrs. Woolfitt showed characteristic kindness to their Scots neighbours, the aged MacKinnies, who had been ill. One day, after school, Don returned to find his mother and Mrs. MacKinnie talking before the kitchen fire. To please the old lady Don recited a poem for her. When he had finished she gave two gold sovereigns to his mother, saying that in gratitude for the kindness that had been shown her, she wanted Mrs. Woolfitt to take the children to the pantomime in Nottingham. Mrs. Woolfitt protested and when her husband heard about it he disapproved strongly, but Mrs. MacKinnie won the day. A week later the family set off for Nottingham by train.

Don bounced up and down with excitement throughout the entire performance. The Theatre Royal, Nottingham, red plush and gold, was one of the most beautiful theatres in the country and it was always to hold a special place of affection in Don's heart. The star of the show was Tom Foy as Simple Simon and that day he conquered one little boy's imagination and made so deep an impression that, forty years later, the little boy was able to remember every word of the opening song:

> 'My girl's promised to marry me
> When I've a hundred pounds—
> Ay a hundred golden pounds—
> To buy a nice little house and grounds
> And it won't be long before I calls her mine
> 'Cos I've got a pound in the bank
> And I only want ninety-nine.'

The days that followed were dedicated to working on an impersonation of Tom Foy. A family friend, a Mr. Harker, owned a phonograph and early Foy recordings; aided by Harker's two daughters, Don painstakingly copied down lyrics and patter. Then he persuaded the curator of the local museum to lend him a smock. All he needed now was a red wig. His eyes alighted on a red skin rug with a thick curly fringe which adorned the Woolfitt drawing-room; bit by bit the fringe disappeared. Some time later, on a wet winter's evening, Don asked for permission to recite and, hardly waiting for a reply, dashed from the room and reappeared, moments later, dressed as his latest god, Tom Foy, crowned with the home-made wig.

There was dead silence; then my youngest sister looked up from her book, murmured 'silly' and continued reading. Only my mother encouraged me with her laughing brown eyes, and with a dry mouth I launched into Tom Foy's monologue called 'Courting'—which in any case was no real subject for a boy of ten or eleven to develop to an assembled and bored family circle.

All went well until his mother suddenly realised where the wig had come from. Don was told to dress properly again and to put an end to the nonsense. His mother, however, stood by him and prevented his father from punishing him too severely.

Not to be properly appreciated was punishment enough. A fear that no one would understand him, that he would never be allowed to achieve his ambition, began to worry him. His sensitive mother detected tension in her son, and was concerned about it. Their relationship was warm and affectionate; Don found it easy to talk to her. When she asked why he was so interested in dressing up and reciting he told her the truth: 'I want to be an actor,' he said. No doubt the reply troubled her. At first, she regarded it as simply the natural response of an impressionable child to his first theatrical outing, and then she hoped it was a passing phase. It is absolutely certain that what was uppermost in her mind was her concern for Don's education: he was shortly to sit for a scholarship to Magnus Grammar School, Newark; it was imperative that he succeeded; a distraction of this kind would be dangerous. Whatever her misgivings she respected Don's confidence and he was much relieved that someone shared his horrible secret, someone who loved and understood him. He had no intention of confiding in his father.

At the best of times, Don was a difficult boy to discipline and it must have been exasperating for his parents and teachers to have in their grasp a bright, intelligent child with an outstanding memory, who could not be made to concentrate on his studies. Few teachers are able to appreciate the gifts of their pupils unless those gifts are scholastic. Don's school life was never easy; to the conventional men who had the task of trying to instil knowledge into him he must have seemed stubborn and lazy, a boy who deliberately refused to make the most of his abilities.

The burden of coping with Don in his early years fell upon the Headmaster of Barnby Road Elementary School, Mr. S. A. Hildage, a small red-faced man with a loud voice and a peppery temper. He it was who kept a firm hand on young Woolfitt and saw to it that the boy knuckled down to working for his scholarship.

It could not have been a difficult conflict for Don, aged eleven, to resolve; he would simply have to do what he was told. Despite the fact that he was passionately consumed by thoughts of the theatre, that he had found an outlet for his energies and, most important, had discovered at this early age his purpose in life which was to be absolutely central to him and with which he was to keep faith for more than fifty years, the standards and pressures of his immediate environment were bound to win the day. Family ties were strong: Don adored his sisters and hero-worshipped his elder brother Philip. The strict, religious, church-going background of his home was a powerful influence. Parental word was law. There was no possibility of provoking a head-on clash at this tender age, nor would it have served any purpose. Young boys of ten or eleven have to learn that purposes in life must be put under dust covers and aired at a later date. Parents and teachers have ever preferred the more docile, malleable children. Don had no alternative. He passed his scholarship in 1913; it was known as the Pupil Teacher Scholarship which implied at least some advance commitment towards becoming a teacher. But Don, as his mother now well knew, had other ideas.

CHAPTER THREE

Extra Curricular Activities

Learning is but an adjunct to ourself
And where we are our learning likewise is.
   —Love's Labours Lost

I

FIVE months after his eleventh birthday in September 1913, Don entered Magnus Grammar School. He was a scholarship boy and therefore expected to justify the grant. But it was with a sinking heart that Don awaited his first examination results. The End of Term list, Christmas 1913, reveals that out of nineteen boys, he was placed three from bottom and as follows in each subject:

	DIV.	LAT.	MATHS.	ENG.	FR.	HIS.	GEO.	BOT.	SCI.
16 Woolfitt	9	13	19	17	15	13	12	8	16

The Headmaster, the Rev. H. Gorse, M.A., wrote sternly to Don's father and threatened expulsion if improvement were not rapidly forthcoming. Don had a great respect for Gorse and thought him 'quite magnificent', but it was the Maths master, Mr. C. W. Percival, who proved to be the bane of young Woolfitt's life; the Term List would seem to confirm the lack of understanding between the two.

Mr. Percival, 'a man with a sardonic sense of humour and stern notions of discipline', was to be the first of many 'bogeymen' Don would encounter in life. It is clear from the boy's recollections that Percival was an unenlightened teacher, a bully who flourished a pointer like a sabre, thrashing the blackboard with it, hoping to elicit the answers to imponderable questions, but

> Far from stimulating my process of mathematical thought this procedure only succeeded in turning me into a dumb stupid dolt without a word or an answer, and the laughing-stock of the rest of the class.

Although caning was only permitted by the Headmaster himself in the presence of a prefect, a system of detention was employed in the school whereby when enough awards were accumulated the ultimate punishment was certain to result. Percival awarded detention upon detention but Don saw in it, not the just rewards for inattention and bad work, but a systematic persecution.

> He [Percival] appeared to wield some power with the rest of the staff and either by conspiracy or over-persuasion he succeeded in getting his colleagues to fall into line with his scheme which was to achieve a really crushing exposure of me to the Headmaster.

The exposure was not long in coming; Don earned thirteen detentions in one week which stood as a school record for all time. Inevitably he was caned and as a result 'was rebellious and mutinous and possessed naturally by a great hatred'.

Then his mother came, once more, to his rescue: she found him crying over his Mathematics home-work:

> This had been frequently completed for me by my eldest sister surreptitiously, but on this morning she had no time to spare and I broke down in real terror.

The story came out; his father was called into the room and 'took my side for once'; a parental visit to the Headmaster followed.

Gorse investigated the affair and must have found, to some extent, in Don's favour for Percival 'became conciliatory' and left the boy in peace. Don, however, was given a long but not unsympathetic lecture and told to forget his 'dressing-up', his imitations, recitations and thoughts of the theatre. Gorse had a profoundly sobering influence on his wayward pupil, and the boy, in turn, regarded him with filial affection.

The following year Percival left the school and Don, to the surprise of all, organised a farewell concert in his honour. It was not, however, without an ulterior motive. Years later, when in Stratford-upon-Avon, Percival visited his former pupil's dressing room, and of the encounter Don remembered

> ... he [Percival] said: 'You know, Wolfit, I always remember that you organised a concert for me when I left Magnus.' In a flash and without thinking I said quietly: 'Oh no, because you were leaving.' His eyes flashed as of old and I knew he realised how complete my revenge had been.

This episode reveals much. The accusations of 'conspiracy', the 'great hatred', the longing for 'revenge' were parts of a pattern that were to be repeated. When, in all periods of his life, Don would find himself up against it, he would fall into that pattern and cry 'conspiracy' and feel 'a great hatred' for critics, theatre owners, other actors, managers, directors. As in the case of Mr. Percival there may always have been an element of justification, but Don was to resort to that defence when blinded to his own defects, or when unable to carry the burden of his own culpability. Furthermore, it illustrates how difficult Don found it to forgive; he would always bear a grudge when wronged. It is clear that the intervention of his father served to encourage this behaviour pattern; it endorsed Don's interpretation of events and furthermore the endorsement came from that remote, austere figure whose approval for anything Don did was welcomed as a sign of affection by his son. Thus, what appeared was a serious flaw in Don's make-up and one that forever caused him a great deal of unhappiness.

The lecture from Mr. Gorse had some effect but not for long: Don simply could not forget his 'dressing-up'; the victory over Percival hardened his resolve: he visited one of his classmates, F. A. Helme, an amateur printer, and asked him to print some cards. In due course they were delivered with their simple inscription:

D. Woolfitt—Actor

II

Thus Don's unhappy schooldays proceeded, it must have seemed to him, at snail's pace. It was now a question of biding his time and of finding a means of fulfilling his theatrical ambition. All he possessed was the absolute certainty that he would be an actor, but it was a certitude based upon faith; what he needed now was something more substantial upon which to build his dreams; this, too, was quickly forthcoming.

When war was declared in 1914, a patriotic fervour swept the nation. Phil, the eldest Woolfitt child, had the previous year gone to Canada to join the Tomlinsons with a view to making a life for himself in the New World. He now returned to join the army and was soon in France. Newark became a garrison town for the Royal Engineers. By the end of 1915 Magnus had formed a Cadet Corps and four times a week Don attended school in khaki and learned drill and how to handle a rifle. Each summer his unit joined thousands of other boys on a two-weeks training camp in Leicestershire for night manoeuvres and rifle-range practice, and each term the school lost the eligible men from its staff who were replaced by women teachers. Help on the farms was required and for six weeks every summer Don went to a large farm at Long Bennington where he learned to handle horses, cut and stook corn and cart it into the stackyard from five in the morning until dark. He developed a love of the land, of the countryside, of rural tranquillity, that was always to form a deep and abiding part of him.

As the wounded returned to convalesce in Blighty, so charity concerts and entertainments were organised; Don was asked to help. Off he would go to Newark General Hospital and perform for the soldiers. His impersonation of Tom Foy was resurrected, red wig and all, and proved a great success at the Town Hall where loud guffaws greeted his opening words, 'Eee I've come!' At the back of the hall stood Mrs. Woolfitt with a group of organisers, amongst whom was Jessie Bond, a great musical comedy star in the 1890s, now married to Lewis Ransome, a local man. Mrs. Woolfitt said, 'Well, Mrs. Ransome, what am I to do with him?'

'I don't know,' replied the actress. 'But one thing I will tell you: you'll never stop that boy from going on the stage and you'd better not try.'

These words helped Don, for they provided an expert opinion and one that could not be ignored. The parental barriers, to Don's amazement, were less formidable than previously, and he found himself permitted to entertain the troops more and more frequently. But it was made clear that his public appearances were being condoned only in the cause of charity and patriotism.

Then tragedy struck the Woolfitt household at a time when few families in England were exempt from grief: Phil was wounded at Passchendaele and died in St. George's Hospital, London. His obituary notice in the *Novarcensian*, the school magazine, exactly captures the national mood:

PHILIP WOOLFITT

There was not a boy in the school who knew Phil Woolfitt who was not cut to the heart when he heard that he too had died of wounds. Leaving us in April 1912, he had spent a couple of years in Canada, and was doing well when the war started. Like so many of our gallant lads he heard the call of the Mother Land at once, and eventually he was sent across to France. It was a joy to see him on his way out: the same bright, cheery, open-hearted fellow that had left us, but developed wonderfully and quite a man. He had not been in France long before he was badly wounded, and he died in hospital in London. It was with sore hearts that we laid him to rest in Newark Cemetry, and we grieve for his parents, but there was a curious thrill of pride and confidence as we looked back on his splendid young life.

Don recalled the sadness of that time on a more personal note, and doubtless more accurately:

I think my mother loved him the best of all her children and the loss of him broke her heart.

III

As a result of the feverish activity that accompanied the civilian war effort, the concerts, the fêtes, the fund-raising appeals, Don was thrown into the hurly-burly of amateur theatricals. His talent and enthusiasm were obvious assets and his natural driving determination was no handicap either. Four people who were themselves in one way or another connected with these activities now entered his life. Individually and collectively they were to make his future possible: an authoress, a musician, a clergyman and a corporal in the Royal Engineers. His sister Norah attributes the discovery of this influential constellation not to the circumstances of war but to Don's own tenacity: '. . . in his teens—his flair for finding all the gifted people in one small market town who could help him towards his ambition—a singleness of purpose which characterised his whole life.'

The four people were Miss Katherine Garner—the authoress; Madame D'Ascanio—the musician; the Reverend Cyril Walker—the clergyman; and Corporal Charles Power, but to Don he was far more than a Corporal:

> he was really a being set apart, a sort of God . . . who had been a Real Live Actor in the Real Theatre.

Between them these four moulded his musical and theatrical taste for the next three years until he left school. Don never ceased to be grateful to them.

The most important influence he attributed to Madame D'Ascanio, a local girl married to an Italian immigrant, who together with a fellow countryman, Cafferata, founded a firm which, from the gypsum pits outside the town, made Plaster of Paris. Madame D'Ascanio, round-shouldered, small and extremely short-sighted, was a pianist of considerable gifts. She had lost a son in the early days of the war and for some time kept to her house in Beacon Hill. In Don, who visited her often, 'she found some strange sense of companionship'. She had the ability to fire penetrating questions which 'did not need an immediate answer but gave one cause for thought', her young pupil wrote. 'Oh yes, your imitations are very funny, but why do you want to imitate anyone? Why not be yourself? You have a good voice, why don't you sing properly? Why don't you recite some real poetry? Have you ever read Shakespeare's plays?' Evidently she was just the person Don needed at that moment; someone who cast a severely critical eye over his amateur, youthful enthusiasm; the one disapproving voice to whom artists, old or young, amateur or professional, are more likely to listen, because it stood out as a discord in the chorus of admirers.

It was her last question that Don took most seriously. He had studied *The Merchant of Venice* and *Julius Caesar* at school; that was the extent of his interest or lack of it. At home he was surprised to discover in the bookshelves, between the Bible and the complete works of Charles Dickens, a set of eight volumes of the plays of William Shakespeare. They were the Tallis-Macready edition, published in 1848, illustrated with full plates of the actors and actresses of that period, including many of the great William Charles Macready himself. Macready, brow furrowed, hands clasped, as Macbeth, intense, earnest, boyish; sombre as Henry IV; as Othello, his flat, unsculptured face quite unaltered by the heavy, dark greasepaint; or as Iago, on the battlements at Cyprus, plumed and pantalooned, eyebrows heightened, a moustache to tug the corners of the mouth into the suggestion of an evil scowl; as Lear, with Helen Faucit the Cordelia lying dead against the kneeling King who looks to heaven as if in the act of cursing the gods. There were prints of other actors, notably Edmund Kean with whom Don would ever feel a deep affinity. Kean, diminutive and wild, as Richard III, Hamlet, Shylock. No other actor, whether in a painting, print, etching or photograph, has ever had his vitality and passion more forcibly projected than Edmund Kean.

'I began to read the plays of Shakespeare,' Don wrote, 'and the more I read the more fascinated I became. Thus my real dramatic education began.' It was also the first stirrings of his love and admiration for the great actors of the past and the great roles they had played. From this moment on Shakespeare's plays would always be associated in his mind with those prints, with those actors and of course with the great roles themselves. He wrote in 1954

I wonder at the inspiration which I gathered from those plates of Macready and Kean in my first volumes of Shakespeare, from the plays themselves. . . .

Thus, in his youthful daydreams Don joined the ranks of Macready and Kean. He was now possessed of three distinct impulses: the first was the need to act; the second an ambition to succeed; the third his aspiration to be a great actor. That phrase, 'great actor', had a special significance and a particular meaning: it was indelibly associated with William Shakespeare's plays and with the mighty roles those plays provided. One could not be a great actor, the boy concluded, unless one acted great parts.

So, with his usual energy, Don began to read, stealing hours after school to sit in the public library: Galsworthy, Pinero, Wilde, Sheridan, Goldsmith. But it was the set of red volumes at home to which he returned most frequently although they 'made tough reading, being Shakespeare; but the plates made all the difference and I could gaze on Macready as Lear, Buckstone as Lancelot Gobbo, Davenant as Malvolio and Charles Kean as Othello.'

Madame D'Ascanio became an important figure in Don's life: not only did she make him read but also introduced him to the music of Beethoven, Bach, Purcell, Byrd, Mendelssohn. He was beginning to glimpse new horizons.

Enter Miss Kitty Garner. 'She had literary ability and some knack of putting lyrics together,' and devised an entertainment entitled 'The Intervention of Santa Claus'. One of the characters was called 'Herr Buffen-Gruffen (not a bad sort of German)'. No amateur in the town wished to play him. It was decided that to cast a boy in the role would render it harmless. Pressure was brought to bear on Mr. Woolfitt. Grudgingly Don was allowed to take part; he was padded with a large cushion, given a pair of thick-lensed spectacles and a walrus moustache, and had a string of sausages hanging from his pocket. He brought the house down when he sang to a twenty-five-year-old woman:

> 'I luff my luff with a true luff
> A luff that will never grow cold
> But it's best to be on with the new luff
> Before you are off with the old.'

The song had special and tender meaning to the young singer. During rehearsals he had fallen violently in love for the first time. Miss Oldrini, who danced the hornpipe, was the object of his silent, shy adoration. Unable to find the courage to declare his love, he nursed a broken heart in secret, plunged feverishly into his school studies, forswore the theatre, and passed his examinations with honours and distinction in two subjects. 'Then I felt better about the theatre.' It was just as well, for as a result of their success in 'The Intervention of Santa Claus', the enthusiastic group of people decided to formalise their association: The Newark Amateur Dramatic Society was formed and Jessie Bond agreed to become first President. The opening production was to be a new play, *Coils*, by Kitty Garner, a rambling Regency story set in the Saracen's Head Hotel, Newark. One of the leading parts was that of an idiot who, at one point in the drama, disguised himself as a sailor and made love to the maids in the house and even to his own mother. The Company also broke into song and dance at several junctures. The part of the idiot had been written for Don. Once more the burning question was whether his father would consent to Don appearing in the play.

With a little more confidence than usual as a result of his good examination results,

... I bearded him in his lair, the lair being the drawing-room whither he retired after high tea to sit in his arm-chair and read the paper. These conversations were always conducted in a very one-sided manner. Having closed the door I would sit down, and a silence would ensue until some three minutes later a voice would come from behind the newspaper: 'Who is that?' Reply: 'It's me. May I please ask you something, Father?' There would follow a long pause after which came: 'Well, go on, I'm listening.' So to the front and back pages of the newspaper I would make my request. At the end would come: 'Well, don't bother me now. I'll talk to your mother about it.' Nothing more was to be achieved after that; the ground was laid and I would retire, never having glimpsed my parent.

During the weeks of waiting for his father's decision, Don cycled over to Hoveringham to stay with his aunt, a Mrs. Tomlinson. He visited, too, her friend, Mrs. Beales, for here he was certain of a sympathetic ear. Mrs. Beales, aware of his father's opposition to the theatre, encouraged Don to 'have a go'. Cheered by these conversations, he would sit her little daughter, Phyllis, on a chair and sing comic songs at the piano, the little girl's favourite being 'When father carved the duck!' Father, doubtless, was much on Don's mind.

IV

Don kept diaries of this period and some have survived. The first is 'Lett's Boy Scout's Note Book and Diary for 1916'. At the back he kept a newspaper photograph of Matheson Lang. He recorded the outstanding events of the war, family affairs, visits to the theatre. Above all the little pocket book is filled with rehearsal times, progress reports on the sale of concert tickets, music lessons and the occasional reference to what he was reading. The 1917 and subsequent diaries contain more intimate information. From time to time there is a cry to the gods:

SATURDAY 20 JANUARY 1917
Will no one get round dad about 'Coils'?

SUNDAY 21 JANUARY 1917
Oh I am getting fed up with things!

But four days later Jessie Bond 'got round dad' and the period of waiting was over. He began to rehearse the play under the stern professional eye of Miss Bond. Thus he was able to record, six days later:

SATURDAY 27 JANUARY
Rehearsal. In my opinion Mrs. Ransome [Jessie Bond] is cutting out too much!

and:

THURSDAY 29 MARCH
Went to rehearsal at 7 o'clock. I wish I could get on a bit with the real thing!

He received a taste of the real thing from Jessie Bond. 'Don't jig about!' she shouted. 'Stand still and command them by being natural. Stand still and just act naturally and you'll be very, very good.' It was the first real direction he had received and he said of Miss Bond 'what an exquisite teacher you were!'

Coils proved to be a great success and was repeated at intervals for Red Cross funds at the village of Collingham and eventually at the Newark Picturedome. It was during one such performance that Don met Corporal Charles Power. The boy, in his make-up as the Idiot was standing at the back of the hall watching his fellows perform, a habit he was later to deplore, when he became aware of a man in khaki standing beside him. The man whispered,

'Just a minute, old man, aren't you the chap who plays the idiot boy in this play?' I mumbled that I was and half stopped. He drew closer to me. 'Well, I've been at the game for some years. How long have you been at it?' Now this was a facer. Was I talking to a real live actor? So I answered him: 'Do you mean professionally?' 'Oh yes,' he replied, 'I was at it for years before this war; you've been at it some time, haven't you?' The truth had to be told so I said that I was sixteen (giving myself an extra six months to gain confidence and thinking that it would enhance his good impression of me), that I was still at school, and that of course I was an amateur. 'Well,' said my khaki friend, 'I watched you play the last scene; you stood so still and made every word tell to such effect that I thought you were a pro and had been years at the game.' . . .
This was a sort of paradise for me. I muttered my thanks and said I must get back. He patted me on the shoulder. 'That's it, old man, back you go on the green again. Pong it over at 'em. You ought to go into the game you know. You'd make a success of it, old man. Cheerio!' With my head buzzing I passed through the door. All those wonderful phrases: 'On the green,' 'pong it over,' 'at the game,' 'a pro' rang in my ears. I acted the remaining scenes in the play that evening feeling that I was treading the boards of Drury Lane Theatre at least, and I am sure I was suffering from a swollen head.

Corporal Power begins to appear frequently in the diaries. With his fund of stories about theatre life, his wise advice and admiration for his young friend's talents, he was an irresistible companion. Typically:

SATURDAY 19 MAY
Went to see Corp. Power. Went to Southwell with him and looked over the minster again. He treated me to tea at Saracen's Head. Rode home and came up home but met him and went to pictures. Had a topping time. He is a sport. Must pay him back if I can. Had a long talk. It rained.

WEDNESDAY 20 JUNE
Went down to see Power in the evening. He made grease for me.

SATURDAY 23 JUNE
Corpl. Power came up for tea in the afternoon. Came into town with him at 6 and went into Library. Got Henry Irving's biography* out. Came home and read.

The introduction of Power into the Woolfitt family circle 'made a great difference to my parents' outlook on the world of the theatre. They found him a cultured, well-educated man, a witty conversationalist.' He had played in George Edwardes' musical comedies, in the old touring melodramas and 'with that great pair Fred Terry and Julia Neilson'. With cuttings and photographs of current London successes from the *Bystander*, *Sketch* and *Tatler* he helped Don make his first scrapbook. In August, at his prompting, Don tried his hand at writing:

MONDAY 27 AUGUST
Settled down.

TUESDAY 28 AUGUST
Started writing play.

WEDNESDAY 29 AUGUST
Finished play.

There was no doubt that Don was basking in his new-found friendship, although life was not all theatre:

TUESDAY 18 SEPTEMBER
Cycled back to school with Mabel and Muriel. Then brought Bert nearly home and then went back and had another fine time!!!!

Towards the end of the year Don met his 'fourth contact with the world of the theatre, the Rev. Cyril Walker, rector of Averham', a

---

* By Bram Stoker, Irving's manager.

village which lay three miles from Newark. In the grounds of his house between the church and the rectory, he had built a small theatre which seated one hundred and twenty people. Besides his passion for private theatricals the rector 'was a regular rider to hounds, drove a very snappy line in dog carts, was a bachelor. . . . He mounted some remarkable spectacles, pantomimes and musical plays, sometimes spending a year on painting the scenery which he did entirely by himself. The village carpenter made the flats; and his valet, Tomlin, was a gifted amateur actor and singer.'

The 1917 Christmas production was to be *Aladdin* with Charles Power as Widow Twankey. Don was invited to play a small part and was captivated by Walker's enthusiasm, the quality of the production, the enchantment of the private theatre.

> . . . the lure of the theatre beckoned me day and night. I read avidly the criticism in the *Morning Post*, collected photographs of London productions, and became aware of the great rhythm of that theatre which, at a distance of one hundred and twenty-five miles, seemed so raffish and uncontrolled.

But, for the moment, London would have to wait.

V

MONDAY 28 JANUARY, 1918
School results. *3rd class Honours*. Distinction in Geog and pass in Spoken French. Cheers! Tea. Went to pictures with Norah to celebrate. Jolly good.

With only eighteen more months of school in front of him, his parents and the teaching staff were much encouraged. Mr. Woolfitt made several efforts to draw Don into some decision as to what his future would be. Clearly, he had no idea of the seriousness of the situation and his son's real intentions were still kept secret from him. But dutifully Don sat for a naval examination, failed dismally 'and I think on my own part deliberately'.

Meantime, performances of *Aladdin* continued into April. In August he was off to the school cadet camp and then to Long Bennington, working in the fields, 'doing a man's work'. He was growing into a strong, well-built young man. His face had a gaunt, muscular appearance, aided by high cheekbones and a determined, square chin. He had emerged from adolescence with little trouble, for the usual uncertainty that accompanies the early teens had been mitigated by his singleness of purpose which had provided a secret anchor. He was possessed of, or at least could give the impression of, worldliness, poise and self-assurance. Girls certainly found him attractive.

SUNDAY 28 JULY 1918

. . . Rotten in afternoon from 6–9 hush—censored—blue pencil.

He developed a somewhat austere, dignified manner that could irritate his friends and family. His brother Bert confessed that 'the only time I saw him at a disadvantage was when we tied him to a clothes post and tickled his feet'.

But whatever his outward show, Don was still nursing a childish excitement for all things theatrical and it was now growing to fever-pitch:

MONDAY 9 SEPTEMBER 1918

Buzzed round in morning and saw them unload scenery for Martin Harvey. In afternoon stayed down at Mikado [a local café] for tea and then saw him in 'Cigarette etc.' Gee he was fine, how I should like to be in his company.

and two days later

. . . went to 'David Garrick'. Gee he was better than ever.

On Saturday 14:

Was bad all day with my dam tooth but cycled to Stratford with Edie and saw Shakespeare's house etc. Had a fine time arrived back about seven and had some music.

That following week the Theatre Royal, Nottingham, presented Fred Terry and Julia Neilson in their repertoire of plays and a secret plot was being hatched by Charles Power spurred on by Don. Power had played in the Terry Company in small parts and walk-ons, and knew that, because of the war, there was a grave shortage of actors of any age or qualifications. He suggested that Don write to Terry's manager, Arthur Garrett, and request an interview with Fred Terry himself.

MONDAY 16 SEPTEMBER 1918

Had no sleep because of the . . . tooth. Stayed in all day. In evening went to 'Royal Divorce' at theatre with Cecil. Jolly fine.

TUESDAY 17

Left at 8.30 for Notts. Rode hard with a swollen face and arrived 2.30. Had tea and stood for 'Henry of Navarre'. Oh but what a show—best I've seen and Fred Terry—gee what a coy to be in! Came home fagged.

THURSDAY 19
Wrote to Fred Terry in morning and posted it! Now we shall see.

FRIDAY 20
No reply from Notts.

But on Saturday morning, Don's letter-box vigil was rewarded. Mr. Terry would see Don that afternoon between the matinée and evening performance. 'He must have been in desperate straits to reply to such a letter, but I did not think of that at the time.' Don set off on what was, up to that moment, the greatest adventure of his young life. Every detail of that day was deeply etched in his memory:

It was raining hard and it continued to rain as I pedalled for dear life through the puddles and downpour as if the devil were at my heels. It was a quarter past three when I leant my bicycle in the narrow brick alley leading to the stage-door. The crumpled letter was wet through and water streamed from my saturated clothing. The letter was handed in. I waited in an agony of fear but I was inside a real stage-door. Mysterious figures came and went, there was the sound of high laughter from dressing-rooms above, and a flurry of costumed figures along the corridor; then a little thin figure, whom I afterwards came to know as Spenser, the invaluable, equable-tempered valet of the irascible but lovable Fred, beckoned me along the corridor into a small room; and there at the end of the room, quizzing me with his light blue eyes shining through his pince-nez, his bald head shining in the electric lights which blazed like a fairy palace round his dressing-table, and wrapped in an old dressing-gown, stood the great Fred Terry, my hero of Sir Percy Blakeney and Henry of Navarre.

'Well, young gentleman,' rang out that beautifully modulated voice, 'what can I do for you?'

I stammered out my request that I might be allowed to join his company (it was a speech I had been well schooled in by Power), and that perhaps there might be a chance to play the part of the little Vicomte de Tournai in *The Scarlet Pimpernel*. During this speech I became conscious of the fact that I was dripping water at a considerable rate and was in fact standing in a small pool. Terry was not really listening to me: he was watching the ever-increasing pool of water on the dressing-room carpet. I must have looked like the rat swimming in the pool in *Alice in Wonderland*; I began to flounder and stopped. 'Where in heaven's name have you come from?' he asked. 'Newark,' I replied proudly, 'it's nineteen miles from here'; and then after a pause: 'You see I cycled.' 'God in heaven,' said Terry, turning away from me and looking out of the little window at the still descending rain. . . .

But he gave me the most wonderful smile when he turned round from the window, said his company was full at present, but if I wrote to him at Christmas he would see me in London, and handed me his visiting card. He patted me on the shoulder (he had the most beautiful pair of hands I ever saw on a man), and I was escorted by the imperturbable Spenser to the stage-door to commence my long journey back home. But the rain did not worry me now; I sang most of the way home for I had a great actor's visiting card in my pocket.

In his diary that evening the cryptic entry reads

... went straight to F. Terry. Had a fine talk with him after matinée. Gee he was fine. Now we know something.

But hope of a visit to London was short lived. Unfortunately, but predictably, considering the nineteen miles in the pouring rain, Don was taken ill the next day with a feverish cold. His mother discovered his wet clothing and an interrogation followed. Mr. Woolfitt called for Power and demanded an explanation and Don 'was sternly refused permission and never reached Fred Terry's home on Primrose Hill ... for the moment, escape was barred.'

As 1918 drifted into November, Don was able to record:

SATURDAY 2 NOVEMBER
Good news from Turkey. She has 'caved' in after Austria and signed armistice.

SUNDAY 3 November
Good news from front. Germans retreating. Good biz.

THURSDAY 7 NOVEMBER
Good news from France.

FRIDAY 8 NOVEMBER
Queer rumours about Peace. It wont be long if things go on like this.

MONDAY 11 NOVEMBER

PEACE—PEACE—PEACE
Rag round town in evening. Some game. Thank God for it.

The year ended with another pantomime at Averham, this time *Ali Baba and the Forty Thieves*. Don played the donkey and was warmly praised by the local critics, one of whom wrote:

A notable feature is the splendid acting of Donald Woolfitt whose presentation of the part of the Donkey gives this talented young

actor an opportunity to display his versatility and he takes full
advantage of it. The continuous merriment which his droll acting
evokes demonstrates his success.

VI

During the first Christmas holidays of peace Don worked in his
father's office at the brewery. He found the dull routine stifling. 'How
on earth dad has stuck it all these years beats me, I'm fed up after a
week.' The dreariness of office routine only served to intensify his
longing for a theatrical career; it was on his mind every waking
moment in all its aspects:

MONDAY 13 JANUARY 1919
In morning went for a walk with Mrs. Thompson and I 'un-
bosomed' (shades of Shakespeare) my ambition to her.

TUESDAY 14 JANUARY
Sir Charles Whyndam [Wyndham] died, aged 82 fine old chap.
There's a pattern for anyone in the profession and then blighters
say 'Oh the stage is full of bad men!' etc etc

The apparent reason for this particular observation is that Don was
going to have to face a show-down with his father sooner or later, and
any paragon might be useful to add weight to the argument. 1919 was
to be Don's last year at school; his future would have to be decided,
for better for worse, in the coming months. When the dreaded interview took place, Don recorded it with a mixture of relief and fatalism.

SUNDAY 19 JANUARY
At last. Had a talk to father and *it* came out. It—dad knows of
course, but he laughs at the idea as if I haven't thought it out long
enough—ah well it's out now so whats the odds.

Disapproval came from another quarter, too:

MONDAY 27 JANUARY
Head gave me a lecture about acting. Said I was doing far too much
and that I must drop it until after the summer etc. Spoke to dad and
asked him to go and see Head but napoo. H wants us to take High
School Certif as well this July. That means a month of exams.

TUESDAY 28 JANUARY
Father went to see the Head and told him about my plans–he said 'I
quite expected it'.

Ruefully, Don copied out the following:

> 'Go my son and shut the shutter
> The father to his son did utter
> The shutter's shut the son did mutter
> And I cant shut it any shutter'

and added

Methinks I am a prophet.

However formidable the opposition now ranged against him, Don seemed able to shrug it off, secretly knowing that no power on earth would stop him from becoming a professional actor. To everyone he knew he talked of nothing else; his friends and family were beginning to find it a bore.

SUNDAY 4 MAY
Peet began saying that he wished to God I was never going on the stage and we had a long talk about it. . . . He said I wanted something behind me (admitted) unless I did it for the honour and glory—well—I don't think that.

And a little later in the month, to his aunt:

SUNDAY 25 MAY
. . . we had a long talk on the inevitable subject—my future career.

He began perfunctorily to work for the all-important examination in July but this in no way prevented him from visiting the Nottingham theatre to see Henry Ainley, or as late as 26 June, writing 'and then the inevitable happened. I began "making up"—my brain refused to work.'

But there was one ray of hope: a practical chemistry examination was to be held in London at the Imperial Institute. Don's spirits rose. He was to stay with a school friend, Nelson, who lived in Enfield. Power, having been discharged from the army, 'was back in London, but in rooms and could not accommodate me'.

On 7 July Don travelled to Nottingham to sit the first part of his examination.

Walked up to the University with the vertical breeze up. Applied Maths in the morning. My God what a paper—I only did about two and a half questions on the paper and I don't know if they were right. . . . Afternoon paper just as bad.

On the fourth day it was all over and Don and his friends celebrated by visiting the Theatre Royal.

Saw H. A. Saintsbury* in 'Edmund Kean'—jove what a show—about 5 calls after Act III and ten about at the final. He is simply fine—never seen anyone like him—beats Martin Harvey I think.

The study, the hard, unrewarding slog was temporarily over; but most important he had London to look forward to; it seems to have made a difference in many ways:

SATURDAY 12 JULY

In afternoon we had House matches A v B and C v D. I made more runs in one innings than I ever made in all my cricket at school. 23. In evening did nothing worthy of mention—its just fine to think that all the swotting is nearly over and we are free for nearly a week.

But during the week the Head sent for Don and instructed him that since he was shortly to be in London, he should make an appointment with Messrs. Gabbitas and Thring, the scholastic agents. It appears from this that all concerned with Don's future now took it for granted that he would become a teacher, for the scholastic agents would, it was hoped, be able to find him a suitable vacancy in one of the many private boarding-schools that abounded on the South Coast. Don complied; no one close to him was suspicious of this sudden docility; secretly, 'it seemed to me a better chance of escaping from Newark than any other'.

The following Sunday, 20 July, Don set off for London. It rained hard all day. Power was at King's Cross to meet the Nottingham train and gave his young friend dinner at Reggiori's, an Italian restaurant outside the station.

Don's first visit to the capital was an unqualified success. Although he stayed with the Nelsons in Enfield, he spent most of his time with Power who acted as guide. Don saw all the sights, and even caught a glimpse of Lloyd George at Downing Street; he sat for the science examination but was pessimistic as to the results. On his second day he paid a visit to Messrs. Gabbitas and Thring, 'rather a farce'. He was told there was a vacancy at St. George's, Eastbourne; the salary was £65 per annum, board, lodging and laundry provided. Don wrote to the Headmaster for an appointment. Thus his days were devoted to practical, tiresome affairs; the evenings were quite another matter.

In that week Don visited the theatre five times. On Monday it was the Palladium

Wilkie Bard, Harry Weldon, Marie Novello, Talbot O'Farell etc a topping programme. Came back and had singing.

---

* H. A. Saintsbury (1870–1939), a popular touring actor. He left £494.

On Tuesday he was in ecstasy

> . . . stood for 'Joy Bells'. George R[obey] was just fine—a simple
> roar all the way through and the scenery and dresses were fine—
> caught tube home—after a topping day—oh London! ah me!

Chu Chin Chow with Oscar Asche was next on the list. Don was
running out of superlatives: 'A wonderful show—simply splendid.'
But undoubtedly the highlight of the visit was Robert Loraine's celebrated performance of *Cyrano de Bergerac*. 'A wonderful show,
Loraine was fine and it quite upset me. I thought I was past that.' In
fact, by the time the Convent scene was played, Don 'was in a state of
high romantic excitement, shivering from head to foot; and so well I
remember emerging from the pit-door after the final curtain had fallen
and being violently sick in the roadside.'

The following day, Saturday, he attended the matinée performance
of *Tilly of Bloomsbury* by Ian Hay. It starred Arthur Bourchier, Allan
Aynsworth and Mary Glynne; Don was 'speechless with delight'.
He wrote in his diary that night, 'A fine day and I feel very much indebted to old Power.'

Before returning to Newark on the Monday, Don was summoned
to an interview with the Headmaster of St. George's, Eastbourne. To
his amazement the meeting was to take place under the big clock on
Victoria Station. He presented himself at noon wearing his best suit,
a pair of gloves, a straw hat and a malacca cane. Presently, while
gawping up at the clock, he was hit violently on the back. Don's
boater fell over his eyes, the cane from his hands. A voice said: 'You
must be Woolfitt!' The voice belonged to Mr. Davies, the Headmaster.

> I gathered myself together and found myself facing a short dapper
> grizzled-haired man who shook my hand, asked me if I played
> cricket and football, if the terms were agreeable . . . and told me
> to be at the school on 14 September. He shook my hand once
> again and departed (the entire interview had taken under three
> minutes) leaving me with my malacca cane in one hand and a
> career in the other.

Later that day Don was on his way home to Newark. As he sat on
the train he must have reflected on the dazzling week he had just lived
through: on the one hand the vivid reality of the theatre; on the other
the already half-forgotten 'torture' of the science papers and the brief
charade on Victoria Station. His immediate future did not concern
him; he well knew that he was plotting an elaborate escape route via
the South Downs.

VII

Don wrote in his diary the night before leaving Newark,

> Is there a proverb 'A boy never knows a mother's love until he leaves home'? If not, I think there ought to be one.

That same evening 'Dad settled money matters with me and gave me my bank book etc. A start in life for me now I see.'

The next day, Saturday 20 September 1919, aged seventeen, Don left home. 'Dear old mother very cut up about it I'm afraid.' Her son had mixed emotions, for, sad though he was to be leaving the family circle, he had managed to fit in three days in London before travelling down to Eastbourne. The excitement of the metropolis soon banished the emptiness he may have been feeling but he confided at the end of the first day away from home, 'So now I'm launched in the open sea and my boat is frail.'

Of course he was off to the theatre again. He had one full day left, and in the afternoon saw the first house at the Palladium, thence to Wyndham's.

> Marie Lloyd and Harry Tate both very good indeed—but the former very common . . . to Wyndham's and saw Gerald du Maurier in the Choice—a fine show. Came home by train after a very enjoyable day—now I suppose I settle down.

He supposed wrongly. St. George's, Eastbourne was not unlike in atmosphere Dr. Augustus Fagan's school at Llanabba Castle in Evelyn Waugh's *Decline and Fall*. Don described it as 'a simple school for some forty or fifty boys, mostly sons of London tradesmen, in a barracks of a large house. . . . The food was simple, two hot joints per week, mountains of potatoes and a plethora of rice pudding. The laundry was execrable and I was housed with another master in a small damp cottage by the gates. The staff consisted of two masters, two mistresses, a matron and Davies [the Head]. I taught at one end of the large school-room, the other master at the other.' The other master was Mr. Nunn, shades of Captain Grimes, 'a queer fellow who has been gassed and I am afraid is not quite normal. . . . Nunn began to fidget and bother—has emptied a case of my fags already and a box of matches—don't know whether he imagines me his batman or what.'

Don was required to teach Geometry, Algebra and a little French grammar. He read out the plays of Shakespeare and some Dickens, refereed football matches 'and took a crocodile of boys, properly straw-hatted, to walk on the sea front'.

In contrast to the flat, open lands of Nottinghamshire and Lincolnshire, he found the Sussex countryside and coast provided a wonderful new environment. 'Then walked to Beachy Head over the Downs. Most glorious views I have ever seen in my life, the sea and the cliffs etc oh!!'

It was only a matter of time before he was turning to the theatre again. Before long he was organising a concert party with the staff, the 'Squibs' they called themselves, and one of his fellow-teachers, Sybil Oldershaw, remembers that Don 'was a very keen producer'.

Somehow, although money was short, he managed 'one concert and one theatre each week'. Eastbourne was a good touring date and to the Devonshire Park Theatre came Sybil Thorndike and Matheson Lang, and visits from concert parties, the 'Brownies' with Charles Heslop and Douglas Furber.

Meanwhile Don was finding Mr. Nunn 'the sort of character that is very useful to introduce into a short story'. In his diary he observed:

One night he [Nunn] mentioned that he was very bothered. . . . He then informed me that he was worried no end because a brother of his in the same family had the same initials and was going round the town running bills up in his name, well everyone can see what he means by that game and already one bill has come in.

Nunn did not last long. Don was happy to record: 'Mr. Nunn left the school Thank God really. Left a lot of his things behind—a simply awful man. "Rome was best rid of him I know." '

By October the young schoolmaster was already making arrangements regarding his real future. Inquiries concerning an elocution teacher led him to Mr. Bernard Streatfield who taught at, among other places, the London Guildhall School of Music, mainly as a singer; but he accepted Don as a pupil twice a week. Streatfield began to work on his pupil's flat Nottinghamshire vowels and 'led me gently into the art of proper breath control and relaxation of the vocal cords'. During the holidays Don returned to Newark and 'for two shillings an hour had lessons in broadsword and épée from a regimental sergeant-major'. He could feel that preparations were well under way.

But at year's end, he was depressed and run down; he took to his bed with a temperature of 102°, was told to rest by the doctor and vented his feelings in private: 'the whole world seems to be in a rotten state just now and it will be for some time to come too I am sorry to say.'

THURSDAY 1 JANUARY 1920

Ushered in the New Year with a cold on my chest. A happy New Year to everyone! and may it further my ambition considerably . . .
I feel very fagged but might be worse!

He recovered quickly enough to record that the next night he attended a party and 'When maidens set their caps at you and escort you carefully into stockyards what is a person to do??' The following evening the mood is less triumphant: 'The aforesaid maiden did not behave herself with such utter abandon as the previous evening but mayhap chance had something to say?' His amorous adventures aside, 'the problem ever before me was how to effect an introduction to theatre'. He wrote a letter to Fred Terry, no doubt reminding him of their first interview, and a week later:

> Refusal from Terry so that's another one cancelled—altho there might be a walk on for me about August 9th if I could come up for one, but I must get fixed up definitely before then.

Then, in the week beginning Monday 28 June, Charles Doran and his Shakespearean company visited the Devonshire Park Theatre. Doran was on his first tour in management but was an actor of considerable experience 'as a supporting artist with Oscar Asche and at Stratford-upon-Avon'. Don was enthusiastic: 'Doran simply fine as Shylock—shall certainly go several times more.' True to his word, he enjoyed *The Tempest*, *Julius Caesar* and *Hamlet* ('A wonderful rendering of a wonderful character').

Don saw his chance and decided 'to try again the method which Charles Power had taught me and wrote to Charles Doran for an interview'.

Suddenly, Don's world changed:

THURSDAY 1 JULY
> Two momentous days here. In evening took boys down to 'Twelfth Night'. Interview with Doran. I said two or three pieces for him and we had a fine conversation. Says he'll take me on with him!! Hurrah. Enjoyed the show very much indeed and returned with boys. Dear kids they are too!

The audition had taken place while Doran made up for Jaques in *As You Like It*. Don recited Gratiano's 'Let me play the Fool' speech. The offer was a studentship in the Doran company for the forthcoming autumn tour as assistant stage manager and to walk on. Railway fares were to be paid but nothing more. It was to be a fourteen weeks' tour, preceded by a week of pastoral Shakespeare in St. Augustine's Close, Canterbury.

'Promising to let Doran have an answer by Friday.' Don's understandable excitement clouded the practical issues, most important of which was that he lacked funds; he also had several weeks of term left ahead of him. 'Would my father advance me a little money, I debated in my mind? Would Mr. Davies release me from my teacher's agreement?' On Friday 2nd, Norah was at home when a telegram arrived:

HAVE JOINED CHARLES DORAN'S SHAKESPEARE COMPANY. PLEASE SEND £30.

She remembers her father's consternation but, to his credit, he sent it at once and unconditionally.* Don's diary confirms this:

FRIDAY 2 JULY
Wired Dad to see if he would advance money. Reply in time for my interview. Saw Lake [Doran's manager] and Doran and agreed to one tour without money and then payment. Returned and Davo [Davies] told me he thought I was very foolish—trust him 'cos he's losing me that's why!

The next day he signed the contract. Shortly afterwards he received a stern letter from his father, perhaps envisaging a series of never-ending demands from his vagabond son, telling him 'that I could expect no more having thrown away my chances'.

But Don brushed the rebuke aside; he was in heaven. Before he left the school to begin rehearsals in London, the boys of St. George's clubbed together and presented him with a small packet containing a briar pipe and the note: 'Dear Sir, We are giving you this pipe because you are leaving. Yours truly, The Fifth Form.' It would be a very long time before anyone called him 'sir' again.

---

* In *First Interval*, Don wrote: 'He replied that he would send me the money, but awaited my letter of explanation.'

CHAPTER FOUR

Inheritance

How green you are and fresh in this old world.
—King John

I

IN 1920, and for a good many years before that, the acting of Shakespeare was the special preserve of actor-managers. The Old Vic was in its infant stages, learning to crawl in the Waterloo Road; the subsidised theatre would have to wait for another war to achieve credibility.

Actor-management had a long and honourable tradition in the English theatre, but its greatest flowering was during the reign of Queen Victoria. Don missed being born into that reign by fifteen months, but as a personality he belonged very deeply to that age, for it was to those standards, to those traditions, that he consciously adhered. Throughout his life he maintained a sincere and loving admiration for the Victorians, nursing a euphoric nostalgia for, as it seemed to him, a well-ordered and flourishing society. In that sense, he may be said to have been born out of his time.

But his talent as an actor was, paradoxically, timeless; although it was often to be wilfully shrouded by him in the trappings of Victoriana, the tradition in which he acted was far older, far cruder, far more profound. The tracing of his theatrical lineage will be done later. To understand him, however, as a theatrical creature, and in another special sense as an actor-manager, we must glance now at the theatre to which he owed his allegiance.

1902, the year of Don's birth, was to be Henry Irving's last year at the Lyceum Theatre. At the matinee on 19 July:

For the last time Irving led Ellen Terry forward by the hand to acknowledge the applause of the Lyceum audience. The eyes of the 'public's respectful loyal and loving servant' were glistening with tears.

Three years later Irving died but the theatre which he had helped to create still prospered and very much on the lines he had laid down.

It has been argued by actors and other interested parties that Irving did 'the profession' a great disservice by conferring upon it a respectability it did not deserve, and certainly had no right to expect. With his knighthood and many other honours, Sir Henry became the first actor to belong, by right, to the Establishment of his day and he accepted the honour, he said, not for himself but for his Art. Before Irving, the actor was nearly a social outcast; in Charles Churchill's *Apology*:

> The strolling tribe; a despicable race.

Or, for that matter, Horace in *Satires*:

> Beggars, actors, buffoons, and all that breed.

When the Queen touched Irving's shoulders with her sword, she inadvertently decapitated the rogue and vagabond.

Irving it was who made a virtue of 'good taste' in the theatre. To attract the 'intellectual and middle-class public', he had found it necessary to eliminate much that he considered vulgar and in so doing confined the actor's art to limits compatible with that society's reverence for propriety.

When he replied to a congratulatory address signed by more than four thousand fellow-players on the occasion of his knighthood, Irving pledged 'to work with a more strenuous endeavour for the well-being of our calling and the honour of our art'. With those words he raised acting from a mere profession to a vocation and surrounded himself with a mystical aura, a priestly aestheticism, so that when he died his disciples talked of 'the mantle of Irving' and speculated upon whom it would fall.

It fell, in fact, on no one; it was shared. Sir Squire Bancroft (who always referred to his wife as 'Her Ladyship'), Sir Charles Wyndham, Sir John Hare, Sir Herbert Beerbohm Tree, Sir Johnston Forbes-Robertson and Sir Frank Benson were the next half-dozen actors to receive the accolade and it was they, in styles that varied from pure lyricism in the case of Forbes-Robertson to the unashamed flamboyance of Tree, who would guide the theatre into the twenties when naturalism, as practised by Sir Gerald du Maurier, took centre stage and the golden sceptre was replaced by the silver cigarette case.

The band of knighted players, all now of course highly respectable, were actor-managers. That is to say they financed, chose and organised a theatrical company which was dedicated to performing plays in which the actor-manager had the best part. Paternalism was at the heart of the actor-manager system. The supporting players were expected to conform to the rules of the family and the first rule was a proper deference to Father both on and off the stage. In return Father took upon himself all the burdens of a conscientious breadwinner with undisputed authority over the children. Discipline was strict but the rewards were great: security of employment, varied parts and the opportunity to watch and learn.

A myth has been fostered that supporting players in these companies did not have to be especially talented so long as they behaved themselves and did as they were told. This would be quite unfair. Irving surrounded himself with a first-class company, many of whom went on to rival him in reputation. Tree had a fine record, as did Wyndham; and Benson over a long period gave work to some of the best actors in England. Nevertheless, it was not the done thing for a satellite to shine too brightly; a good notice for a small-part player was hardly, if ever, welcomed, not even by the small-part player himself; others had been dismissed for much less. Advancement in the profession was not achieved overnight by sudden bursts of brilliance; rather was it a painstaking ascent, step by step, observing always the strict hierarchical structure inherent in such companies, where actors of a certain standing were contracted for a range of parts commensurate with their status.

The actor-managers had two arenas. The first and most important was London where, if they were lucky, they had their own theatre. The second was the provinces, and the Prince of Provincial Shakespearean Managers was Sir Frank Benson, in many ways the archetype of all actor-managers; in fact, he was known to his company as 'Pa'.

F. R. Benson (Winchester and New College) had served his apprenticeship with Irving, playing Paris to 'The Chief's' Romeo in 1882, but as an actor-manager, Benson was, throughout his career, deeply committed to the provinces. The actors he employed included Henry Ainley, Harcourt Williams, Oscar Asche and Matheson Lang; they were proud to be known as Bensonians.

Benson's love of sport was legendary and stories abound; it was said, affectionately, that his company was engaged more for its sporting prowess than its dramatic gifts. An actor, the tale goes, once received a telegram from Pa which read: 'Can you play Rugby week beginning November 3rd. F. R. Benson.'

This placed the actor in a quandary: should he travel north, or learn his lines in *The Merry Wives of Windsor*, or start training as a wing three-quarter?

Benson had an illustrious career. Both C. E. Montague and James Agate accounted him a magnificent Richard II, and a fine Hamlet, a part he played until the age of 72. Of another of his performances,

Agate wrote: 'I have seen one first-class Macbeth and one only—Benson. Benson was a superb Henry V and an exquisite Richard II, and his Thane was a result of adding the two together.'

But by 1920, the year Don joined Doran, Benson was already sixty-two, the ageing leader of a theatre that was fast fading, its edges frayed. The London critics, like superior interior decorators, treated it with a certain condescension, for decorators are only interested in externals.

'Poor players or begging friars,' Benson said, 'we go up and down the length and breadth of the land . . . that the country may never go without an opportunity of seeing Shakespeare played by a company dedicated to his service.' 'Dedicated,' 'service,'—these words were at the true heart of Benson's mission, not to speak of the extraordinary training ground he provided for two generations of actors, enriching their art with the traditions from the past. The major role in creating the theatre at Stratford-upon-Avon was played by Benson and in concluding this brief assessment of his actor-management, it will be well to quote his biographer, J. C. Trewin:

> They have celebrated Benson now in a memorial window at Stratford-upon-Avon; but there should be a memorial tablet to him in every theatre . . . where he was accustomed to return year after year in the classic repertory.

The provincial theatre of England had then a life of its own and was not on the whole fed by the metropolis. Admittedly, there would be the Grand Tours of the London actor-managers, taking with them several plays to be presented in repertoire; there were too the Number One, Number Two and Number Three touring companies who would present recent West End commercial successes, revivals, romantic dramas, each on a different circuit, categorised according to size. The provincial theatre, on its own behalf, provided entertainment for the Lancashire and Yorkshire 'smalls'—towns and villages too insignificant for the bigger managements—the Welsh mining villages, the hamlets of County Durham and Northumberland; there were melodrama companies, Shakespearean companies, musical comedy companies, all crossing and criss-crossing the British Isles, all changing trains at Crewe on Sundays. Never was there so much theatrical activity, never so much exuberance or vitality. The truly popular entertainment was the Music Hall, which abounded with artists who toured week after week, year after year, perfecting perhaps one routine which their audiences loved and welcomed.

Into this hurly-burly, sometimes serving the highest ideals of man, sometimes not, young Don Woolfitt now entered. He was not just a young man alight with personal ambition: he genuinely worshipped

Shakespeare; he believed in Irving and Benson; he was convinced that he had answered a vocation; the words 'dedication' and 'service' were part of an incantation he understood. His career was to be played out against this backcloth and he never noticed that the back-cloth needed renewing from time to time. By force of circumstances, Don's first professional steps were taken through the unfashionable stage-door, into a theatre where 'good taste' was equated with effeminacy, where the *mise-en-scène* and supporting players were secondary to the leading man. In this theatre, he played out his professional life; it was a theatre sniffed at disdainfully by the theatrical Establishment, snug and cosy in London; it was labelled vulgar and second-rate. It may have been both those things, but nowhere better than in the unfashionable theatre were the words 'service' and 'dedication' understood. The provincial life of Britain was greatly enriched by its existence. And it is worth repeating that Don's extraordinary gift for acting on the grand scale transcended time and again the setting he chose to give it, which is a measure of the gift itself.

If, from his family, he inherited nothing theatrical, then it was from the society into which he was born, to which he belonged, that he inherited a vast, ready-made theatrical tradition which was to provide him with all the advantages he could want and, like any abundance, some of the disadvantages, too. His talent was a thing apart.

II

So it was, in a state of some excitement, that the eighteen-year-old ex-schoolmaster made arrangements for a place to live in London during the brief rehearsal period for his first professional engagement.

A school friend had an aunt, a Mrs. Madge Merrett, who kept a boarding-house in Mortlake and she agreed to take Don in. She 'kept a raffish Bohemian household of some seven or eight lodgers consisting of her brother, a violinist, . . . two or three giggling secretaries, a teacher of elocution, a business man, . . . and an effete Australian.' To this colourful group would now be added a young actor, one for whom Mrs. Merrett provided a London *pied-à-terre* for many years. 'She moved frequently from district to district, from Bloomsbury to Brixton and the poorer districts of West London, selling a little furniture each time. . . .' Don adored this short, round little woman with her infectious, high-pitched laugh. 'She was a twentieth-century Mistress Quickly.' Thus, with accommodation suitably befitting his new profession, he presented himself at the first rehearsal of Mr. Charles Doran's Shakespearean Company at the Jewish Girls' Club, London.

Charles Doran had been born in the city of Cork in 1887 and

educated there. He made his first appearance with Frank Benson's company in Belfast and later rejoined the company at the Lyceum Theatre for one of their rare London seasons in 1900. He played Captain MacMorris in *Henry V*. He had an unspectacular career as a supporting actor to the Terrys, to H. B. Irving ('The Chief's' son) and to Oscar Asche and Lily Brayton. After much touring both in England and abroad, there followed London engagements, but not of any major importance. In 1920, however, aged thirty-three, Doran had gone into management, forming his own Shakespearean company and playing the parts he had not previously been allowed to play under the management of others. His repertoire included Hamlet, Shylock, Prospero, Petruchio, Falstaff and Henry V. Like many actor-managers, he presumably considered his own range to be unlimited, doubtless believing the old actor's adage: 'If ye can play the Dane, laddie, ye can play 'em all.' He was short and stocky and had about him a vague facial resemblance to an overfed Henry Irving.*

That summer of 1920, after six months' touring, Doran briefly re-rehearsed the company in London before journeying to Canterbury for the so-called 'Pastoral Week of Shakespeare', which meant playing in St. Augustine's Close, out of doors.

Don was now to receive his first impressions of life in a touring company, that enclosed society of professional actors with their own private language, their private jokes, their generosity and jealousy, pettiness and grandeur. It was to be a way of life he loved from the first.

Because most of the actors were already familiar with their roles, rehearsals were perfunctory. Nevertheless, Don watched every move, listened to every word. It must be appreciated that he was not yet a fully-fledged member of the company, but rather in the position of an apprentice, in his case a serious, conscientious student driven by a fervent determination to act, and to succeed.

On the Sunday, he attended his first train call, the assembling of the company on the station platform in readiness for the journey, and was bewitched by 'the glorious exhibitionism, the flavour of the circus parade, and the general exuberance of the actor in transit. The arrival in Canterbury, the searching for the theatrical quarter, the bargaining with the landlady for the bed-sitting room which I shared with another actor, were all new and exciting details.' There followed that first thrill of seeing where they would perform, receiving their costumes from the wardrobe mistress, and having to dress in a classroom for the costume parade, followed by the dress rehearsal.

---

* In the last years of his life he could be seen in the Green Room Club, forever doing sums involving large amounts of money on the backs of envelopes. He died in 1964, aged seventy-seven, and left £36,037.

The company opened with *Julius Caesar*, Doran as Brutus. Don 'howled with the rest of the Roman mob to the full extent of my lungs', and then hurriedly changed into the costume of a Roman centurion, one of three who were to carry the dead Brutus from the plains of Philippi.

My helmet was large but an old actor hissed: 'Put your grease towel inside it'; I added an enormous brown crêpe-hair moustache which was totally out of period and none too secure on my shining cheeks. Thus accoutred and looking more like a music-hall edition of a fireman than a Roman, I took up my position whilst the noble Brutus expired. Then, as rehearsed, I stepped forward to hoist the defunct tragedian on my shoulders. Whilst lifting him up a far from Roman voice hissed at me: 'For God's sake mind my toupee.' I had not until that moment realised that our Brutus was not the possessor of a full head of hair, and in a flash I knew that the whole dignity of this final procession of seven majestic figures depended on me. So taking the by no means slim Brutus on my right shoulder, I proceeded to pat the toupee gently with my right hand whilst with my left I clutched firmly some yards of Roman tunic and a large portion of human flesh beneath it; and thus did I make my first long exit from the professional stage to slow and solemn music.

The rest of the week was devoted to alternating *Julius Caesar* with *The Tempest* and *The Merchant of Venice*. Nothing further untoward occurred except that Portia, on delivering 'it droppeth as the gentle rain from heaven', was greeted by a deluge. 'It was clear,' wrote Don, 'that pastoral Shakespeare had its drawbacks.'

When the week was over, Don returned home to Newark to face his parents for the first time since taking the plunge. They were 'perplexed and worried'. Two of his aunts were more severe, and warned him that he must expect the fiery furnace as his just desserts. But Don's resolve could not now be shaken, for in the weeks that had just passed, he had glimpsed the gates of heaven; neither parental disapproval nor the threat of hell could prevent him from wanting to enter them.

Soon he was back in London rehearsing for the tour proper which was to open later at Bridlington. Two new productions were to be added to Doran's repertoire: *The Taming of the Shrew* and *Macbeth*.

'There is, and always will be, an element of sheer luck in an actor's life,' Don wrote years later. 'It is not in his power to command recognition but only to seize the opportunity when it comes, and such a slice of luck, pure luck, came my way on my very first week inside a theatre.'

On the Wednesday, at Bridlington, he was greeted at the stage door by a distraught stage manager.

'You,' he screamed, 'do you know the second grave-digger and the second player in *Hamlet*?' I said I was doubtful. 'Well, anyway, you play them tonight and tomorrow night. Reginald Jarman has been taken to hospital with diphtheria. . . . On Friday you will play Biondello in *The Taming of the Shrew*, on Saturday afternoon Sylvius in *As You Like It*, and on Saturday evening Ross in *Macbeth*. Here are the books with the cuts. Rehearse now and go home and study.'

It is the kind of nightmare that young actors welcome with all their hearts. Every available moment of the day, Don studied the lines in an intense, feverish heat. As is usual in theatrical crises of this nature, his colleagues were more than helpful, and did all they could to encourage the young man who had found himself thrust into 'the glorious company of speaking actors in one fell swoop'. When the time came for the evening performance, willing hands helped him to make up, dress, adjust the wigs that did not fit him.

Despite the terror of the occasion, despite the feeling that his voice did not belong to him and that, unaccountably, the opening lines of *How They Brought the Good News From Ghent To Aix* were pounding ceaselessly through his brain, Don survived and did well. In that week, and the one that followed at the Theatre Royal, York, he played Second Player, Second Gravedigger, Biondello, Sylvius, Ross, Sebastian, Octavius Caesar and Marullus. As a baptism of fire it was not unusual for those days;* by contemporary standards it simply could not happen, for there are not the companies geared to so tightly-packed a repertoire.

Doran was pleased with his young apprentice, and sent for him to explain that the salary of the absent principal was to be halved and that Don would receive two pounds per week.

With what high hopes now he faced the future! Not only was he doing what he most wanted, but was also being paid for it. 'I was a Real Live Actor at last,' he wrote, 'and grew my hair very long.'

III

Real Live Actors were obliged, in those days, to provide for themselves certain necessary equipment. Out of his meagre resources, Don set about acquiring black and brown tights, black and brown shoes,

---

* Sir Henry Irving in his first three years in the theatre (1856–1859) portrayed four hundred and twenty-eight characters.

two ballet shirts, a half-flow wig, grease paints and a small hamper or skip, which the theatre baggage man transported to his rooms and collected for sixpence a week—if required. Don also bought a plain black exercise book into which he could paste his press cuttings. Each week the local reviews were carefully preserved, and headed with the name of the newspaper and the date. Wherever the name Donald Woolfitt appeared, and gratifyingly it appeared frequently, the pertinent passage was underlined in ink. He kept these press books, the good notices and the bad, until the last year of his life. They provide a fascinating record and, in the early stages, not only of Don's career, but of others, giving fleeting glimpses of a host of young hopefuls whose names are now familiar to playgoers: Cecil Parker, Barbara Everest, Edith Sharpe, Norman Shelley, Hilton Edwards (of Gate Theatre, Dublin, fame), Abraham Sofaer were all with that first Doran company. And, among others, the critic of the *Cork Examiner* on 18 December 1921 was gracious enough to note that 'Mr. Ralph Richardson was an efficient Lorenzo'.

Don himself was regularly praised for his performances in those roles already mentioned. It became apparent that he had a decided gift for comedy and, as is true of many young actors who are not blessed with outstanding physical grace, was far more at ease hiding behind an eccentric character than being exposed to the public unadorned as a conventional lover or bloodless juvenile. He confessed later, '. . . and although I studied and watched the great tragic roles, it was not then within my compass, or indeed my ambition, to essay them'.

Don's energy, which, when properly harnessed in later years, was to unleash a mighty histrionic power, was at first expressed in a slightly uncontrolled, perhaps uncontrollable, exuberance and vitality on stage. The *Belfast Telegraph* critic observed: 'The clown, Young Gobbo, was rompingly, quizzically acted by Mr. Donald Woolfitt.'

And the *Northern Whig and Belfast News*: 'Sir Toby Belch and Sir Andrew Aguecheek had inimitable impersonators in Mr. Arthur Young and Mr. Donald Woolfitt respectively, although the latter was on occasions inclined to exaggerate the part.'

But Don was learning and working hard at his new craft. He was discovering that Shakespeare 'was an exacting but very rewarding taskmaster. . . . Above all I found the joy . . . in the music and beauty of both his prose and verse.'

Possessed of a naturally powerful voice, he was now learning how to use it with better effect in the more lyrical passages. It had, even then, an extraordinary range, being able at one moment to plummet to the lower bass register and at the next to swoop to the nasal, almost falsetto, high notes, while always maintaining resonance. The flat Nottinghamshire vowels were being ironed out slowly but surely, and he was developing a pure, forthright diction that was totally without any kind of affectation. Once he became an actor, Don never took formal voice lessons; he acquired self-knowledge of his instrument by trial and error, and, of course, by nightly practice in performance that, with the passage of time, was to strengthen his vocal cords sufficiently to withstand, in the future, the enormous strain of the English classical repertoire. He was acquiring many skills, not least the ability to speak at speed, a necessary attribute for Biondello in *The Shrew*, with his fast speech just before the wedding of Petruchio and Katherine. The art of movement and of dancing he picked up as he went along, but there was another practical side to touring that had to be learned: the 'get-in' and 'get-out' of scenery, the setting of lights, the folding and packing of costumes and properties week after week, theatre after theatre.

Doran recognised Don's worth both as a useful young actor and as an enthusiastic assistant stage manager; he engaged him for a further spring tour and raised his weekly salary to three pounds. 'On this,' Don recorded, 'I could live easily.'

Life on tour never failed to excite Don. He loved the closed world, the self-containment, the exclusiveness of the company; he loved train-calls and the constant change of scenery. Touring provided a framework for the restlessness that Don had inherited from the Tomlinsons, his mother's family.

It was undoubtedly true that the touring company proved to be, in Don's words, 'the travelling academies for the student,' offering more freedom than any university or college. In the summer the actors formed a cricket XI; in the winter they played hockey. There were opportunities to explore the beauties of England on long country walks when rehearsals permitted, there were museums and galleries to be visited and, on the south coast, concerts where one could listen to fine music. '. . . and always the excitement of the next town to be visited and the experience of facing a different audience each week in six or seven plays by Shakespeare.'

Perhaps best of all, Don loved theatrical digs. Even when leading his own company, he rarely stayed in hotels. He preferred the private house, run by that special breed, now almost extinct, the theatrical landlady who provided bed, breakfast, lunch, tea and dinner after the performance in return for astonishingly little payment. When the towns to be visited were notified to touring actors, the first thing they did was to write off to their landladies, reserving accommodation. A touring actor's digs list was a valuable, closely guarded document and Don began his in 1921 and maintained it scrupulously for many years to come, commenting on the quality, the price and any special features. In Worcester, he adjudged Mrs. Smith's establishment as

POOR (SMELLS)

The Villa Marina in Douglas, Isle of Man was

DAMN BAD

But worst of all, in Swansea,

BAD (BUGS)

However, for the most part, they were

GOOD

or

V. GOOD (BATH)

He loved the hours after the performance. Tired, but still exhilarated, the actors would repair to the local public house nearest the theatre, where autographed photographs of distinguished visiting artists often lined the walls. There, they would down their pints, discuss the performance, tell their favourite stories and then disperse into the night, back to Mrs. McKergo, to Miss Flake, to Mrs. Bent. After supper, they sat before the fire in the sitting-room reserved for them, and nightly held 'the long discussions on the state of the drama and the art of interpretation'. It was an attractive life for any young man after the rigours of a conventional upbringing. It bred companionship, fierce friendships, fiercer jealousies, cliques, romances, gossip, and to anyone of an energetic temperament, was never dull. Don rejoiced in it. 'I have struck gold,' he wrote.

But he nearly lost all on two occasions.

Doran's scenery had been used by the late Henry Herbert in South Africa. It was delivered in two consignments, the second arriving when the tour was already under way, and had to be stored under the stage without close examination. The consignment included the sets and properties for *Hamlet*. On the first night of their use, during Ophelia's burial, Don, as 2nd Gravedigger, removed the purple pall as the coffin was lowered into the grave-trap. On the lid of the box, facing Claudius and his Queen, was the printed label: 'PICKFORDS. NOT WANTED ON THE VOYAGE.' Don burst out laughing, or 'corpsed' in theatre slang, and the moment the scene was over, was dismissed from the company; minutes later, he was reinstated.

The second occasion was at Newport, during *Macbeth*. A full house saw one of Macbeth's servants rush on with a lighted torch after the murder of Duncan. Unfortunately, an electrician, thinking everyone had passed, pulled tight a cable across the entrance. Don caught his foot in the cable, hurtled through the air to land at Macbeth's feet, his wig having been set alight by the blazing torch.

> 'Who can be wise, amaz'd, temperate and furious,
> Loyal and neutral in a moment? No man:
> Th' expedition of my violent love
> Outran the pauser reason. Here lay Duncan. . . .'

The audience rocked with laughter. Someone seized Don's wig and stamped out the flames. After the scene, with tears of shame running down his cheeks, he was called into the presence of the irate tragedian. Again he was dismissed, again the dismissal was rescinded. Presumably, when the 'pauser reason' usurped the actor-manager's anger, he realised that he would be hard put to find so willing a recruit as the unfortunate Woolfitt at such short notice, in Newport on a Saturday night.

It was true, too, that Doran regarded the young man with genuine affection. Early in 1921, Don was sent for and examined as to the desirability of Newark as a suitable date for the company to play. Don replied that he thought the people of Newark would give Doran a fitting welcome. In due course, the Palace Theatre was booked; on 4 April the company played *The Merchant of Venice*. The *Newark Advertiser* observed that 'Mr. Woolfitt, the promising Newark actor, made him (Young Gobbo) an important personality in the play'.

Doran behaved with great generosity towards the most junior member of his company. After the performance, he stepped forward to make his curtain speech, so beloved by all actor-managers. The *Newark Herald* reported him as saying:

> It is also gratifying to see the way in which one of your own townsmen, Mr. Donald Woolfitt, who has played Lancelot Gobbo this evening, has been received. (Applause.) Mr. Woolfitt has allowed me to play Shylock this evening—(laughter)—but at the same time I have held the threat out to Mr. Woolfitt that if we do not do well at Newark he will be hanged at the next town. (Laughter.) But joking apart, I am pleased to say that Mr. Woolfitt shows every promise of becoming a good comedian, as his performance and your applause has indicated.

Don glowed with pride. In his diary he was pleased to record that the company 'drew good houses all week. Great reception.' He lived that week at home, and he commented:

> Newark-on-Trent.
> Good digs for this week. Landlady does your washing for you and cheaply too!!!

What endeared Don to his employer was the young man's un-disguised enthusiasm. Don displayed an enjoyment of acting that knew no bounds. Given William, the yokel in *As You Like It*, Don, after a long rehearsal, patted himself on the back: 'William was a scream!'

But to many of his fellow actors, both then and later, this love of performing was suspect. His Doran colleagues found him likeable however, even if he regarded himself rather too seriously. Certainly, the more lighthearted of his fellows, and those too old to care any more, viewed his keenness with suspicion, and decided that he was remote and often pompous. It was difficult for some of them to appreciate the depth of his feeling for the theatre, the genuineness of his dedication. He believed firmly that self-discipline was an essential ingredient for success, and this was also a handicap to being easily accepted as 'one of the boys'.

From his diary:

17 FEBRUARY 1921

Got really blotto for the first and last time. Know how far I can go.

There was, too, a prudish side to his nature.

19 SEPTEMBER

Wrote letters in evening whilst Jerry took a bird out or rather a lady—can't one degenerate into loose expressions.

Although this was expressed half-jokingly, he genuinely disliked be-having incorrectly. But what his fellows observed in him was a young man driven by intense personal ambition and the will to succeed at any price, a brooding, introspective figure who seemed only to come alive when performing before an audience. All this was true, but the external show concealed a sensitive youth, desperately unsure, his pride easily bruised, and one who lacked the ability always to laugh at himself. Inwardly, he would excuse all his shortcomings by pleading the seriousness, the single-mindedness with which he approached his art. He expressed that seriousness, those youthful longings, those inner conflicts in a short essay written in the back of his 1920 diary:

BY THE SEA

Isn't the sea just like human nature, ever restless, ever trying to do as much as it can, doing very little and failing miserably. A wave is just like a being. It begins far out at sea, with hundreds of others, just as a little ripple, laughing, content and with nothing big about it. Then it increases in ideas, its top begins to rise and it crests and foams towards its goal: the shore. Sometimes it spends itself before it reaches its destination, flounders into a mass of foam and pushes other waves on and helps them but it fades away and is never found or noticed again. Then many waves all join and make one huge array that takes the beach by storm and looking very fine for a period it throws itself away. But where has it gone? It made very little impression on the goal it was aiming for. Sometimes they bring up valuable things as a human being searching in the sea of knowledge tears out fragments and offers them to the world—oh but what a mass of baser material he brings up too just as the sea does and casts it on the goal which makes it all the harder for the other waves to reach their end. It's a failure, just as life is a failure! Look at the sea, notice how many big waves there are compared to the hundreds of smaller ones that are never even looked at—oh what is life? is it a farce—is it something real or a jest of the Gods?

Certainly by July 1922 he must have decided that life was, after all, real, for the Doran company was temporarily disbanded and Don found himself faced for the first time with the worst reality that confronts an actor: he was out of work.

SUNDAY 2 JULY 1922
Finished with Chas. Doran after two years work.
Arrived town 1.0
Lunch with Norah.

No doubt brother and sister discussed Don's plans for finding work. Knowing no one in the London theatre who could lend him a helping hand, and after only two years' experience with one management, the prospects could not be regarded as bright.

For the next two weeks Don 'trudged the staircases of the agents with hundreds of other artists' only to discover that, to his dismay, he was being labelled a Shakespearean actor which was, to most London agents, a decidedly limited field of employment. It is an old theatrical adage that the second job is the most difficult to secure; it was certainly proving true in Don's case. He was not a juvenile in the accepted sense of the word, that is to say he was not handsome enough, or indeed, for those days, gentleman enough to be cast as the tennis-playing son of an upper-middle-class suburban household, so beloved of West End dramatists. Even then, the idea of Don and French windows did not somehow go together; he was built to enter through archways.

His savings were fast running out; he allowed himself two shillings a day for breakfast, transport to and from the West End, and a late evening meal at Mortlake, where Mrs. Merrett continued to provide him with reasonably priced shelter.

So, in mid-July he returned to Newark for a short holiday and, presumably, to alleviate the pressure on his meagre resources. Although in his autobiography he wrote, 'I dared not go home for that would have been to admit defeat,' but, from his diary:

TUESDAY 18 JULY 1922
Arrived home 6.52
Very happy.

Don, as the above suggests, was clearly pleased to be back in New Balderton; perhaps he shielded his pride with airy talk of future engagements. His mother, like all mothers, was little concerned with her son's pride. She was glad to have him home, to feed him three decent meals a day, repair his clothes, and generally see that he was properly cared for.

During his short stay in Newark, he wrote countless letters for work. He tried Fred Terry once more and journeyed to London at the end of the month for an interview.

FRIDAY 28 JULY
Returned to town for appointment with Terry.
Refused walk-on.

In refusing Terry, he was doing his best to hold out for the opportunity of taking a step up the ladder, to find work with a company superior to Doran's; he was to be sadly disappointed.

Mr. Naylor Gimson, described as 'a Hebrew music-hall artist', needed an actor to play the part of an Irish policeman in a fifteen-minute farce entitled *Pollock's Predicament*. The tag-line of the sketch tells all: 'Rebecca, if ever I am unfaithful to you again may all the pictures fall off the wall'—whereupon all the pictures fell off the wall, and down came the curtain.

Because he had learned the trick of arriving at the agents' office before anyone else, Don was offered the part. He was now too short of funds to refuse. He rehearsed for five days and opened at the Empire Theatre, Chatham.

Don did his best to look on the bright side. After all, here was another new world to discover, 'the world of acrobats, singers, carnival acts and front-cloth comedians, bustle and blaring brass'. In this milieu, so far removed from the statelier atmosphere of Shakespearean actors, Don played and stage-managed for five weeks. During the last week, at the East Ham Palace, the place at the top of the bill was occupied by Bransby Williams, the celebrated impersonator of Dickens's characters, and an old friend of Naylor Gimson. Williams was a popular entertainer. His act began with him making up in full view of the audience, which was followed by recitations from Dickens, changing his make-up for each character. Don watched and learned. He also noticed, with some puzzlement, unusual interest shown by Williams in the sketch, for he watched it from the wings for three performances. On the Friday night, his motive was revealed. When Don went to call Gimson for the second house, Williams emerged from his own dressing room made up and dressed exactly like the Jewish comic. 'There was a rush on to the stage of two identical figures. Gimson was shouting, "No, Bransby, you can't do it," but Williams answered that he knew the sketch intimately.' The action was very fast—the set contained five doors which were in constant use—and Don never knew with whom he played the sketch that night; nor did the audience.

Just as this engagement was coming to an end, Don was sent for by an agent and offered a tour with Alexander Marsh and his wife, Carrie Bailie, in a repertoire of Shakespeare, to play some of his old parts. In September, he travelled to Ipswich with his small hamper of properties and make-up to begin one week of rehearsals for a repertoire of six plays.

On reflection, Don accounted Marsh a competent actor. 'A man of small physique, good voice, and unbounded enthusiasm.' He had played leads with Frank Benson and, whereas in Doran's company the actors had been encouraged to make broad effects, Marsh insisted on a greater attention to detail, good inventive business, 'and a more subtle searching for true characterisation'. Marsh, however, possessed one further asset: his wife, Carrie Bailie. Of her, Don wrote that she 'had great quality and should have been a leading lady in London; her Rosalind, Katherina and Paulina were among the best I have ever seen. She had gaiety and wit, and at that time was undoubtedly the finest actress it had been my fortune to encounter.'

Don's range of parts was extended to include Salanio, Rosencrantz, Demetrius, and his first villain, Tybalt. He had now to unlearn many of the effects he had acquired with Doran, to distort his body less, to discover the value of relaxation and to keep his head up and his body erect. In short, he was learning to be more economical as a performer; he was also learning repose on stage, and it would never come easily to him.

The Marsh company played smaller theatres than Doran, so Don was exposed to yet more of the British Isles: to the north, the mining villages of Durham and Northumberland; to the south, the Channel Islands.

Marsh advertised a mammoth repertoire of forty plays, but in fact prepared no more than fourteen. Even so, the list was formidable enough: in the six months that Don remained with the company, the repertoire comprised *Romeo and Juliet, Hamlet, The Merchant of*

Venice, The Taming of the Shrew, As You Like It, Twelfth Night, The Winter's Tale, A Midsummer Night's Dream, Macbeth, Julius Caesar, The Tempest, in addition to *David Garrick, The Bells* and *The Orphans of The Storm.*

Marsh's bluff was called on one occasion when a certain school chose from the advertised list Sheridan Knowles's verse play *Virginius*, made famous by Macready. 'Consternation reigned. No one but Marsh had ever played it.' The company made a brave try to study the turgid verse, but eventually rebelled. Finally, Marsh's manager 'threw himself at the mercy of a stern headmistress', and a performance of *Romeo and Juliet* was given instead.

These early, formative years were crucial to Don's development, not so much as an actor, but as a theatrical figure. True, he was gaining a knowledge of Shakespeare in what he always considered the best method: playing the plays. His prodigious memory stored up not only his own lines, but also all the others as well. He was entering into an intimate relationship with the intricacies of Shakespearean language, and he grew to deplore the intrusion of business that could not be justified by the text, or the injudicious cutting of the plays to support intellectual theories put forth by scholars and that new band of theatrical creatures, directors. The distortion of the balance of the plays, as practised by many an actor-manager, could always be justified by historical tradition, for the history of these great plays was, more often than not, the history of the great actors who performed them. And it was by acting in the plays that Don's instinct learnt to sniff out the very heart of the drama, to seize on those tensions which, when projected, brought the characters vividly to life.

But it is the other side of the coin, the purely theatrical side, that has to be considered and there were three distinct lessons for this young, eager student to absorb.

Night after night, be it Doran or Marsh, Don would see the actor-manager step forward to make his curtain speech. Night after night, theatre after theatre, they would repeat the phrases so beloved by Henry Irving. Doran, for example, confessed to the Bournemouth audience that his most cherished ambition was 'to keep the best alive of our drama'. At Worcester, he was 'serving the genius of the greatest poet-dramatist who has ever lived'. In Folkestone, Doran 'pointed out that they were all animated in the desire to educate the nation in what were undoubtedly the works of England's greatest playwright'. Marsh, in Kidderminster, was 'the public's humble and respectful servant' whose chief aim was 'to take Shakespeare to every corner of our beloved realm'. The sense of higher purpose thus projected brushed off on young Don, and it must be remembered that whether or not from motives of personal aggrandisement, whether or not every actor-manager imagined there was a knighthood in his knapsack, these men performed an inestimable service to the community. The fact was they *did* take Shakespeare into every corner of the British Isles; they gave people who would otherwise have been neglected the opportunity of seeing and listening to a most important part of their cultural heritage.

The second lesson was loyalty. The closed world of the touring company engendered, amongst the actors themselves, a fierce loyalty to the management. In practice it meant that between themselves they could criticise and complain to their hearts' content, but let an outsider once, just once, make disparaging remarks, and the faithful would spring to the company's defence like feudal serfs. Don was endowed with a great sense of loyalty; in him, it was one of his greatest virtues, and paradoxically, as will be seen, one of his greatest failings. Whatever private reservations he may have had about the men he worked for, he would never voice them in public. It would be wrong to diagnose this form of loyalty as a symptom of toadying to the management. The life of actors has ever been precarious, and they felt, rightly or wrongly, a sense of gratitude to their employers for being allowed to practise their art; that gratitude was expressed in the form described. A similar passion was voiced by Stephen Decatur when ending his famous toast in Norfolk, Virginia: '. . . but our country right or wrong.' The drawback was, of course, as G. K. Chesterton pointed out, that it was like saying, 'My mother, drunk or sober.'

The third lesson of Don's early career was that he was being steeped in the traditions of English acting that reached back to Irving and before. Many of the older actors would certainly have played with 'The Chief' and it was conceivable that Don talked with men who had seen Samuel Phelps whose last performance, as Cardinal Wolsey, took place as late as 1878 when the eminent tragedian was 74, the year of his death. Charles Kean, the son of the legendary Edmund, died in 1868, and he, after all, played Iago to his father's Othello in 1833, a memorable, tragic occasion when in the last act, the ailing father whispered to son, 'I am dying—speak to them for me'. Don loved stories from the past and had a genuine, deep respect for old actors. He liked nothing better than to hear tales of bygone days, to discover the links in the chain: the passing on of business from one actor to the other, the idiosyncrasies of the great, the means they employed to gain their effects. This was the stuff of which he never tired.

The theatre buildings themselves were like ancient monuments. Many of them had housed Macready, Kean, Kemble. For Don to tread the same boards as these dead heroes was to step into a living reality; such connections with the past produced in him genuine excitement. He had only to touch a dagger or a snuff box used by some celebrated artist of the past for his eyes to glaze as if with religious wonder.

Audiences in those days were, to say the least, less sophisticated than their modern counterparts. At Consett, County Durham, for example, Don playing Salanio in *The Merchant of Venice* saw four women in the front row suckling babies at the breast. The local stage manager informed the bewildered young actor that the front row was always reserved for nursing mothers as they could not be over-looked. On another occasion, in a theatre on the outskirts of Birming-ham, as Portia said, 'The quality of mercy is not strained', a loud voice rang out from the gallery: 'Well, good night all,' and heavy boots clumped down the gallery steps. At the Theatre Royal, White-haven, while performing to an audience growing increasingly hostile, Marsh, as Mathias in *The Bells*, hissed at Don as the Mesmerist, 'Get up stage, you fool!', just as a shower of bottles smashed on the fore stage.

On the debit side, there were bad habits to be acquired, too, and chief of these was the actor-manager's insistence that maximum attention was focused not on the play but on the leading actor. There were a number of ways in which this imbalance was achieved: brighter lights on Lord Hamlet was an obvious one, so too the placing of minor and not so minor characters down stage while the Prince occupied an up-stage, and therefore more commanding position. Often, the actor-managers were the only ones with properly finished costumes, adorned with glittering jewels which, catching the brighter light at the most desirable moment, drew the audience's attention away from whoever happened to be speaking at the time. There were subtler methods, too: the instructions to supporting players to keep the pace of the play going by speaking as quickly as possible, thus enabling the leading man to take his time; the age-old trick to keep on the move, so that, during a weighty speech by a lesser character, the actor-manager would set off on a long, meaningless prowl, more often than not circling the unfortunate player who, feeling the need to address his fellow artist, would find himself with a stiff neck at the end of the week. All these malpractices, and many others, Don learned at the outset of his career, and like everything else, he never forgot them. In time, he would add one or two of his own.

IV

Two days before his twenty-first birthday, on 18 April 1923, in Guernsey, Don woke and was unable to rise from his bed. A doctor was summoned; he diagnosed pleurisy, and according to his patient, 'a complete nervous breakdown'. The illness marked a turning-point in Don's young life; it was a crisis partly brought on by the enormous strain of playing, in the previous six months, thirty-one parts, and of stage-managing Marsh's large repertoire. But there was another contributory cause to the collapse, and by far the more serious. Some months before, Mrs. Woolfitt had undergone an operation for cancer. The knowledge that his beloved mother was in the clutches of a fatal disease plunged her son into a deep despair. The bond between them, upon which he had relied so heavily in the past, was now ominously threatened. Don's love for his mother, and more especially hers for him, was the most stabilising influence on his highly charged temperament.

He was facing the problems of growing up; to all but his family who continued to use the childhood abbreviation of his name, he was now known as Donald.

Writing of his own illness so many years later, the phrase 'a complete nervous breakdown' is unquestionably an exaggeration. Besides his concern for his mother and the strain from overwork, Donald was paying the severe penalty for taking such pains to conceal his own vulnerability. Few believed then, or later, that he was sensitive, not in the trivial sense that he responded badly to adverse criticism—he did—but in the sense that small events affected him disproportionately to their importance. The shield of self-reliance Donald had built around himself, the outward show of strength and ambition, had cracked, and he was now suffering for it. There would always be the element of the psychosomatic about his illnesses; often a great mental strain manifested itself in a physical ailment, and no one was better at exaggerating a limp or a cough or a sore throat. In the years to come it would not be unknown for him to cry 'Wolf'. But this is not to make light of the illness which incapacitated him on the eve of his majority. It was serious enough for him to be kept in Guernsey for some weeks while the Marsh company continued their tour. He tried to rejoin them at Weymouth, but again collapsed. He had no alternative but to write to his parents to tell them he was coming home.

It was an unfortunate year for the Woolfitt family. Illness had struck Donald's father too, for he had recently been operated on for a duodenal ulcer, but by the time his son returned to convalesce, he appears to have recovered.

Luckily, both daughters were at home to nurse the invalids; the weather was fine; mother and son recuperated side by side in deckchairs in the small garden. Typically, Mrs. Woolfitt showed more concern for her son than for herself; she was an extremely courageous woman who must have known she could not have long to live, yet it was she who most helped Donald through this anxious time; his sisters and Nature took care of the rest.

It was a time for reflection. Donald looked back over the preceding three years with a mixture of pleasure and a feeling that he had not done as well as he had hoped. He had formed one important relationship that was to endure beyond the usually fleeting friendships of company life. Frank Milray, fourteen years Donald's senior, was 'a most excellent comedian and a fine water-colourist whose studies of Bedfordshire later became very well known'. The two men, both working for Marsh, had taken a liking to each other. Milray, himself highly strung and nervous, detected in his younger colleague the strain that resulted in Donald's collapse. While in the Channel Islands, he persuaded Donald to sketch and cycle, and the two became close friends.

As Donald's strength returned, so he thought once more about trying to find work. He wrote, 'The outlook was grim and although I could have written to either of my former managements for re-engagement, I did not feel disposed to do so but was determined to make some progress.'

Re-enter 'my beloved Jessie Bond'. Perhaps at his mother's prompting, Donald cycled out to Farndon to see her. With customary generosity she wrote two letters of recommendation on his behalf: one to Frank Curzon, the manager of Wyndham's Theatre; the other to Fred Terry. At this point in Donald's affairs, his financial resources were very slim indeed, and so it was decided that when he returned to London he would stay with his sister Norah, who had rooms in Maida Vale, while she studied at the Royal Pharmaceutical College. Using her address, he enclosed Jessie Bond's two letters and wrote off to Curzon and Terry.

In July, after three months' rest, he set off once more for London 'with six pounds in my pocket and . . . my banjo and a very heavy raincoat'. One week and countless agents later, he had pawned the banjo for a pound, but could not pledge the overcoat since the weather was warm and the pawnshops piled high with heavy coats. Just as he was despairing of ever finding work again, he received the long-awaited reply to one of his letters: Mr. Fred Terry would be pleased to receive Mr. Woolfitt at 4 Primrose Hill Road the following morning at eleven o'clock.

'I was on the doorstep at eleven sharp. The butler showed me into the drawing-room and there sat the gracious and beautiful Queen of the theatre, Julia Neilson.' Presently, Fred joined them. Donald did not remind them of their previous meetings, clearly a wise decision, for the interview ended with Donald being offered the part of Armund

St. Juste in *The Scarlet Pimpernel* on the autumn tour, salary four pounds ten per week. '. . . I was shown out into a London that had changed completely. The birds sang, the grass was green and the trees whispered in the breeze.'

He was no longer a Number Three Touring Actor. In one jump he had become a Number One Touring Actor, 'playing with the most loveable pair of stars in the country'. Nor was he required to work as a stage manager; the engagement was the step up for which Donald had been waiting. He never knew what Jessie Bond had written in her letter, 'but I suspect it must have been pretty strong to enable me to take so many hurdles in one stride'.

Donald's love and admiration for the Terrys never dimmed. It was the attraction, perhaps, of opposites, for Terry was everything Donald could never be. He came from an illustrious theatrical family, brother of Ellen, and had made his first appearance at the Theatre Royal, Haymarket under the Bancrofts in 1880, aged seventeen. Terry was a romantic actor, with a magnificent presence and a fine voice. His wife, Julia Neilson, in her memoirs described him as

> tall, taller than I; handsome as a picture; ardent about the theatre. He had all the gay charm of his already famous family, beautifully courteous manners and a passion for hard work.

Donald idolised Fred and Julia: 'They were adorable and great.' But they inhabited a quite different theatre world from the one Donald knew, or would indeed himself inhabit. Certainly, the quality of the productions, the sets and costumes, were far superior to anything the young actor had encountered previously. Terry was a rigid disciplinarian, and their latest recruit marvelled at the care he took with actors who were, like himself, new to their roles. Above all, the Terrys had style. Sir John Gielgud* was reported to have defined style as 'knowing what play you're in'. That definition was certainly true for his grand-uncle and aunt. The plays they were in were the ones their audiences wanted to see, a vitally important factor in the actor-manager's reckoning, for there was no state aid, no room for experiment, since every company had to pay its way. The Terrys presented bold, romantic dramas and comedies, a world of exquisite costumes, of handsome, noble men, and gorgeous, virtuous women. It was a world of escapism, of passionate throbbing love scenes in which a touch of hands sent shivers down the audience's spine, where men smiled in the face of death, dismissed incredible dangers with a brave laugh, and ladies in distress were somehow always gay and were never seen with a hair out of place.

* Himself a Terry, Fred and Ellen's grand-nephew. He made his first appearance under the management of Fred's daughter, Phyllis Neilson-Terry.

But on that autumn tour, Terry's judgment seems to have been at fault. Besides presenting *The Scarlet Pimpernel*, their most celebrated success, the Terrys toured *The Borderer*, a drama of Mary Queen of Scots and Bothwell. Marguerite Steen, who was then a member of the company (playing Lady Portarles in *Pimpernel*) wrote in her fine history of the family *A Pride of Terrys*, that *The Borderer* 'offered [Julia Neilson] the best part she had ever had a chance of playing under her husband's direction. *The Borderer* was another piece of hack writing, of contrived situations and unlikely dialogue.' Yet, Julia was able to bring to the role of the unhappy Queen a truth and reality that was not apparent in the text. Miss Steen continued, 'She . . . proved herself for what she was: a great tragic actress. . . . Naturally, the public detested it.' It was quite out of the run of plays their audience had come to expect of them. 'There was not a laugh from start to finish.'

The production, in this particular play, was not all it should have been either. Julia's taste was more at fault than Fred's whose 'performance was impeccable'. It was left to Fred's sister, the incomparable Ellen, to go to the heart of the matter: 'All those veils you all wear, and Julia's white stuff all over her head; one can't see what she's *doing*!'

Donald, who endearingly always lacked judgment where people he loved and admired were concerned, saw none of this. His loyalty knew no reservations; the Terrys could do no wrong. What the young actor, fresh from less glamorous engagements, reverenced was, in Marguerite Steen's words:

> . . . the First Company of the Road: the last of the great stock companies inheriting the traditions of Kean, Garrick, and the 'circuit players'. . . . We travelled in the Grand Manner; on our long journies we were entertained *en prince* by 'The Chief' and 'The Missis'. The best of theatrical lodgings were taken for granted as 'Terry's'. We were fêted wherever we went. As 'Terry's' we were given preference. There was an uproarious party at the end of every tour, with wine flowing like water, and Fred and Julia shedding their light on the most insignificant members of the company.

Protocol was as strict as in a royal palace; Donald was awed by the fact that, '. . . unless a senior member nodded or waved to him a young actor never dreamed of addressing him between dressing-room and entrance on the set'.

There was much else to admire. Observing Terry, Donald saw for the first time the enormous courage and obstinacy of stars. In great pain from gout, when it was agony for him to touch the stage with his foot, Fred, aged sixty, insisted on finishing the performance on walking sticks. 'It was a lesson in fortitude for any young actor,' Donald recorded, 'and so beloved was he by his audience that they would rather see him on two gout sticks than not at all.' The cynics could attribute Terry's obstinacy not to his courage, but to his monstrous ego. This would be to belittle him, and all other stars who play in the face of illness or personal tragedy. The fact was that they knew full well that the audience had paid to see them perform, and not an understudy, however gifted. It was a sense of responsibility unquestioned by that generation of actors.

If Donald perceived the less valuable aspects of the Terry company, he either suppressed the criticisms inside himself, or excused his idols in public. To him, the Terrys' virtues far outweighed their faults; their past achievements were sufficient to mitigate their present failings.

But 'the wind had changed', as Miss Steen observed. By the time she and Donald were in the company, 'Terry's lambs' were considered too stylised by the fashionable theatre. A new, quite different approach was needed for the works of Noël Coward and J. B. Priestley. Fred's injunction to Donald would be of little use in a play like *The Vortex*:

> Don't sound so sad. God in heaven, you are playing with the most beautiful woman in Europe. Why sound sad? Be gay, my boy, be gay. Throw your arms around her and kiss her.

Miss Steen concluded that 'most of Fred Terry's people, who knew "the job" down to the flick of an eyelash, were coldly regarded when they went for interviews and auditions'.

But as far as Donald's own talent, his own skills, his own developing style was concerned, he had an unfailing instinct for gleaning only that which was useful. It was not a conscious approach to his art, far from it. His talent was master of that choice; and when he was true to that talent, he was an unstoppable, majestic force. Marguerite Steen, in summing up the Terry company of that time, most of whom were never heard of again, wrote:

> A notable exception was an eager and ambitious young actor named Donald Wolfit, who had stayed with the old firm only long enough to profit by its excellences, not long enough to get bogged down by its apparently inescapable idiom.

Donald looked back on that year with the Terrys as the most glamorous of his career. They played principal theatres in the large provincial cities and crossed the sea to Dublin and Belfast, then in the grip of rebellion. Apart from two understudy rehearsals a week, Donald was free to swim, to play tennis, golf and, above all, to read.

He was catching up on his neglected education and avidly devoured the works of Hardy and George Eliot. He wrote plays too, and read them aloud to Marguerite Steen, another with whom he formed a friendship that lasted long after the engagement. It was during this period that he first encountered the plays of Henrik Ibsen, and a life-long fascination began with the works of the Norwegian dramatist.

The Christmas of 1923 saw Donald back in Newark, for the Terry company were rested over the holiday period. He was cheered to see that his mother, if no better, was at least no worse. He did not know the intense pain she was suffering, for she was outwardly cheerful and the disease had not yet begun to drain her of energy.

Because of his rise in status to the Number One circuit, Donald had felt it necessary to dress the part. Accordingly, he had ordered two new suits and found he could not pay for them; he had not yet enough confidence to play the gentleman and keep his tailor waiting. Ever resourceful, he hit upon the idea which was to be a useful stand-by both now, at the start of his career, and many years later, at the end: he decided to give a Dramatic Recital.

Together with his old music teacher Madame D'Ascanio, Donald assembled a programme of poetry, recitations and impersonations, with musical interludes by Madame D'Ascanio, Miss Vincent Robinson and Mr. A. Smith. The last item on the programme is of special interest, for it illustrates just how impressionable Donald was.

5. IMPERSONATIONS FROM CHARLES DICKENS
    (a) Uriah Heep—'David Copperfield'
    (b) Jingle—'Pickwick Papers'
    (c) Old Grandfather—'Old Curiosity Shop'

This was precisely the sort of performance Bransby Williams pre-sented, the one Donald witnessed while working with Gimson, the year before, watching Williams make up for each character on stage, in full view of the audience. This Donald now reproduced in Newark. It was a pattern that would be repeated. Time and again, under his own management, he would recall these early years of his career and choose plays that the actor-managers of his youth performed, adding them to his own repertoire.

The *Newark Herald* was full of praise:

Hearty applause punctuated all the items and merited congratula-tions must be extended by Newark to Newark's actor.

Donald paid his tailor.

In the Spring of 1924, Terry put a new play, *The Marlboroughs*, into rehearsal, with Julia as Sarah Churchill, Fred as the Duke. Some of the dialogue, which he only heard rehearsed, Donald never forgot:

THE DUKE: Has the Queen been here?
SARAH: Yes.
THE DUKE: What did you say to her?
SARAH: I told her to go to Hell.
THE DUKE: Well, when you have told the Queen of England to go to Hell, you must be prepared to do a little travelling yourself.
SARAH: No, I stay here. London's my battlefield!

At which Julia made her exit, sweeping through the door in fury, and to ecstatic applause.

It was a small-cast play and there was no suitable part for Donald but he had, during the course of his year with the Terrys, made friends with a fellow actor, Frank G. Cariello, who was soon, under his own management, to tour Ireland with an old drama called *Bought and Paid For*. He offered Donald the part of the Japanese servant.

Cariello had played Chauvelin, the French envoy in *The Scarlet Pimpernel*, and Donald had understudied him; often the two men shared digs together. He was typical of the type of actor Donald met in his early days, and one to whom he was loyal for more than twenty-five years. Cariello had been 'bred in the old drama days'. Short and square, he intoned rather than talked, in a deep, trembling voice ideally suited to melodrama and he used it with equal *fortissimo* both on and off the stage. Cariello was like a caricature of an 'actor-laddie', except that he was never well-off enough to afford an astra-khan collar. Indeed, Donald once confessed that Cariello was one of the few actors he had ever heard actually use the word 'laddie'. He was voluble and exuberant with a kind of old-fashioned charm and good-manners that he reserved for pretty women. The most lavish term of endearment he could bestow on a man was 'bloody villain!' He had a fund of theatrical stories that always seemed to begin, 'On the Saturday night, in Rochester, we played as I remember, alas, to only £19.14.3. etc.' The theatre and cricket were his passions; his prejudices were rather more numerous. He disliked homosexuals, 'gentlemen of the Hebrew fraternity', and ugly actresses. Of the latter he confessed to seeing no use for them 'except to play landladies and prison wardresses, and God knows why *they* should be unattractive!' To Cariello, all men born on the Continent of Africa, black or white, were 'Scotch-arsed Zulus'. John Martin-Harvey, with whom he had played Laertes, was a 'four foot six ponce' (Cariello was not much taller himself). He once proclaimed in a theatre foyer, he thought intimately, 'I have been a member of the Labour Party all my life, but I utterly despise the British working class'. A performance by a distinguished modern actor as Shylock he described as 'the finest portrayal of a Jewish lesbian I have ever witnessed, but by Christ, laddie, not quite what the Bard of Avon intended, was it?' All this delivered with a great display of vocal pyrotechnics and in such a way that it was impossible to take offence.

Julia Neilson-Terry, in a letter to Donald written in 1941, clearly remembered him well: 'Dear Cariello! Is he still as stocky!?! I used to find him *very heavy* to *MOVE!*'

Donald fell under the charm of this endearing man; he was one of the actors he never forgot and would always feel a debt towards; loyalty of this kind was not always beneficial to both parties, as will be seen.

For three weeks Donald travelled Ireland with Cariello in *Bought and Paid For*, mostly one-night stands. Thirty years later, the present author heard the two men discuss that tour. Donald said, 'And I remember, Frank, we played to eleven pounds seventeen on the Monday night.'

'Twelve pounds seventeen,' corrected Cariello. 'Forgive me, dear boy, and pray continue.'

It was quite a plunge from Fred Terry to Frank G. Cariello. Yet for all Donald's anxiety constantly to be bettering himself professionally, he preferred to work, rather than not. On his return from Ireland, in 1924, Donald was two months without work during the hot summer, traditionally a bad season for the actor unless he had previously fixed an engagement with one of the seaside companies that flourished round the coast of Britain.

Only one offer came his way, to tour in the chorus of a musical comedy, but, no doubt wisely, he declined, feeling that musical comedy was not the direction in which to steer his career.

The spell of unemployment was temporarily broken by a short tour of a current West End success which had starred Athene Seyler, Frank Cellier and Leslie Banks, entitled *The Mask and The Face*. With a somewhat less brilliant cast it met with little success in the provinces. A Dublin newspaper warned:

LUGUBRIOUS COMEDY: MIRTH IN MOURNING AT THE GAIETY THEATRE.

Early in October, Donald was back at Mrs. Merret's. He could not have found himself out of work at a worse time: the autumn tours were all cast, and only the prospect of a pantomime at Christmas offered any hope at all. Donald was dispirited; news from home was depressing too, for his mother was growing weaker with each day that passed.

Then, one of those 'sheer pieces of luck' occurred. In the Salisbury Public House in St. Martin's Lane, a time-honoured sanctuary for out-of-work actors, Donald met an old actor called Patterson who, during the course of conversation, mentioned that Matheson Lang was to revive *The Wandering Jew* because of the failure of a modern play, *The Hour and The Man*. Patterson suggested that Donald try Lang's offices which were not far away in Gerrard Street, on the off-chance that there might be parts still to be cast. Donald was reluctant and pessimistic, for there was a great gulf between the unfashionable provinces and fashionable London, and touring actors never found it easy to break into the West End. But old Patterson was encouraging; Donald realised he had nothing to lose by trying.

'Taking my courage in both hands,' Donald remembered, 'I ran to Gerrard Street, up five flights of stairs, and before my courage failed me found myself in a small outer office facing a large man, Mayor Cook, Lang's manager.'

Cook asked the young, breathless actor to write out a list of his previous engagements and then, taking the piece of paper, disappeared into an inner sanctum. Presently, Donald was beckoned to follow and found himself face to face with Matheson Lang.

Lang's first question alarmed Donald somewhat.

'Do you strip well?' he asked.

Donald mumbled something about golf and tennis, and did his best to look athletic.

'Would you be prepared to black yourself all over?'

Donald replied that nothing would please him better.

'Very well,' said Lang, 'you can play my black servant in the tent scene. Your contract will be sent on, four pounds ten, rehearse on Tuesday, at the New Theatre.'

They shook hands and Donald found himself once more in Gerrard Street, 'blessing the name of Patterson, of Lang and of all the gods. . . . I had vaulted the final hurdle with incredible ease. I was to be a West End actor. This time I had my hair cut.'

The boy from New Balderton must have felt that fame and fortune were lurking round the corner. He had served a tough, demanding apprenticeship that, in many ways, had moulded his theatrical taste for the years to come. He was now to learn about acting from a very able master of the art, but he could not have known that the struggle for recognition would continue for a great many years yet. With high hopes and a profound belief in his destiny, the young actor determined to make it easier for the London critics to report his success, as surely they must: to avoid the constant mis-spellings of his name that he had suffered over the years, he decided to simplify it. From now on he would be Donald Wolfit.

Part Two

DONALD WOLFIT

1924–1937

CHAPTER FIVE

London and Points North

For now sits Expectation in the air.
—Henry V

I

'I want you to carry the Cross past the window in this first scene. It must be done reverently.'

Thus, Donald made his first entrance on the London stage, himself unseen, but the Cross bobbing on his back, passing the window of Matathias, the Wandering Jew, on the road to Calvary. 'It was an inspiring moment,' wrote Donald.* The scene was, of course, Jerusalem, on the day of the Crucifixion. Matathias, whose wife lies dying, rushes out to spit on Jesus because He cannot come to the house to heal the dying woman. Matathias thus invokes the punishment to wander the earth until he finds redemption in Seville at the stake.

The Wandering Jew was one of Matheson Lang's most famous roles. Lang made his first appearance in Wolverhampton in 1897, aged eighteen. Tall, heavily built, he was exceedingly handsome, with a fine, resonant voice. He had appeared with Mrs. Langtry and with Ellen Terry, with Frank Benson and in the Vedrenne-Barker season at the Royal Court Theatre in the plays of Shaw and Ibsen. His first outstanding success was in *The Christian* at the Lyceum Theatre in 1907, when he also won high praise for his Romeo and Hamlet.

Matheson Lang was certainly successful, but he was never taken seriously enough to be regarded as an important actor who had a contribution to make to his art. The *intelligentsia* of his day did not approach him with the same respect they reserved for Johnston Forbes-Robertson, or even Lewis Waller. Ivor Brown, writing of one Lang performance, is typical:

Mr. Lang's acting is, as ever, a large and capable affair. . . . All

*For Wolfit's own choice when he came to revive the play in 1953, see page 225.

restlessness vanishes when he takes the stage; these are catarrhal
times, but his masterful control of an audience silences coughs in
a way that should make the houses of Veno and Owbridge rage
jealously together.

Theatre historians of the 1900–30 period either mention Lang *en
passant*, or not at all. As an actor-manager, some of the plays he chose
to be seen in severely limited his gifts, but in his most celebrated success, *Mr. Wu*, he played the least sympathetic of villains ('a Chinese
scoundrel' according to *The Era*), and allowed Owen Nares the part
with the most appeal to the audience; it was a brave choice for an
actor-manager to make, and it paid off. *Jew Suss*, the adaptation of
the Feuchtwanger novel, was another unlikely role, but again he
scored a success. Lang gave Peggy Ashcroft her first chance in this
production.

In 1920, during the run of a play called *Carnival*, a back-stage story
in which Lang portrayed an actor playing Othello with more cause to
be jealous of his wife off stage than on, Lang presented on Wednesday
matinées a production of Shakespeare's *Othello*. Those who saw it
acclaimed it as undoubtedly Lang's finest performance.* Yet it
missed being one of those celebrated events in the theatrical calendar,
and is hardly ever mentioned in the same breath as Forbes-Robertson's Hamlet or even Waller's Henry V. W. A. Darlington, for many
years the critic of the *Daily Telegraph*, in his book *Six Thousand and
One Nights*, solves some of the mystery:

> . . . Matheson Lang, during the run of *Carnival*, acted Othello at
> a series of matinées. He gave, as it were, the performance in
> Shakespeare's tragedy that the hero of *Carnival* might be supposed
> to be giving, using the costume and make-up which that character
> wore in his backstage scenes. Given the choice between seeing
> the same favourite player in a second-rate machine-made modern
> part and in great tragedy, the audience never hesitated. To them,
> *Carnival* had reality and *Othello* had not; it was as simple as that.
> They continued to crowd the modern play, and allowed the special
> matinées to languish. Perhaps it was a sign of the times that my
> editor, Sir John Le Sage, did not think fit to send me to see Lang as
> *Othello*.

Nor did Darlington think fit to see it of his own accord, acclaim it,
and urge his readers to attend. Be that as it may, he rightly lays the
blame at the feet of Lang's public, which in turn, reflects on Lang
himself, for his taste in plays, apart from the two already mentioned,

---

* In a recent conversation with the author, Ernest Milton said unhesitatingly that
Lang's Othello was the most outstanding performance he had ever seen.

was for romantic melodrama, inhabited by cardboard characters who appeared in a series of 'good scenes'.

Lang was endowed with every natural advantage to scale the heights. Born in Inverness of a family that was to produce another eminent member of society—Cosmo Lang, the Archbishop of Canterbury was his cousin—Lang, like Lewis Waller, was one of the first matinée idols, given to engineering elaborate first entrances, and to attracting hordes of female admirers. Perhaps he was too handsome, the voice too beautiful, the success apparently too easy for him ever to be regarded as anything more than just a popular actor-manager. He was also guilty of two further unfashionable crimes: he spent much time in the provinces and on long foreign tours, and his wife Hutin Britten was also his leading lady. Like many an actor-manager, before and after, he was notoriously tight-fisted, yet to his eternal credit it was Lang who lent the infant Old Vic a helping hand, donating a large part of his wardrobe to the new, struggling theatre in the Waterloo Road. In 1914 he inaugurated the productions of Shakespeare there with *The Taming of The Shrew*, *Hamlet* and *The Merchant of Venice*, but it must be remembered that the Old Vic was far from being the fashionable institution it later became.

The Wandering Jew, in that 1924 season, was followed by a revival of *Carnival* and *The Tyrant* by Rafael Sabatini, with Lang as Cesare Borgia. Donald's description of Cesare's first entrance, which came in the second act, gives a good indication of Lang's ability to create a startling theatrical effect, and captures something of his personal magnetism:

At the height of the brawl in the ante-room the double doors were flung open and the magnificent Borgia, his savage eyes glinting and narrowed until they were like a panther's, and carrying in his right hand a lily which he delicately passed across his quivering nostrils, stood in silence surveying the scene.

The engagement with Lang lasted well into 1925. Donald moved to a basement room at 12 Markham Square in Chelsea, and paid a rent of seven shillings and sixpence a week. Although he was only playing small parts—Phirous, the servant in *The Wandering Jew*, a Player in *Carnival* and a Swiss Captain in *The Tyrant*—he was at last a West End actor. It was the first time that he had appeared in a new play and his classical training was given a sharp jolt at hearing the alterations to script discussed, so that the lines suited the actors, or juxtapositioning of the text, the cutting of speeches, the general shaping of the play. It was also the first time that he had ever had a costume specially made for him. All in all, he found the life of a London actor decidedly agreeable.

Then, in February 1925, the dreaded news from Newark arrived. Emma Woolfitt, his mother, died on the eve of her fifty-seventh birthday, having suffered with great fortitude her long and desperate illness. She had lived long enough to know that her son had found work in London. Lang allowed Donald to absent himself from a rehearsal to attend the funeral. On that bleak winter's day, his heart breaking, Donald travelled north and returned the same evening in time for the performance. The young man had learned the lesson of responsibility well from Fred Terry.

His mother's death was a dreadful moment in Donald's life. Although he had been away from home for five years, family ties were strong. Eva, his sister, recalled Donald's 'utter devastation on Mother's death. She had encouraged, inspired and upheld him throughout his early struggles.' The wound left by his mother's passing would take several years more to heal.

II

For weeks after the funeral Donald suffered a kind of inertia; he brooded and mourned. Then, with what was perhaps a conscious effort to overcome his grief, he plunged himself into the work of the Sunday Societies. The work of these Societies was to present plays, thus enabling actors settled in long West End runs to keep their names before the critics and managers, to practise their art, and to alleviate the boredom of a long run; they also served as a valuable shop window for the out-of-work. 'Sometimes a guinea was paid for the labour,' Donald remembered, 'sometimes not, but the financial reward was not of paramount importance.' The Sunday Societies revived old, neglected plays, and found new ones, English and foreign. *Journey's End* began life on a Sunday, and so did *The Man with a Load of Mischief*. Donald with customary energy and enthusiasm, entered into this bustling activity, walked-on if there were no parts, made friends and played important roles; in this way he lightened the pain of the loss of his mother.

In the early summer, Frank Vosper,* newly engaged by Lang for *The Tyrant*, and also at the beginning of his career, told Donald of a chance he had refused from J. T. Grein, founder of The Independent Theatre Society, to play the part of Joseph in Ernest Rhys's translation of *Joseph and His Brethren* by a Latvian poet, Rainis; Vosper suggested that Donald should offer his services to Grein. In May

---

* Frank Vosper (1900–37), actor and playwright. Agate wrote of him 'As an actor Vosper was versatile and interesting . . . his two best pieces of acting were Mr. Dulcimer in *The Green Bay Tree* and the murderer in his own play *Love from a Stranger*.' He was also the author of *People Like Us*, a dramatisation of the Thompson-Bywater case.

1925, Donald attempted his first leading role before a London audience which included his old mentor Corporal Power, at the Scala Theatre.

'At least eight papers reviewed the performance,' Donald wrote with some pleasure. The words 'strength', 'heroic' and 'virile' occur more than once, and *The Era*, the trade newspaper, summed it up by announcing that 'it was a good performance without being a great one'. Nevertheless, it was apparent that Donald had shown flashes of power, however immature, which he was later to develop and intensify. 'The performance even reached the ears of Matheson Lang and I was quizzically complimented and encouraged.'

In July, Lang announced a forthcoming tour of Canada and the United States, but Donald's minor roles did not warrant his inclusion in the company, and he was again out of work.

If he had imagined that once being a West End actor he would trot from London theatre to London theatre, he was to be sadly disappointed. Work was hard to come by. He tried the Old Vic but it was closed until late autumn. The familiar round of agents' offices followed with, hopefully, interviews and auditions resulting. At last, he was engaged to understudy and stage manage the tour of *The Man with a Load of Mischief* by Ashley Dukes, which was then running at the Theatre Royal, Haymarket with Fay Compton, Leon Quartermaine and Frank Cellier. Donald felt he had taken a step backwards and was unhappy for the duration of the engagement with not enough to do.

In Manchester, one evening, he was the guest of the Arts Club after the performance. Although Donald writes, 'I was *invited* [author's ital.] to perform', a fellow guest, C. D. Harvey, remembers a young man springing to his feet and 'launching *unannounced* [author's ital.] into a riveting rendition of *The Lady of Shallot* by Alfred, Lord Tennyson'. This account would accord with Donald's eagerness to perform at any opportunity; if there was a ready-made audience assembled, he never showed the least reticence in seizing the chance to entertain them. Mr. Harvey continues, '. . . the young man was intense, almost violent in his manner when performing. He recited two or three other works, though I cannot now remember them. I was, however, greatly impressed and never forgot the Tennyson or the young man's name: Donald Wolfit.'

Another, equally impressed, was 'a large florid man with a long wisp of hair trailing across his forehead', Donald recalled. His name was Arthur Belt, by profession an undertaker, by inclination a theatre manager who ran the Manchester Repertory Theatre in the old tramway depot in Rusholme. It was a convenient arrangement, for Belt's funeral parlour was nextdoor to the depot. ' "Right from the shoulder," Belt enthused, "No fancy nancy business about that, none of your West End actor stuff." ' He gave Donald an open invitation to appear in the company. ' "If you're ever out of a job come straight to me and I'll shop* you. Is that a bargain?" ' Two months later, Donald put him to the test and Belt was as good as his word. Donald appeared in *The Rose and the Ring* and *Hindle Wakes*.

He spent Christmas at home in Newark, then returned to London, once more to audition for the Old Vic, once more to be refused. It must have seemed that being a London actor was no more than a hollow boast, and so it proved, for he was shortly to travel north again, playing small villages and hamlets, as far north indeed as the remote Highlands of Scotland, in the company of eleven other actors, on one of the most valuable and courageous ventures in the history of the contemporary English theatre. Like that other great enterprise in the Waterloo Road, the driving force behind Donald's new engagement was a woman, determined and energetic, with a burning sense of duty and the avowed motto 'to bring the Arts into everyday life'. If there were nothing else fashionable about her enterprise, at least she lived in Adelphi with James Barrie and Bernard Shaw for neighbours, and there Donald presented himself to begin a year with the Arts League Travelling Theatre and its guiding spirit, Miss Eleanor Elder.

III

A dozen actors, none of them of note, who find a single lorry sufficient to support them and their simple belongings from village to village, give a performance which for sheer beauty and innocent mirth has not been matched since The Follies were in their prime.

In those words the *Morning Post* accurately described the bare bones of the venture. Eleanor Elder, who had been trained by Frank Benson, and as a dancer by Margaret Morris, was a competent performer, but more important she was a cultural missionary. Her vision was to take the Arts to those people who would not normally have the opportunity of seeing them. Encouraged by her neighbours, Barrie and Shaw, and with help from Lord Cavendish-Bentinck she obtained an annual grant from the Carnegie Trust, and in 1919 founded the Arts League of Service. She bought a reconditioned Lancia bus with twelve seats and filled it with twelve actors. She sniffed out the most promising designers and painters, bullied well-known directors from the London theatre, and covered the country with a programme of one-act plays, folk songs and dances.

---

* Theatre slang, now obsolete, not to be confused with the phrase's other usage, 'to inform on'. 'Shop' meant also a theatrical engagement, a 'berth'.

In each village or town the artists were given hospitality for the short duration of their stay. 'On an average,' wrote Donald, 'we visited five halls a week.' In the rear of the bus they took ladders, curtains, costumes, properties, acetylene outfit and footlights.

Donald described the routine:

The journeys were seldom more than twenty-five or thirty miles. We loaded the van at nine-thirty prompt, travelled, unloaded and generally set up our outfit by lunch-time. The afternoon was occupied by rehearsals, or otherwise was a free time to be spent with one's host or hostess. After the performance all was packed up and laid ready by the door of the village hall or institution for loading on the morrow; and then back to supper and bed. I have never lived in such perpetual motion as during this year. We tumbled in and out of baronial halls, Scottish castles, manses, rectories, vicarages and simple miners' cottages, meeting wonderful kindness and enthusiasm day after day, for the work of the Arts League Travelling Theatre was an inspiration to those outlying places which had no other form of entertainment from one year's end to the next. . . . Thirty items were travelled, six one-act plays, eight or ten folk-songs, four or five absurdities, eight dances and mimes.

For the 1926 season they had Reginald Denham, Ernest Milton and Leslie French to produce one-act plays by Laurence Housman, Clifford Bax, Lennox Robinson and Allan Monkhouse. Miss Elder herself 'had a genius for taking a folk-song and so interlacing it with movement and mime that it became a thing of delight'.

The dancing was supervised by a young fifteen-year-old girl with blonde hair and clear blue eyes. She was known as Rosalind Patrick then. She was rather nervous and timid, but with a dazzling smile when she relaxed. She was terrified of Donald, overwhelmed by his blatant masculinity. Many years later, they were to meet again, but by then she had changed her name to Rosalind Iden.

It was hard, exhilarating work. No Terry protocol here: everyone helped where they could, setting props, changing scenery, singing, dancing, acting.

'I think I never spent a more wonderful year in the theatre,' Donald confessed. 'We travelled the roads and lanes of England and Scotland the cycle of the seasons, hedgerows aflame with blossom and berry and stark in the grip of winter.'

Donald gained much from his year with the Arts League. Rosalind Patrick remembered his ceaseless energy, his untiring propensity for hard work. No one moved more scenery, set more props, packed more costumes than Donald, in between playing in nine or ten of the items with the attendant quick changes of costume and make-up. The Arts League blew the dust and cobwebs of the past momentarily from his mind. Miss Elder's fresh air blessed his spirits. And it is surprising, in view of his later reputation, how well he fitted in with the others, how much he enjoyed and valued the *esprit de corps*. Gone were the accusations of remoteness and aloofness that had been levelled at him previously, and would be levelled at him again. He was relaxed and happy and, in Rosalind's words, 'enormous fun'. The significance of that year was that Donald was at last being stretched almost to the limits of his physical capacity; he hated to be idle; he liked to have his nose in every corner of the organisation; the bustling activity ideally suited his restless temperament. From the daily travelling off the main roads, he obtained an intimate knowledge of the British Isles, and a deepening love of the countryside. Most important of all, he learned about the people of Britain, that those outside London and the big provincial cities had a right to partake in their cultural heritage and it was a duty to provide the opportunity. He wrote:

Every evening we encountered an enthusiastic, unjaded audience, many of whom had travelled for miles, often on foot, to see the performance. The whole conception was an inspiration. In some villages, when the hall was crowded boxes would be placed outside the windows for people to stand on, and often there would be several faces peering in at each opening.

It also brought Donald into contact for the first time with the English aristocracy. For five days the company stayed as the guests of Lord and Lady Aberdeen at the House of Cromar. Here the actors attended prayers in the drawing room, listened to His Lordship read the lesson and Her Ladyship play the harmonium. 'My sister loves a lord!' declares Mr. Stirling in *The Clandestine Marriage*; so did Donald. He held the nobility in awe and later, as he himself grew more notable, he thrilled at meeting with them. In Miss Elder's words:

They were brought into touch with people on every rung of the social ladder, and had brief but illuminating glimpses of the problems of agriculture, of education, of justice; the fascination of big industries, mines and factories—sometimes from the house of the director or home of the worker. The host one night might be a Justice of the Peace and a police inspector the next. The rector, the doctor and the schoolmaster were invariably on the list of those who had offered hospitality wherever the company went. A tour with the Travelling Theatre might be likened to a documentary film on British architecture. Everywhere there was kindness and hospitality, whether you dined with a footman behind your chair, or helped your hostess to wash up after high tea in the kitchen.

In return Miss Elder gave those very people an exciting, lively theatrical experience, and offered them the opportunity of partaking in the other arts as well. The programme announced:

THE ARTS LEAGUE OF SERVICE ENDEAVOURS TO FURTHER ITS AIMS THROUGH ITS TRAVELLING THEATRE, TRAVELLING PORTFOLIOS OF PICTURES, LECTURES ON ART, MEMBERS' LENDING LIBRARY OF PLAYS, 'AT HOMES' FOR MEMBERS AT WHICH ENTERTAINMENTS ARE GIVEN AND ADVICE ON PLAY AND STAGE PRODUCTION.

In miniature, it was a more comprehensive service than the modern Arts Council provides. But by the mid-thirties the cinema and amateur societies had taken over the work, or so it seemed to the Carnegie Trust, who withdrew their support. The dying agonies of the Arts League did not go without protest. St. John Ervine, the playwright and critic, wrote to Eleanor Elder in the summer of 1937 a long and encouraging letter. It is reprinted in full, for it so fully captures the meaning of the Arts League, and pays just tribute to its founder.

Honey Ditches,
Seaton, Devon.
May 11th, 1937.

Dear Miss Elder,

I am shocked to learn that the Carnegie Trustees are thinking of withdrawing their grant from the Arts League of Service on the ground that your work is now finished—as if work, such as yours, is ever finished. They might as well propose to shut the British Museum on the ground that we now know everything! I can speak of the value of your troupe of players better than most people, because I live in the country and have several times seen the pleasure they give the country people. If it were not for the visits of the Arts League of Service to Axminster, the only dramatic entertainment that people in this district would receive, year after year, would be moving pictures in the local cinemas. On each occasion that I have seen your players in Axminster, the uncomfortable hall in which their performances were given was packed. If the Carnegie Trustees withdraw their grant and your troup is unable to visit us again, we shall be left dramaless all the year round, except for the twice-weekly debauch at the pictures where our country people will be taught that the only desirable ambition for any boy and girl is to get rich by any means so that they may lead lives of unparalleled luxury.

I regard your work as most important because it enables the mass of people to obtain some satisfaction of their deep desire for drama. The depth of that desire is being made apparent to me at present, for I am visiting repertory theatres throughout the provinces, and I am greatly impressed by the persistent love of the theatre which remains in our countrymen despite the fact that it is discouraged in almost every way. I went the other night to see a play at Colwyn Bay where, in the season, a cinema which has been converted into a theatre was packed to see a play performed. Your organisation is keeping this love alive in places where, even in the hey-day of the drama, plays were seldom or never seen.

But that is not your only function. Your travelling theatre is an invaluable training school for young players who not only obtain experience such as they cannot obtain elsewhere, but obtain it in the right way, that is to say, by frequent changes of play and frequent changes of audience. Your players act every night in a variety of works, plays, mimes and dances and, by changing their locality several times in a week, they are made to undergo the ordeal of adjusting themselves quickly to totally different populations. A young player who has to interest an audience of colliers tonight, an audience of agricultural labourers tomorrow night, and an audience of retired Anglo-Indians on the third night has learned something about his job that no performance in one piece in the West End will ever teach him; and it is, I think, a proof of the value of your organisation to actors that when I went to Stratford-on-Avon the other day, I found two young players from the Arts League of Service in principal parts, Mr. Clement McCallin and Mr. Donald Wolfit, and very good they were. Their quality was acquired in village halls while acting with your organisation.

I sincerely hope that the Carnegie Trustrees will renew their grant and would even suggest to them that they increase it. They will be doing the drama a grave disservice if it is discontinued.

Yours sincerely,
St. John Ervine.

Predictably, the drama was done a grave disservice, and the Arts League vanished from the scene.

CHAPTER SIX

Sheffield

For, boy, however we do praise ourselves,
Our fancies are more giddy and unfirm,
More longing, wavering, sooner lost and worn,
Than women's are.

—*Twelfth Night*

I

THE Christmas of 1926 Donald spent at home in Newark. He wrote that it was 'one of the last of the many gatherings so dear to us as a family'. His two sisters had both graduated: Eva from Manchester University, Norah from the Royal Pharmaceutical College. Because of the uneasy affection between father and son, Donald would only re-visit his home in the future out of a sense of duty. 'Homeleigh' would never be the same to Donald now that his mother's warmth and love were no longer present to welcome him.

The passing of 1926 marked not only the dispersal of the Woolfitt family, but also Donald's entry into a new phase of his life both as an actor and as a man.

When Eleanor Elder had invited Donald to continue for another year with the Arts League, he had declined; he consciously decided that he needed to broaden his experience. What he most wanted was the chance of playing leading roles, which he rightly felt would test the technique and skills he had acquired over the years, and the only way he could see of fulfilling this aim was to join a repertory company.

The two leading repertory theatres in England at that time were Birmingham and Liverpool, but the idea of a repertory company had first been realised at the Gaiety Theatre, Manchester, before the First World War. The conception of the repertory movement was of a permanent resident company, presenting different plays at weekly, two-weekly or three-weekly intervals, largely depending on the size of the town. The merits of such a system had obvious advantages over the touring company: it cut costs, for neither the company nor the sets had to be moved week after week, yet it continued to supply the audience with a varied bill of fare. Furthermore, the actors became familiar to the audience so that, on a small scale, the star system, so beloved by the British theatre-going public, was inadvertently sustained. But without doubt the greatest virtue of the repertory company was the training ground it provided for young actors. Birmingham and Liverpool between them would serve as nursery for some of the most outstanding actors of the post-war period.* But it is not surprising that when Donald came to be engaged by a repertory company, he did not find himself in the fashionable cities of Birmingham or Liverpool. Instead, he was cast in the role of pioneer and helped pave the way for a permanent professional company to be formed in the city of Sheffield.

In January 1927, Donald met Maxwell Wray who, the year previous, had been appointed producer of the Sheffield Repertory Company. Donald described the set-up as 'spartan and peculiar'. He continued:

> Originally an amateur group, it had as chairman and vice-chairman respectively Professor A. E. Morgan, the principal of Sheffield University, and Professor B. Ifor Evans, of the Department of English. . . . Under their leadership, the Carnegie Trust were persuaded to provide a small annual grant on condition that the company became fully professional within two years. . . . In the slum district of Hillsborough we had a workshop and rehearsal room as headquarters, and on The Moor, at the other side of the city, in the South Street Hall (a parochial building with a balcony and wooden pews) stood our theatre. It was not permitted to use the theatre on the Sabbath, and one or two nights a week choir practice in one of the adjoining rooms overlapped our starting time by half an hour. The seats were wooden, of course, but the audience sat on their coats or brought cushions if they were wise. We played alternate weeks as the supporting cast was amateur with a smattering of ex-professionals, and could only rehearse in the evening.

Donald was engaged as leading man; Chris Castor, an attractive versatile actress, was leading lady. These two were the only professionals.

Donald spent a year at Sheffield, playing long leading roles week after week in a variety of plays that included *I'll Leave It To You* by Noël Coward, *Zack* by Harold Brighouse, *Windows* by John Gals-

---

* The list is very long and very distinguished, but among those who began at Birmingham are Laurence Olivier, Paul Scofield, Margaret Leighton. And at Liverpool, Michael Redgrave, Robert Speaight and Rex Harrison.

worthy, *A Doll's House* by Henrik Ibsen, *Dear Brutus* by J. M. Barrie and *Widowers' Houses* by Bernard Shaw.

The year at Sheffield was an important period for Donald's development both professionally and privately. On the professional front, it was not simply that he was playing long leading parts. He had, in Maxwell Wray, an enthusiastic, intelligent director who diligently guided him into the complex realms of 'pacing' a performance, of not giving too much too soon and leaving nothing for the end; of discovering those essentials in a character that when projected breathe life into the drama; of hammering away at personal mannerisms which, because of the short rehearsal period, all young actors are apt to rely on in time of doubt and nervousness. Donald was beginning to understand what it meant, in terms of sustained concentration, to play parts at the very centre of the dramatist's work, thus shouldering the responsibility of making that work viable. He was fortunate in another respect. The drama critic of the *Sheffield Telegraph*, Charles Cameron, was a perceptive analyst of the art of acting. First and foremost, he treated the Sheffield Repertory Company with a seriousness that it undoubtedly deserved, and of course welcomed the showing of the cultural flag in his city. He was tireless in seeing to it that the company maintained the highest possible standards, always taking into account the difficulties under which they laboured. He was severe if they fell short of those standards, and generous in his encouragement if they achieved them. It was Cameron who bullied and badgered the people of Sheffield, in Donald's words, 'to look on the founding of a professional repertory theatre as essential to the dignity and pride of the steel city'.

The bullying and badgering paid off, for soon the company, and especially its two leading players, were the toast of the devoted Sheffield playgoers. They 'opened their hearts to us', wrote Donald, 'the small hall was crowded, we became the fashion'. Donald worked hard, showed his accustomed interest in every aspect of the company's operations and wallowed in the experience of being a big fish in a little pond. He wrote an article on the Arts League for the *Telegraph*; Chris Castor contributed another entitled *Are State Theatres Needed?* They were the centre of attraction.

The company worked long, arduous hours under trying conditions. The stage was small so that sets were built close to the back wall; if a character had to exit one side of the stage to re-appear on the other, he was obliged to make his way along a muddy passage outside the building, shielded, when necessary, by umbrellas and mackintoshes. This was Donald's element, and always would be: the greater the obstacles overcome, the greater the feeling of achievement.

His performances at Sheffield revealed his versatility, his gift for make-up and an extraordinary ability, an instinct, to aim at the heart of a character. After the years with the actor-managers, where the small part players were little helped, Donald was genuinely struggling and often succeeding with the problems of attempting to act, and to be, all that the character demanded. Here was no leading player showing himself off, but rather a serious-minded young professional coming to grips with the complexities of his enormously difficult art. Cameron accounted his Dearth in *Dear Brutus* his finest performance, and was full of praise for *Zack*, and Anthony in *Anthony and Anna* by St. John Ervine. Donald failed, on his own admission, as Helmer in *A Doll's House.* The character, he wrote, 'eluded me—I could not find the right mood for the complacent, pompous husband . . . and strove too hard'. Good or bad, Donald was learning what was for him, perhaps, the most difficult lesson of all, self-criticism.

There is a more important assessor of those Sheffield performances than either Cameron or Donald himself, and that is Harold Hobson, the drama critic of the *Sunday Times.* Then a young man of twenty-three, he regularly attended the South Street Hall and many years later was to admit that the leading man 'was one of the greatest influences on my theatrical tastes that I have ever known'. In the years to come Hobson would write often of Donald; their professional relationship would sometimes be stormy, but the bond forged at Sheffield, unknowingly, for the two men did not meet then, would prove stronger than either the petulance of a wounded actor or the harshness of a London critic. And, on one occasion, some thirty years later, the critic would come generously to the aid of the actor and help him to achieve, by direct intervention, a resounding success.

In a letter written to Donald in 1949, Hobson wrote:*

> Memories of the superb performances which you gave in the 1920s at the Sheffield Repertory Theatre are still fresh in my mind. Often I think of how I used to walk home to Nether Edge, excited, exalted and aglow after some performance of yours in Shaw, Galsworthy or Barrie.

Later, about those same performances:

> I was as much moved by some of them as I have ever been by any actor in the theatre.

And:†

> When we were both in Sheffield he laid on me an enchantment against which in later years I sometimes rebelled, but whose power I have never doubted.

---

* For the full context of this letter see pages 183-4.
† To the present author.

There were private reasons why Donald was able to make this sudden leap forward as an actor, and why his powers developed so freely: he was in love with his leading lady, Chris Castor.

No record exists to show whether or not Donald had any deep emotional attachments prior to this time, but having regard for his passionate and intense nature, it would not be fanciful to suppose that he had. He was not, however, a promiscuous man; he was a romantic. For him to engage in a serious relationship with a woman, he had to be in love with her, to set her on a pedestal and worship at her shrine. In return, he required to be worshipped without reservations. There was also an element of provincial puritanism about his standards of morality, so that if he did ever entertain casual affairs, and there is no evidence either way, it is certain they would have had to exist on an emotional plane in order for him to justify them. He loved fiercely and passionately, and was jealous with equal intensity. But what made this side of his life fraught with difficulties and pain was that his highly-charged feelings were extremely volatile and changeable. He fell in and out of love with sudden savagery, and he would have to wait until his late thirties to achieve stability and calm in this respect. Women, in these early years of his life, were attracted by his immense vitality, and the positiveness of his personality; all his life he engendered an uncompromising, forthright virility; there could be no mistaking Donald for anything but a full-blooded man.

Chris Castor was four years older than Donald. An experienced actress by the time she joined the Sheffield company, she had played minor parts in Robert Lorraine's celebrated production of *Cyrano de Bergerac* (the one that had affected young Don so deeply), and better ones with Mrs. Patrick Campbell, whom she understudied. Now, in her first engagement in repertory, she was playing the female leads opposite Donald. For the whole year, they saw each other every day, every evening; the relationship deepened, and soon they declared their love for each other. It was the first time since his mother's death that Donald had found emotional security.

II

In the autumn of 1927, Donald's erstwhile employer, Matheson Lang, visited the Lyceum Theatre, Sheffield, on his annual tour. Donald asked if the actor-manager would send someone to see *The Silver Box* in which he was playing the villainous Jones. Donald remembered:

On Tuesday evening Mrs. Lang herself came. On the Thursday I was sent for and asked to read the script of a new play by Ashley

Dukes called *Such Men Are Dangerous* and especially to note the part of Stepan, a Russian serf who assassinated Czar Paul Alexander at the instigation of Count Pahlen. I was offered the part.

This chance was the turning-point in Donald's career. He had been offered a very effective part which appeared at the most critical moments of the drama, and it was made all the more telling because Donald was to share the death scene with Matheson Lang, as his master, the Count; in addition, the play was scheduled for London.

The remainder of the year at Sheffield, Donald spent in the reflected glory of the Lang contract and in the glow of his romance with Chris. By year's end, they had made plans to be married; the wind was set fair.

It was typical of Donald's energy and enthusiasm that, the moment the contract with Lang had been settled, he should begin to prepare for the role of the Russian serf. His reading list, entered into the fly leaf of his 1928 diary, names three works: *Crime and Punishment*, *The Brothers Karamazov* and *The Lower Depths*. In his autobiography he recalls also studying a tetralogy entitled *The Peasants* by Ladislas St. Raimont. Not content with this thorough immersion *à la Russe*, he sought out a teacher of the language at Sheffield University and learned a folk song which Stepan was required to sing as he faces his master with loaded pistol, in the final scene of the play. He also saw to it that he was word-perfect, a habit he would continue throughout his life, and an unusual one, for most actors are accustomed to wait at least until the moves have been set before committing their lines to memory. But Donald liked to get the lines out of the way early, so that he could train his concentration on the characterisation of the part, and because, with the text learned, he felt more confident when facing a newly-assembled company.

At year's end, Donald and Chris took their leave of Sheffield and returned to London; they carried with them their audience's gratitude and wishes for a successful and happy future.

Donald began rehearsing for *Such Men Are Dangerous* at Wyndham's Theatre, early in January 1928; Chris, meanwhile, had joined Barry Jackson's company which was to present, among other plays, a modern-dress *Macbeth* at the Royal Court Theatre. The couple planned to marry in April when Donald returned from the pre-London tour with Lang.

A fine cast had been assembled for Ashley Dukes' play, principally Robert Farquharson, Isobel Elsom, Gyles Isham, John Garside and Harcourt Williams, who was shortly to render Donald an important service. In February, the company travelled to Edinburgh to begin the tour, but no sooner had the production been launched than Lang was disturbed to learn that another play about Czar Paul Alexander was scheduled for a London production. After tense and lengthy discussions with his advisers, Lang decided to continue the tour but to postpone the London opening. To Donald it looked as though he would have to face a long, indefinite wait, a distressing prospect to one who was shortly to take on the responsibilities of a husband. Fortune, however, smiled: towards the end of the tour he was offered another fine supporting role in a play called *The Enemy* by Channing Pollock, an anti-war tract that suffered, according to Donald, from a certain lack of originality.

In April, he and Chris were married at St. George's, Westminster. Five weeks later, the bridegroom was once more in Edinburgh to begin another pre-London tour. From the very start of their married life, the newly-weds were undergoing the strains of a theatrical marriage: the long separations; the one partner rehearsing by day while the other played in the theatre by night; both experiencing exciting but quite different *milieux*. Donald, as if suddenly realising his new responsibilities in the uncertain world of his chosen profession, wrote to Chris of his loneliness, of his misgivings about the future. He felt isolated and helpless and spoke of himself and Chris 'fighting our way upwards with no relatives behind us and very few influential friends'. The sentence is revealing of Donald's attitude that would persist all through his career. He saw life as a fight, a struggle; he saw himself, even then, as one who stood alone. He suffered not only from self-doubt, but also from the understandable insecurity that resulted from choosing an insecure profession. Donald envied young men with private incomes and university degrees and, even more, those with a theatrical background and connections. The idea that, if he was to succeed, he would have to rely on his own resources, without expecting help from anyone, appears to stem from this time.

The Enemy opened at the Strand Theatre, London, in July, to a distinguished audience which included Randall Thomas Davidson, the Archbishop of Canterbury, members of Mr. Baldwin's cabinet and high-ranking officers of the three services; neither their presence, nor the fine performance of Horace Hodges in the leading role could save the play; it received a disastrous press, and ran for only four weeks. But Donald was more fortunate. It is an oft-stated theatrical maxim that it is better to be acclaimed in a series of flops, than to go unnoticed in a long run. Donald played the part of a young, shell-shocked student, who returns from the front a nervous wreck, clearly a part to test the actor's emotional resources. The *Daily Sketch* critic was not alone in reporting that 'Donald Wolfit, a new name to me, made a hit in a small part.' The timing of these personally favourable notices, in a play that was shortly to close, could not have been better. *The Enemy* was withdrawn just in time for Donald to rejoin Lang for the opening of *Such Men Are Dangerous* at the Duke of York's Theatre. He was to have two first nights before the London critics in the short span of six weeks.

III

Such Men Are Dangerous opened at the Duke of York's Theatre in September 1928. The undisputed highlight of the evening was the death scene between Matheson Lang as Count Pahlen and Donald as Stepan; its staging belied many of the accusations made against this actor-manager that he was ungenerous to supporting players and jealous of his own position. He allowed Stepan to face him, loaded pistol in hand, not in the down-stage, weaker position, but on the same level, actor to actor. They wait, silhouetted, for the clock to strike which is the signal for the shot to be fired. A tense pause ensues, broken by Pahlen, who says, 'Sing me a song, Stepan.' Gently, the servant sings a folk-song, dreading the moment when he must kill his beloved master. The clock strikes. Stepan fires. The curtain falls.

It was, by any reckoning, a gift for a young actor and ever afterwards Donald wondered if Lang really knew what an opportunity he had handed to what was, after all, a minor character. It is more than likely that Lang, a very experienced judge of theatrical effect, realised only too well, but because of the demands of the play, knew too that there was little he could do about it. From the modern viewpoint, when actors are supposed to be unselfish, caring only for the dramatist's work, and deeply committed to ensemble playing, this particular analysis of motive and effect may seem outlandish. In 1928, however, questions of this kind were much more overt than in the 1970s; leading actors held centre stage by right, whatever the demands of the scene. Even today, it is not altogether rare to hear prominent players complain of a lack of discipline among the young, or to see them take the director aside for a whispered conference, the result of which may be to rearrange the furniture in such a way as to make the prominent player more prominent. In Donald's case he would, as in all things, favour the overt manner.

Such Men Are Dangerous had a tumultuous reception from the first-night audience. Next day, the press were equally enthusiastic. Most newspapers mentioned Donald; indeed, the *Evening News* acclaimed him for giving the best performance in the play, but it was James Agate, the drama critic of the *Sunday Times* who, for the first time, set the seal on Donald's success; it would not be the last. He described the performance as remarkable, and continued: 'One read in his [Stepan's] sombre, faithful eyes that if he had been a dog he would have died on his master's grave.' Upon which, Donald in his autobiography, commented,

> That, indeed was how I felt about Matheson Lang who had given me the chance of a lifetime.

It must not be imagined that this was overnight stardom; on the contrary, the general public were still unaware of his name, but the success turned him, within the ranks of his profession, from a completely unknown actor into an actor who could be identified. Professional recognition, at this stage, was more important to him than to capture the public's fickle imagination; it would be a great help when it came to finding work. Donald had taken an important step forward.

The play was off to a good start and looked as though it would run well into the New Year. In his private life, too, Donald had cause to rejoice: Chris was pregnant.

Then, in November, King George V became gravely ill with septicaemia. London, already fog-bound, was plunged into an even deeper gloom. Rumours spread that the King was dead. Crowds gathered before Buckingham Palace to read the bulletins and, nightly, the B.B.C. gave news of the King's perilous condition. According to Donald, people stayed home to listen to the wireless, '. . . theatres everywhere were half empty'. By Christmas 1928, the King had recovered a little, but the play not at all. Lang wisely replaced it in January 1929 with another success that he had toured, but which had never been seen in London, *The Chinese Bungalow*, in which he played Yuan Sing, hoping to repeat, no doubt, his triumph as *Mr. Wu*. Ivor Brown was at his wittiest in *The Observer*:

> . . . this particular Chinese junk puts to sea rather slowly and then lumbers along amid the storms of Oriental passion to the haven of Happy-ever-after-landing tickets for Europeans only. . . . His [Lang's] cellar is complete from cocktail to brandy; indeed his very voice is like a bad liqueur, at once sweet, sticky, and full of bodeful fire. . . . If there had been a competition for best-dressed bungalows in the furthest East, Sing would have won the offered sports saloon or the month at Monte Carlo every time.

After praising the acting in general, he concluded in particular: '. . . And Mr. Donald Wolfit, as a Malay, is dentally sinister.'

Once more Lang had gathered together a fine company which included Nona Wynne as the Ayah, Marjorie Mars as Sadie Sing and Austin Trevor as the whitest of white men, Richard Marquess, whom Donald understudied. During the run of the play,

Donald forged a friendship with Austin Trevor that was to span almost forty years.

Four days after *The Chinese Bungalow* opened, Trevor was taken ill with influenza. Because rehearsals had been hurried, Donald was not fully conversant with the part, and after only an hour-long run-through of the main scene with Lang, appeared at the matinée. 'In all my experience in the theatre,' he wrote, 'that was quite the most terrifying time I have known.' Somehow, he bluffed his way through, with Lang prompting him from behind his gently fluttering Oriental fan. When Trevor returned to the cast, he presented Donald with an expensive pipe; the gift was received ungraciously by the under-study who let it be known that he thought presents in the circumstances unnecessary, when all he had done was fulfil the terms of his contract. Doubtless, he was suffering from a twinge of conscience for not knowing the lines well enough, but in the dressing-rooms his colleagues smiled indulgently, called him 'pompous' and concluded that Donald had 'a chip on his shoulder'.

With Austin Trevor back in the cast, Donald found himself once more playing a small part that demanded little of his vast energy. Again he entered enthusiastically into the activities of the Sunday Societies. Among the many performances he gave, one was of particular importance to his future career: the Provost in *Measure for Measure*. Harcourt Williams who had first met Donald in *Such Men Are Dangerous* and was impressed with his ability, had just been appointed director of the forthcoming autumn season of plays at the Old Vic. He attended the Sunday performance and was pleasantly surprised to find that the young actor had a talent for speaking Shakespearean verse. Donald was invited to meet Lilian Baylis and to discuss a line of parts for the season. The meeting went well and, with final details still to be settled, he was engaged to play Tybalt in *Romeo and Juliet*, and Lorenzo in *The Merchant of Venice*; his other roles would be decided later. After several earlier attempts to enter the stage door in the Waterloo Road, Donald now found the way in with surprising ease. But he did not allow himself to enjoy the prospect as fully as might be expected. By a quirk of personality, Donald was never able wholeheartedly either to trust or delight in good fortune; it was as if he suspected that any advantage could be snatched away as rapidly as it had been gained. Now, with the Old Vic contract secure, his mind filled with the practical problems that faced him: the run of *The Chinese Bungalow* was scheduled to end on 20 April, his twenty-seventh birthday; the Old Vic season would not begin until the autumn; the baby was due in June. He was faced with having to fill the five-month gap; the financial pressures, the impending responsibility, weighed heavy.

For the first time his diaries, like his father's before him, were consumed with financial details. Each week, his salary was entered, and around April, his total earnings for the year; more often than not there was a note on savings. Donald, having read his Dickens thoroughly, heeded Mr. Micawber's homily on thrift: 'Annual income twenty pounds, annual expenditure nineteen nineteen six, result happiness. Annual income twenty pounds, annual expenditure twenty pounds ought and six, result misery.' In many respects, that could be described as Donald's own economic creed. Obsessed as he was by insecurity, the nightmare of not being able to feed his family, or himself ending up impoverished in a home for aged actors haunted him and, as will be seen, he never exorcised the spectre. For this reason, his economy was always well-disciplined; he would never indulge in a flamboyant or an extravagant way of life so often associated with actors. In good times or in bad, he did his best to maintain the same simple standard of living.

As Stepan he received £9 per week;* for *The Chinese Bungalow*, Lang raised his salary to £10. During the run, he wrote a light comedy called *The Worm* which he persuaded the Sheffield Repertory Company to perform and received a royalty of two guineas. The moment the Lang season ended he was off to the Everyman Theatre, Hampstead, for a week to appear with Elaine Inescourt in a new play, *Smoke Persian*, for £5. He produced two one-act plays for Eleanor Elder at six guineas a time. Unable to find immediate work in London, he offered himself as leading man to the Hull Repertory Company, salary £7 per week; this engagement would take him through to the autumn. The first year of their marriage, husband and wife earned between them £531.5.0. Expenditure £433.5.0; saving £98; result happiness.

He experienced a more profound happiness on 2 June 1929. At 4.29 p.m. Chris gave birth to a 7lb 6oz girl. The father, having listed forty-six possible boys' and girls' names in his diary, agreed to call the baby Margaret, the parents being influenced in their choice by pleasant memories of Dearth's daughter in Barrie's *Dear Brutus*. So joyful was the young father that, after seeing mother and child in the nursing home in Maida Vale, he ran all the way home to their flat in Earl's Court in a state of frenzied excitement. Six days later he was off to Sheffield to see a performance by amateurs of his play *The Worm*, only to read in the *Sheffield Mail* that 'some parts of this play will not bear too close an examination' and that the critic acclaimed the set as the most outstanding feature. The next day, Sunday, he crossed Yorkshire to begin the engagement with the Hull Repertory Company

* Equal to approximately £35–£40 per week in 1970.

for their summer season at the Theatre Royal, Huddersfield. During the following six weeks, his most important roles were Sir Anthony Absolute in *The Rivals* and Diego Spina in *Lazarro* by Luigi Pirandello. Meanwhile, in London, Chris and Margaret were doing well and had left the nursing home at the end of June. In July, the family were reunited in Newark for the christening. The marriage was constantly under the strain of enforced separations precipitated by the necessities of professional life.

The christening was a family affair, but not without a touch of theatrical glamour. When it came to godparents, a promise by proxy was made on behalf of Mrs. Patrick Campbell.

The family spent a week in New Balderton before returning to London for Donald to begin rehearsals. It is certain that he saw the forthcoming engagement at the Old Vic as a great opportunity to rise higher up the tree. The intensity of his ambition at this time is well illustrated by a story of a young girl, Muriel D'Arcy Mumby, an acquaintance of Donald's, seeing him one day in Newark on a shopping expedition. Donald alighted from his bicycle and said to her, without greeting or preamble, 'I start at the Old Vic next week, and I mean to get to the top!'

The real struggle for recognition was about to begin.

CHAPTER SEVEN

The Old Vic

To wilful men
The injuries that they themselves procure
Must be their schoolmasters.
—*King Lear*

I

BY 1929, the Old Vic had been presenting the plays of Shakespeare, as a matter of policy, for fifteen years. The foundations for this remarkable enterprise were laid, unpromisingly, in 1880 by a determined crusader, Emma Cons, the first woman member of the London County Council. Appalled by social conditions, an affirmed enemy of drunkenness and prostitution, Miss Cons, in an effort to lure the drunkards and whores off the street, purchased the freehold of the New Victoria Palace in the Waterloo Road with the intention of turning it into a temperance music hall. In a short time she raised enough money to convert the theatre into the Royal Victoria Hall and Coffee Tavern. Miss Cons, as a bait to the 'wicked', offered good clean entertainment: lectures, penny-readings and any other form of recreation that she considered respectable. Refreshments were no less wholesome: coffee and buns. It was an early experiment in environmental improvement, and it succeeded. Miss Cons employed a succession of managers to watch over her crusade; one man who lasted two years, which was a longer period than most, was a thirty-six-year-old ex-actor called William Poel,* who had some outlandish ideas about restoring the original Elizabethan style of production to the plays of Shakespeare, to rid them of their then fashionable encumbrances of realistic settings and declamatory acting. Although he did not have the opportunity of trying out his ideas during his term of office in the early 1880s, he was to be an important influence on the theatre in general, and on the Royal Victoria Hall and Coffee Tavern in parti-

* See page 103 et seq.

cular, which the English public, with its unfailing knack for deflating pomposity, nicknamed the Old Vic.

Miss Cons had many valuable attributes: a crusading spirit, a social conscience, grim determination and, perhaps most important of all, a niece named Lilian Baylis. In 1895, Lilian, aged 21, was living in South Africa teaching music and dancing. She had recently been ill and was making a slow recovery; Aunt Emma invited her to visit England for a holiday. Aunt and niece discovered a great bond between them, for they were both inspired by profound religious beliefs that coloured every aspect of their lives; the elder woman was satisfied that the girl had also inherited the family's crusading zeal and she appointed Lilian Baylis manager of the Old Vic.

The rest is history: how Lilian Baylis encouraged opera recitals, and later obtained a dramatic licence to present the operas in full; how she introduced film shows, and how, when funds were low, she turned in despair to the works of William Shakespeare. Her devotion and single-mindedness is legendary. Harcourt Williams in his book *Old Vic Saga* recounts:

> Emma Cons died in 1912. Her portrait . . . used to hang in the vestibule. . . . Nearby, hung a portrait of King George V. 'Not quite so large as Aunt Emma's,' Lilian Baylis once explained to Queen Mary, 'because your dear husband has not done so much for the Old Vic.'

Lilian Baylis ruled her enterprise like a benevolent Head of State until her death in 1937. Her Prime Ministers were numerous and each, in their way, made an invaluable contribution to the Old Vic and, in turn, to the British theatre. Some of them enter this story again, in other capacities: Sir Philip Ben Greet, Russell Thorndike, Robert Atkins, Andrew Leigh, Harcourt Williams and Sir Tyrone Guthrie. Individually and collectively they established a style of Shakespearean acting and production that earned the admiration and envy of the world; they transformed the out-of-the-way building in the Waterloo Road into a fashionable centre-piece of the English theatrical scene. They were served, in turn, by some extraordinarily gifted actors and actresses, many of whom found the transition from the Vic to the West End difficult to make. On the whole, the women fared better than the men, as Sybil Thorndike and Edith Evans prove, but few of the men received the recognition that was their due: Ion Swinley, Baliol Holloway and, perhaps the most gifted of all, Ernest Milton. He too enters this story again but in this brief account of the Old Vic his contribution cannot be made too much of. In a letter written to him in the early 1930s, Lilian Baylis stated unequivocally that his Hamlet was one of the chief turning-points in the Old Vic's fortunes.

It was, and is, universally regarded by critics, fellow actors and play-goers as a dazzling display of the highest quality, and is thought by many to be one of the truly great performances of this century. Certain it is, that it caused a good deal of attention to be focused on the Old Vic, for it seemed that in Milton's Hamlet the torch of the purely lyrical tradition of English acting had been rekindled. That particular flame was to burn even more brightly in the 1929–30 season for which Harcourt Williams had recruited a company that many leading critics thought to be without any particular strength or merit: Martita Hunt, Adele Dixon, Margaret Webster, Gyles Isham, Brember Wills, Richard Ainley, Donald Wolfit and John Gielgud.

The richness of English acting is well illustrated by that list, for Wolfit and Gielgud represented the two extremes of the wide spectrum of styles, and confirm that England, with the liveliest theatrical tradition in the world, suffers that most pleasant of cultural maladies, an *embarras de richesses*. Wolfit embodied the heroic, earthy force; Gielgud the lyrical and aesthetic. Between those two extremes existed a whole range of performers embracing styles that, to a lesser or greater extent, combined the two.

It was predictable that they would not take to each other. As far as Wolfit was concerned, Gielgud was all that he disliked most: a member of a distinguished theatrical family, the Terrys, brought up in the comfort of the upper middle class, educated at a public school, Westminster, and trained for the stage at the Royal Academy of Dramatic Art. He seemed to have every advantage. It was, to some extent, an irrational judgment which blinded Wolfit to Gielgud's exceptional gifts: his superb voice, his grace of interpretation, his perceptive intelligence and, above all, a soulfulness that was capable of encompassing noble passion in the finest sense. Wolfit was unable to appreciate that there was room for them both and, furthermore, never understood that it was extremely important for the theatre that there should be. As men they had only their love of the theatre in common, and it would not be enough to form the foundation of anything more than chilly politeness, and sometimes not even that. Disagreements were plentiful and throughout his life Wolfit would, at the mention of Gielgud's name, inhale deeply and noisily through his nose like an enraged bull, which was his way of signifying enmity.

At least, at rehearsals, both wore the actors' uniform of the day: black Homburg with a snap brim, blue shirt, red tie. Wolfit never discarded the Homburg and would regularly visit a well-known hatmaker in Piccadilly, fling his worn headgear on the counter and say, 'Another one of these, please'.

On Waterloo Tube Station, after the first meeting of the company in August, a young student, Susan Anthony, who was paying £40 per season for the privilege of walking on, saw Wolfit waiting for his train. His stance, his manner caused her to reflect, 'Now there's an actor.' She would, in time, come to know him better, but in the early days she was an objective observer of the scene and was aware, even in her humble capacity, that Wolfit was very much aloof from the rest of the company, one apart from the other leading players, John Gielgud and Martita Hunt.

Rehearsals began full of expectation. The seal of national approval had been placed on the Old Vic's efforts at the beginning of the year when Lilian Baylis was admitted to the Order of the Companions of Honour. The theatre was about to become fashionable, for John Gielgud was to embark on a series of performances that would bring him deserved fame and honour, and attract the sophisticates across the river by way of Waterloo Bridge.

The first production was *Romeo and Juliet*; Gielgud as Romeo, Adele Dixon as Juliet, and Wolfit as Tybalt. The production was not well received. From *Punch*:

> They are such resolute Bardolaters at the Old Vic that, acting (I imagine) on a bare hint in the Prologue—'the two hours' traffic of our stage'—they raced through their romantic unsophisticated tragedy and were just beaten at the post.

Of the acting:

> Mr. John Gielgud was not, I think, quite the ardent lovesick stripling of our imagination. He was adequate in elocution (occasionally a little noisy), spirited in movement; but there was no quality of rapture in his wooing. . . . The rash *Tybalt* (Mr. Donald Wolfit) more plausibly Italianate than the rest, spat the venom of vendetta through passionately compressed lips and was pleasantly in the picture.

The new company was clearly having difficulty in finding its feet. *The Merchant of Venice* followed with Brember Wills cast, in the headline of the *Morning Post*, as A MAD SHYLOCK. Wolfit, as Lorenzo, earned praise from Harley Granville Barker, who wrote to Harcourt Williams extolling the actor's poetic gift. Williams himself wrote later, 'Young Donald Wolfit as Lorenzo spoke the verse in the last act exquisitely.'

'Nonetheless,' Wolfit observed, 'I was not happy in the list of parts that was being assigned to me and, having proved my worth in the team was promised Mowbray and the Bishop of Carlisle in *Richard II*, and Cassius and Touchstone.'

The above indicates that Wolfit must have complained to Harcourt Williams, who seems to have placated his unhappy actor by acceding to some of his demands. This kind of action, however, would not make Wolfit popular with either the producer or the company. But Wolfit was always insistent upon what he saw as his rights, and was doubtless encouraged by being the only member of the company to be warmly praised in *Romeo and Juliet*, and by Granville Barker's mention of him as Lorenzo.

The first two plays of the season then, were not popularly received; the accent had been on pace, coupled with speed of action so that one scene followed another with as little pause as possible, a direct influence but a misunderstanding of William Poel's methods. The complaints voiced generally in the Press against speed must have sunk in, for a more temperate pace was achieved for the next production, *Richard II*, and it was the company's first outstanding success, due almost entirely to Gielgud's fine acting in the title role. Only one critic had reservations: James Agate in the *Sunday Times*, headed his review, 'Half a King' and complained that:

> Mr. John Gielgud does not give us anything at all of the artist-half of Richard, though he does perfect justice to what I would like to call the elegaic-half.

Agate considered the company less than first-rate, though he admitted that Martita Hunt as Queen Isabella and Wolfit as the Bishop of Carlisle 'made some amends'. Agate's review, however, did not detract to any great extent from the considerable acclaim that Gielgud received. But it did confirm Wolfit's admiration for Agate as a critic. In the next twenty years the actor would have cause to admire the critic even more.

The company capitalised on the success of *Richard II* with Molière's *Le Malade Imaginaire*, Wolfit as Dr. Purgon, and at Christmas *A Midsummer Night's Dream*, in which he was cast as Demetrius. For both roles he was noted for his 'gusto'.

Wolfit was deeply unhappy during this period of his life. His marriage was floundering, but because of their love for Margaret, both partners made efforts to preserve a façade of stability, but as both were constantly in work and often apart, these attempts were subject to serious set-backs from which the marriage never recovered. Professionally, there were tensions within the Old Vic company; Wolfit's private and public life were always dependent the one upon the other. He found a friend in Margaret Webster and, as a result, was befriended by her parents, Dame May Whitty and Ben Webster; Wolfit was grateful; he wrote: 'their friendship gave me tremendous encouragement and delight at a time when I was in sore need of it.'

It would seem probable that much of Wolfit's need stemmed from seeing Gielgud so elegantly ascending the ladder of success. Wolfit was two years older, with a wife and child to support; for nine years he had worked hard at his trade; his own ascent was slow and, at times, so painstaking that it seemed to be at a standstill. John Gielgud, on the other hand, after four years in the profession, had taken over from Noël Coward in *The Vortex* in 1925, and the following year had succeeded the same actor as Lewis Dodd in *The Constant Nymph* at the Strand Theatre; he had later appeared in New York in *The Patriot* and in 1928 played Oswald in Ibsen's *Ghosts* at Wyndham's; after a series of plays in London he arrived at the Old Vic, 'in the very May-morn of his youth, Ripe for exploits and mighty enterprises'. To Wolfit, Gielgud's success appeared effortless and privileged. His own path had been pitted with obstacles; the struggle to overcome them had intensified his insecurity which, in turn, expressed itself in over-assertion, and in sinking all his vast ambition into each role as it presented itself.

Mid-season saw the end of the decade; the 1920s passed into history as the Jazz Age. The 1930s entered in the misleading guise of a lamb. For Wolfit, the hope that his struggle for recognition was over must have been uppermost in his mind, and in January he may have been encouraged to think that his time had, indeed, come.

In *Julius Caesar* he played Cassius, with Gielgud as Marc Antony and Harcourt Williams substituting at the last moment for Gyles Isham as Brutus. The critics were unanimous in their praise for all and, as far as Cassius was concerned, could have been privy to a conspiracy of adjectives: 'fiery', 'tempestuous', 'impetuous', 'vehement' recur in all the notices. Wolfit was pleased to record that it was for this performance that

> I was now to be the recipient of a signal mark of favour from the gallery of the Old Vic. . . . During each season they had a custom of presenting a laurel wreath to the actor or actress who had pleased them most, and they had decided to bestow this honour upon me for my performance as Cassius.

Wolfit drew enormous comfort from this show of the gallery's affection for him. As far as he was concerned, the smart, sophisticated set could like whom they pleased, for he was the favourite of the ordinary theatregoers, those members of the audience who had queued for hours on end, the working people of London, untouched by fad or fashion. It was an omen of things to come.

On the last performance of the play, he was told he would receive the wreath across the footlights. His own recollection of this event reveals the tensions as he sensed them:

> . . . I thought it would create very bitter feeling if I took the gift on

the curtain call with Brutus and Antony on either side of me. On the other hand, I could not offend the gallery who were paying me a high compliment. The calls at the end of the play were rearranged and taken separately and so I took the coveted prize to a tumult of applause. . . . Oh, that laurel wreath! It hung on my sitting-room wall until it fell to pieces, the proudest trophy of my life; but alas—it caused me much trouble, and in certain quarters I believe it is not entirely forgotten to this day. One person to whom it gave great pleasure was Lilian Baylis who was always delighted when one of her boys or girls made good.

There was yet another incident that certainly caused him further unpopularity. *Julius Caesar* was followed by *As You Like It* in which Wolfit played Touchstone. At a matinée of schoolchildren, their chatter became so loud that the actors, by mutual consent, played the beginning and end of scenes, cutting the middle section. In the last scene of the play, Touchstone has his famous 'If' speech; as Wolfit began to speak, the other actors hissed, 'Cut the speech!' but Wolfit insisted on giving it in full, the reason being that if he had cut the speech, Martita Hunt as Rosalind, would not have had time for her quick-change from boy back to girl, and be ready to re-enter with Hymen for 'Then is there mirth in heaven . . .'. His colleagues were irritated; Wolfit's response was to argue that Shakespeare was a master-craftsman who had put 'a brilliant speech . . . into the mouth of a clown and so precisely timed as to turn wit to a practical purpose'. Beady mutterings of 'pompous' and 'silly ass' greeted this rationale, but that would be too facile a way of explaining Wolfit's behaviour. Lest the occurrence should seem trivial, let it be made clear that it was one which Wolfit recounted often in later years, as if still trying vehemently to justify his action.* His unpopularity with certain sections of his profession was founded on just such incidents. Wolfit could never be light-hearted enough on stage to cut a long speech; he fought, as it were, for hard-won possession of what was rightfully his, be it to a matinée of school-children or a glittering first-night audience; he approached all performances with exactly the same seriousness. And, of course, the point must be made that he was right: to cut the speech would have left Martita Hunt struggling out of breeches into petticoats. It was not a happy time.

The season received a sharp jolt in March when the Old Vic presented, for the first time in its existence, two short plays by George Bernard Shaw: *Androcles and the Lion* and *The Dark Lady of the Sonnets*. Wolfit played Ferrovius in the first, and took enormous pains with his costume and make-up, adding two-inch lifts to his

---

* He wrote of the incident in his autobiography.

sandals and a two-inch pad to the crown of his wig, giving himself an overall height of six foot three. Lilian Baylis, in an interval during the dress-rehearsal, called him over, eyed him up and down, and said: 'Isn't it wonderful, my dear boy. You are making such wonderful progress with us. It's like having a tender little plant; we water it and watch it grow.'

Three weeks later John Gielgud gave his first performance as *Macbeth*, received a thunderous ovation and was highly praised. Agate surrendered to his power: '. . . the actor carried us away', he wrote and also had a warm word for Wolfit: 'Macduff was magnificently given by Mr. Donald Wolfit.'

The final play of the season was *Hamlet*. The performance by John Gielgud as the Prince, which grew in stature over the years, has gone down in theatrical history as a very great performance and with it another Terry took his rightful place in the front line of English actors. This Hamlet was the renewal of all that was best in lyrical acting by one whom Agate described as 'a perfectly graced actor', capable of sustaining passions on a high, poetic, emotional plane, commanding a voice of great beauty, rich and flexible, expressing exquisite pathos and profound intensity. Gielgud's Hamlet stands beside Irving's and Forbes-Robertson's and, if they were fashionable, Benson's and Ernest Milton's.

The Old Vic company had, by the time this play was produced, come together as an ensemble and the Prince was well-supported. It is an important landmark for one other reason and that is that Wolfit, as Claudius, discovered his own style of acting, a style that would depend on a mighty inner power which was to swell to such enormity that the actor would have difficulty in containing it. For the first time in his career, Wolfit had achieved 'size' in performance and it is, in part, due to the fact that the line of characters he had played that season, culminating in Claudius, was like a well-planned training session for the real thing. Tybalt allowed him to exploit villainy; Lorenzo gave free rein to his poetic gifts; in Cassius he explored venom and bitterness; playing Macduff he was obliged to portray a man of action in turn horrified at the death of Duncan and shattered at the murder of his own family. Harcourt Williams wrote, '. . . Nor have I seen a better King than Donald Wolfit', and that was the general view of most of the important critics. 'Donald Wolfit was as fine a King as seen for many years in London,' declared the *Daily Sketch*, and in *Truth*: 'For me the best performance of the evening was Donald Wolfit as Claudius.' The critic of *Punch* dealt with the role in more detail:

Mr. Donald Wolfit (*The King*) struck a new note and I thought gave an attractive and plausible performance. The *prie-dieu* soliloquy was particularly well done, nor did he forget to fawn upon the Queen in such wise as to give colour to the report of his character and edge to his nephew's rage. Nor, again, did he make himself so personable a man as to render ridiculous the 'Hyperion to a satyr' comment.

Wolfit looked back on this performance as an important signpost in his inner development as an actor. He remembered, in conversation with Roy Walker, many years later, the dangerous excitement he felt after the play scene on the first night. 'Give me some light!' cries Claudius, and Wolfit, on giving voice to that terror, discovered inside himself a reservoir of power, vocal and emotional, of which he had until then been but dimly aware.

The production was an unqualified success. The London sophisticates, ever a lazy breed, decided that to make the arduous journey south of the river was now the 'done thing'. Later, in June, the play transferred to the Queen's Theatre, Shaftesbury Avenue, which, had they known, would have saved them the trouble.

Next door, at the Globe, C. B. Cochran presented an international season which included another Hamlet, Alexander Moissi, the distinguished German actor, and there was yet a third Hamlet playing in London during the summer of 1930: Henry Ainley as the Prince, Gwen Ffrangcon-Davies as Ophelia, Cedric Hardwicke as Claudius and Irene Vanbrugh, 'gloriously miscast', according to Agate, as the Queen. Despite the formidable array of names, the Vic's performance benefited by comparison; the Haymarket version was so clumsily cut 'as to render nearly all the latter half of the tragedy meaningless'. Wolfit, too, must have scored, for Agate wrote: 'As for the King, Mr. Cedric Hardwicke will also, I hope, forgive the suggestion that when one wants to see Churdles Ash one visits another play.'

Of the three Hamlets, Moissi was closest to Wolfit's heart. Here was a kindred spirit, an actor in the great European tradition of unashamed, unembarrassed passion, the display of which has always been inclined to make Englishmen feel a trifle uneasy. Wolfit thought Moissi's Hamlet

. . . a very great performance indeed. . . . His beautiful tenor voice, fraught with agony, soared to the roof of the theatre. The moment when he took the huge branch candelabra from the guard and thrust it into the King's face in the play scene was great theatre, and the sight of the tiny black figure thrown into the air to land on the shoulders of the six-foot-tall soldiery at the final curtain was a never-to-be-forgotten experience.

Wolfit never apologised for admiring sheer theatrical effect; to him it was part and parcel of the theatre's function, and he despaired at the trend that later developed to reduce the drama to life size.

His good notices for Claudius, his awareness of increasing emotional resources did little to compensate for the disappointment he was to feel 'at not being invited to return to the Vic for a second season'. He wanted so much to continue there, to extend his range of parts, but it was not to be. Ralph Richardson joined the company, playing Prince Hal, Caliban and Bolingbroke. Gielgud was again leading man. To Lilian Baylis, after the last performance of *Hamlet*, Wolfit remarked how sad he was to say good-bye. She replied, 'Well, don't say it then, dear boy. Just make it *au revoir*.' Wolfit wrote: 'I think she knew my very real sadness at departing from this remarkable theatre.'

It is of importance in Wolfit's life that his engagement at the Old Vic coincided with the theatre's elevation to the fashionable ranks. Wolfit was never at ease in these circumstances, and certainly less so because of his supporting role in the success, but even that was not so important a factor when one considers that, twenty years later, he returned in leading roles and experienced similar unhappiness.

The pattern, however, of Wolfit's relationships with his fellow artists had begun to emerge. He was, considering his ability as an actor, a very bad dissembler; he lacked both the inclination and the guile to oil the workings of social and professional intercourse. He had no means of disguising his feelings, of suiting his mood to the mood of others. His absorption with self, with the serious purpose of the theatre, and with his vaulting ambition made him a difficult proposition within a company, and these preoccupations were all the more intensified in the eyes of his colleagues by his discovery of 'size', for it showed itself not only in performance. He appeared even then, at any rate in the eyes of the young student Susan Anthony, larger than life, as if all human qualities, good and bad, were in him exaggerated.

II

Not long after he left the Old Vic he again met that young student, and a friendship began and soon became serious for them both. She was twenty-three, the daughter of a well-to-do City metal broker, educated at a public school. A handsome young woman with a mind of her own, she displayed a striking personality and a character quite as determined as that of the young actor with whom she was in love. Wolfit's marriage to Chris was still formally preserved for the sake of the child, Margaret, but even the formality was soon to be set aside.

Susan introduced Wolfit to a certain style of life of which the boy from New Balderton knew little. Until he met her, Wolfit considered the height of *gourmandise* was to eat tinned red salmon with tinned green peas. Susan advised him otherwise. He admired her self-assurance and *savoir-faire*; she was extremely practical and forthright, and they shared a deep love of the countryside and of nature.

It was in the countryside, or anywhere far, far away from the theatre, that another side to Wolfit's character appeared; a gay, inconsequential, ridiculous side that delighted in childish jokes, elaborate word-games and nonsense rhymes, for which he had a particular facility. Something akin to a switch being thrown occurred as Wolfit entered a stage door; all the darker aspects of his nature bubbled to the surface; but set him down on a riverbank, or in a country lane, or in the company of close and intimate friends and the burden lightened: he could be expansive, warm and devastatingly charming. This lightness Susan also encouraged.

Professionally, another figure of major importance entered Wolfit's life at this time: William Poel, whom Wolfit remembered as 'a picturesque old man in a black Inverness cape and a Churchillian hat. A tall gaunt man with a slight stoop, he had a massive noble forehead, a wide mouth and a pair of piercing light-blue eyes. These features I remember well, also his long delicate hands and beautifully modulated voice.' More vividly, the actor was reminded that as he, Poel, approached down the street, 'one got the impression that Professor Moriarty disguised as the Archangel Gabriel was on the move'.

Poel is, without doubt, the most important reformer of English Shakespearean acting and production of the past hundred years and takes an honoured place beside Gordon Craig and Harley Granville Barker, whose *Prefaces*, in the words of Robert Speaight* 'were a brilliant application of Poel's principles'. As may be expected, he was labelled a crank by his contemporaries. Born in 1852, and judged to be too delicate to be sent to university, he became an actor in 1876, manager of the Old Vic 1881–3, and Benson's stage manager in 1884, then for many years general instructor to the Shakespeare Reading Society. In gratitude for his work, the Society made a donation, and together with one from Mr. Anthony Dillon, Poel founded the Elizabethan Stage Society in 1894. Through the work of this Society, Poel laid the foundations of an approach to Shakespearean speaking and staging that is still being built upon.

Speaight, in assessing his contribution and comparing it with Granville-Barker's, who on his own admission was a disciple of Poel, wrote: 'The magnificent thing about Barker was his mind and his power of expressing it on paper. His monument is the *Prefaces*,

* Poel's biographer.

and any producer will always break his teeth against them in vain. The magnificent thing about Poel was his vision . . . which he never began to express on paper and only expressed in flashes on the stage.'

Wolfit always publicly acknowledged Poel for teaching him all he knew about speaking verse; and another who acknowledges a great debt to Poel is Dame Edith Evans; in 1912, while still a milliner, she appeared in his production of *Troilus and Cressida*, which brought her to the attention of London managements.

Of Poel as a teacher, Dame Edith said that she considered him the first man to discover the importance of correct emphasis in speech. The traditional method of speaking Shakespeare had always favoured the declamatory style, 'full of sound and fury, signifying nothing'. Poel preferred the words to be spoken 'trippingly on the tongue'. His pupils were instructed to go for the 'key words' in a speech, thus bringing out the true meaning and rhythm of the verse. This method, Dame Edith was certain, produced a new kind of vitality and life in the words themselves. One may summarise Poel's methods by concluding that he insisted on sense *and* sensibility. An example of his methods was given by Ben Iden Payne, Miss Horniman's producer in Manchester. Iden Payne knew Poel well and admired him; he remembered for almost sixty years an emphasis Poel had required in his production of *Measure for Measure* at the Gaiety; the first speech of the Duke, in Act I, Scene One:

Of government and properties to unfold,
Would seem to me to AFFECT speech and discourse.

According to Dame Edith and to Wolfit, Poel was extremely gentle; he taught, not in the classroom, but through directing in the theatre, although he confessed to Iden Payne that, 'I cannot do anything with good pro actors'; of Dame Sybil Thorndike and Sir Lewis Casson he complained, 'They cannot take the *tones*.' Sir Lewis himself had a curious method, an extremely rigid one, of giving inflections to actors, reducing words to rhythmic sounds. Thus, in *Oedipus the King*, 'In Thebes, City of Light,' became, Da-*da*, da-da-da-*da*!' Dame Edith agreed that Poel gave direction rather like Sir Lewis, but 'was much less strict'. Poel never interfered with the comic parts, and liked to employ competent performers who could manage without his help in these roles; doubtless the fact that much of Shakespeare's comedy parts are written in prose had something to do with his attitude.

Poel's other contribution concerned the production of the plays. Once more, Dame Edith:

He was also the first man to produce Shakespeare so that each scene followed naturally on the next, without break, in the Music-

Hall tradition. He rejected the Beerbohm Tree method of great set operatic pieces.

And Harcourt Williams:

> It was Poel who made the first attack on the over-upholstered, pseudo-archaelogically correct way of staging Shakespeare, which had led to the drastic cutting of the plays and the general slowing up of the tempo to fit all into the elaborate scenery.

Poel's theories, which he himself first put into practice, were, according to Williams, 'to find expression in the work of the Old Vic'. Apart from the style of production, Poel, as the name of his society implies, thirsted to renew the Elizabethan shape, the wooden O, and thus directly influenced contemporary theatrical architects who have modelled their buildings to accommodate the very Elizabethan concept that Poel strove for. Theatre building today, pushing at the eighteenth-century proscenium, like Samson in the temple, has much to thank him for.

His work was secret and unheralded, but made itself felt, both in England and America, and struck at the very roots of all that was considered fashionable. Sir Tyrone Guthrie summed up Poel's work, coupling him with Granville Barker,

> . . . who between them revolutionised British, and therefore American ideas of Shakespearean production. The text must be inviolate. If realistic scenery cannot—and it cannot—be suitably adapted to the constant changes of environment and atmosphere indicated in the text, then realistic scenery must go. Poel's productions were given on a bare stage. . . . I agreed with Poel and Barker that the first consideration must be the text, that Irving and his contemporaries were wrong to subordinate this to scenic convenience, and that Shakespeare must not be tied to literal realism.

Literal realism was anathema to Poel, both as far as settings and acting were concerned. At the heart of his beliefs was the contention that since Shakespeare had written for the most part in verse, the realistic school had poor foundation for an argument. This does not deny, as Guthrie so rightly insisted, that the actor must be identifiable as a real, living being, but nor does it mean that he was to reduce the size of the character and what he said to the level of everyday ordinaries. Size was demanded from the actors commensurate with the dramatist they served. In Wolfit's vocabulary, which Poel taught him, King meant King, and Prince meant Prince. To seek contemporary significance by straining either the text or the context was to distort the work, and undermined the eternal nature of the themes of Shakespeare's plays, which were pertinent to each generation because they were eternal; they needed no director to re-upholster them in whatever fabric of the day happened to be most fashionable. But because the statement of eternal themes seems irreconcilable with the demands of fashion, the pressures have been for the theatre to adopt the opposite approach. Throughout Robert Speaight's fine biography of Poel, the impression of the outsider, the solitary worker, the lonely revolutionary standing aside from the mainstream of accepted thought and practice, is endorsed. Perhaps this was part of the reason why Wolfit was so powerfully drawn towards him, and the influence teacher exerted over pupil, as the latter's acting grew in stature, may be easily discerned.

There was much to like about Poel himself. If not exactly eccentric there was certainly something about him of the scholar, self-contained in his own world, which is likely to lead to personal mannerisms and curious predilections that could be interpreted as eccentric. Iden-Payne remembered that the first shock one received on meeting Poel, well known as he was for his insistence on correct speech, was to be assailed by an odd mannerism that was somewhat disturbing. 'I . . . urrah . . . would . . . urrah . . . like you to . . . urrah . . . be in my . . . play . . . urrah,' and doubtless this is what he said to Wolfit after seeing him as Prus in a production of *The Marcopulos Secret* by Karel Capek at the Arts Theatre.

Poel invited Wolfit to play Cato in *Julius Caesar the Dictator*, which the latter described as 'an episodic compilation consisting of extracts from *Julius Caesar* and Chapman's *Caesar and Pompey*'. The play was presented during a glorious July, for one Sunday night, aptly at the Globe Theatre, Shaftesbury Avenue. Both production and actors elicited enthusiasm and, in particular:

> Mr. Donald Wolfit gave a fine performance of Cato. His elocution was admirable, so devoid of histrionic declamation that every line he spoke was natural.

Some days after the performance, Wolfit was to be photographed as Cato. For some reason Poel had arranged the sitting in Snaresbrook. Wolfit wrote a letter describing the episode to Susan, and not only does it present a delightful picture of Poel, but also gives some clues to Wolfit's private life at the time:

Earls Court.
In the Heat.

Dear Susan,

Thank you for your letters—they do cheer a body up! And a body needs it in this heat.

First of all I must tell you about the expedition with Poel. He arrived at Nathans [theatrical costumiers] at 2.30 (it was 92° if you remember). Then he discovered he'd lost his stick that he lent me for Cato so nothing would do but we must go to the Globe Theatre to find it. We set off, I with a parcel, and a heavy leather suitcase. We arrived in due course at the Globe; it was not there. Then he said we walked to Leicester Square (only a few minutes and the Globe was on our way!!) I murmured something about a taxi as I heard the sweat landing on my suitcase in rending wallops—but no—we must walk, only a few minutes. There he took two tickets to Liverpool Street. We changed at Holborn with the dear bag. I murmured faintly something about wanting to go to Barking to be 'took'. Oh no—we weren't going to Barking. It was still 92° and like a nightmare. We got into a train, a steam train at Liverpool Street and then I discovered we were really going to Snaresbrook. My bag was behaving very well at this point, it just sat and got dry on the floor of the carriage—dear bag.

We arrived in Snaresbrook, in the distance, on top of the hill I saw a row of houses and shops, the road was bright and sunny up the brow of the hill. The bag became a little difficult, evidently desiring an umbrella. Poel said would I like a cup of tea if we saw a shop before we came to the studio. I murmured I would, but we got to the studio first. I collapsed in a chair and called for water, murmuring that I didn't stand the heat very well. He said he had noticed that and stepped quietly out of the pool that was gathering round his feet. I changed, or rather stripped and put a towel round my loins. He stepped over to me and said 'Would you like an orange, it might refresh you.' He went out and bought me two. Bless him. It was then 4.30. I was posed and taken for an hour. Then we had a cup of tea and returned to Snaresbrook. I arrived at the flat at 7.45. It was still 92° and the bag was very good on the way home.

Today I have been over to Colchester, there is a big opening for a repertory theatre there. When next I see you I shall have some news for you—it's a grand chance if I can raise the money.

Yes. I know the Canterbury ground, it's fine, I saw several matches there some years ago when I played pastoral plays there in Comem. week with Charles Doran.

I am so glad to have been the means of introducing those books to you, it is a real joy to me and Susan, let us hold on to this friendship. It is very difficult and there are days when circumstances forbid me writing to you but I will write whenever I can, and it seems fair.

It is cooler tonight thank Heaven. Had a fine run down to Colchester today out of London's swelter and heat.

My love,
Donald.

P.S. Spent yesterday aft. in the Serpentine—a great swim.

In August, having taken time to consider the performance, Poel wrote to Wolfit:

I am sure that my thanks over and over are due to you for your admirable impersonation of the part of Cato. I always contend that the English actor can't impersonate and I expect that you have not exactly what we call the English temperament. When I put the part into your hands I shuddered at the idea of giving it to a boy to act. But the impersonation was masterly. Because it *was* Cato with Cato's idiosyncrasies. The play was worth producing simply that we might for the first time realise Cato in the flesh. All the business too was done with admirable restraint, and the effect of the sword following you into the tent was also most effective. I think you have a brilliant future before you if only you are lucky to go with intelligent actors. Best wishes and renewed thanks.

William Poel.

III

1931–6 were, professionally, uninspiring years for Wolfit. True, he was little out of work but his employment advanced his ability hardly at all. He accepted any work that was offered him with one reason in mind: he was still saving money, but now with an added incentive. As the letter to Susan about Poel makes clear, Wolfit was already entertaining thoughts of setting up on his own. The idea of running a repertory company in Colchester came to nothing because he could not raise the money. His unhappiness at the Old Vic no doubt contributed to the fact that the only way he could see of gaining the heights was if he was hauled to the top by his own determination. To this end, he saved with increased vigour. In 1931 he opened a deposit account, and soon he was investing in gilt-edged securities, debentures, applying for new issues of shares, and generally building up his capital. Wolfit invested with a canny instinct, as time would tell. He endured the treadmill of the early thirties because he knew he was going to be able to hop off, to buy himself, as it were, out of servitude.

December 1930 found him at the Embassy Theatre, Swiss Cottage, in a repertory season, the brain-child of Alec Rea and A. R. Whatmore. The season is noteworthy for the talents of its two leading men: Wolfit and Robert Donat. They became friends. Both hailed from the North—Donat was born in Manchester in 1905—from similar backgrounds, and both had experienced a thorough, hardworking apprenticeship. Wolfit nursed a great affection for Donat; he admired the younger man's carefree personality and often repeated Donat's standard response to any request from a director: 'There will be no extra charge.'

The last play of the Embassy season was an adaptation by Edward Lewis of Mary Webb's novel *Precious Bane*, containing two fine male parts: Gideon, the chief protagonist, and Beguildy, a sorcerer. While waiting for the cast list to be announced, Wolfit said to Donat, 'Whoever plays Gideon will be the first to get to the top.' Donat agreed, but added, in broad Lancashire, 'Aye, and t'other'll not be far behind.' Wolfit was right. Donat was cast as Gideon and scored the first outstanding success of his career; soon after, he was besieged by film offers and became an important cinema star. Donat's life was crippled by chronic asthma. When he died in 1958, aged fifty-three, Wolfit said, 'If Bobbie had had his health, he'd have knocked us all into the middle of next week. He was a very wonderful actor.'

In the early summer of 1931, Wolfit, aged twenty-nine, played Solness in Ibsen's *The Master Builder* for the first time. Agatha Kentish was Hilda, Margaret Rutherford Mrs. Solness, and Stringer Davis Brovik. So began an obsession with a play that Wolfit was to perform, on and off, for the next thirty-five years. His fascination for the part will be examined later; his first performance at the Greyhound Theatre, Croydon was rapturously received by local critics and audience. From the *Surrey County Herald*:

> He took six curtain calls and it was not until the orchestra played the National Anthem that the applause died down.

The following month an event occurred dear to Wolfit's theatrical heart. He returned to the Embassy Theatre to play opposite Sybil Thorndike in a pre-West End try-out of Steve Passeur's *Marriage by Purchase*; for the leading lady—SYBIL THORNDIKE MISCAST screamed the *Daily Telegraph*—it was a disaster but she had some compensation: in the Birthday Honours List which was published during that week, she was created a Dame of the British Empire; Wolfit was the first person to kiss her on the stage, and it was the sort of theatrical moment that he relished.

But he was not really happy, either professionally or privately. He wrote:

> At this period my performances were suffering from an intensity that sometimes went over the border-line. I was not being allowed in the parts that were coming to me to develop my vein of comedy and was rapidly acquiring a reputation for brooding psychological studies in repression and bitterness.
>
> It may well be that my unhappiness was largely responsible for this state of affairs. After my departure from Sheffield, seeking for a domestic background that would give me a sense of permanence, I had plunged into a hasty marriage in the profound hope that a successful theatre partnership would develop into one more lasting.

Alas, like so many others in my profession, the conflict of tempera-ment and ambition proved insurmountable. In a vain effort to forget this I undertook every scrap of work that was offered to me.

Concealed between the lines of that passage was the very real and intense pain Wolfit was experiencing. The conventional standards of his upbringing exerted a serious influence over his actions, and caused him to falter. He had not, at that time, yet made the break with Chris, but it was constantly in his mind, for, by then, his relationship with Susan had matured, and he now returned her love. Outwardly, how-ever, he was concerned about the welfare of his daughter Margaret, and inwardly assailed by twinges of guilt, activated by his own stan-dards of social behaviour. The conflict was resolved by an offer from Sir Barry Jackson to tour Canada in a repertoire of plays; it meant he would be away from England for six months. He used the tour to ease the break-up of his marriage. When he returned to England, Susan found him a flat in Chelsea, and he set up on his own.

The Canadian Tour was to provide Wolfit with his first opportunity of going abroad; it was an unqualified success. He listed its virtues:

the overwhelming hospitality so that one became short of sleep by accepting invitations from enthusiastic theatre-goers; the joy of being allowed to play five good parts; the sense of financial security.

He might also have added that the tour had enabled him to rational-ise his private life, which doubtless contributed a feeling of relief to his personal burdens.

In Canada, he played Browning in *The Barretts of Wimpole Street*, Young Marlowe in *She Stoops to Conquer*, Joe in *Yellow Sands*, Coade in *Dear Brutus* and Shakespeare in *The Dark Lady of the Sonnets*. The company included Sophie Stewart, Daphne Heard, Julian D'Albie, Andrew Leigh, Gordon Green and Nora Nicholson. They were enthusiastically received wherever they went.

Wolfit, in the country of his mother's birth, felt very much at home. He learned a good deal from the way the tour was organised, and stored the information for later use. He had some criticisms—their seasons in the larger cities he felt were too long—but accounted the tour a personal triumph for Barry Jackson, the founder of the Birmingham Repertory Theatre.

Before returning to England, Wolfit spent four hectic days in New York, then in the unsteady grip of Prohibition; he was looked after by Dame May Whitty who plied him with a home-made brew 'which she made in her bathroom from grapes and other mysterious ingredients'. This no doubt contributed to the fact that he found New York 'bewildering'.

On his return to London in April, 1932, he took up residence alone in Jubilee Place, Chelsea, and continued to work under Jackson's management; for the remainder of the year his talents were devoted to the work of George Bernard Shaw.

Wolfit was engaged to portray the Doctor in Shaw's latest play, *Too True to be Good* at the New Theatre, London, to be followed by playing the leading role of the Parson-Burglar (created at the New Theatre by Sir Cedric Hardwicke) on a lengthy tour of the provincial cities. His co-star on the tour was a stunningly beautiful young woman, Greer Garson.

Too True to be Good ends with one of the longest speeches ever written: 'it exceeded ten minutes in length and was indeed a sermon.' The best possible judge of his performance and of the delivery of that sermon is the playwright himself. After seeing a matinée in Brighton, he wrote:

> 4. Whitehall Court, S.W.1.
> 17th Oct. 1932

Dear Mr. Wolfit,

I was delighted with your performance at Brighton. The final speech has never been better done.

In the first act, at your entrance, make a marked difference between your tone when addressing Sweetie—'D-n it: she's awake' &c &c, and your manner to the patient, which should be extremely polite and seductive.

In the second act, the business with the parasol at 'no commandments and no God' was quite wrong. You presented the parasol to Sweetie *on the line*. Do not do this. Declaim the speech, parasol in hands, with impressive seriousness. Wait for the 'no God' to make its full effect on the audience. Then, to relieve the tension, suddenly wake up and present the parasol to Sweetie. In this way you will get the double effect. You mixed them at Brighton and got none.

In the third act, at the cue 'empty your own slops', you must instantly utter a yell of disgust and rush back shuddering to your O.P. side. He must be violently revolted by the way the women rub in his squeamishness.

I think you will find both these points work satisfactorily.

Many thanks for your admirable study of the part.

> faithfully,
> G. Bernard Shaw.

Wolfit was to nurse a suspicious admiration for Shaw; on the one hand, he was in awe of the man's fame; on the other, he detested the playwright's view of actors as marionettes, and questioned his true love of the theatre. But in 1932, Shaw was one of the most famous men in the world and praise from him was irresistible. What Wolfit did as the Parson-Burglar was to display his gifts for organising complex thought patterns, to make a long didactic speech clear, and, therefore, interesting. But he did not take all the credit. He wrote:

> Every paper throughout the country bestowed praise on me for that speech, but they should in all fairness have given the praise to William Poel, for I spent days and days with him at Howards Lane, Putney, hammering out the stresses, reducing the redundancies and carrying some if not all the music that Poel found in this cry of a disillusioned post-war parson turned burglar.

The tour saw out the remainder of the year. The New Year, 1933, Wolfit welcomed with influenza from which he quickly recovered, for on Wednesday, 11 January, he was invited down to the New Theatre by Bronson Albery. From Wolfit's diary:

> Albery rang up at 3.15 with the result that I shed the flu. Met Gielgud in the New and settled to play Mowbray in *Richard of Bordeaux* at my terms.

He was a last-minute replacement for the part, for the very next day Wolfit records:

> First rehearsal of 'Richard of B.' at the New Theatre.
> Mowbray a poor part but hope to make him effective.

The play had been tried out up the road in Great Newport Street, at the Arts Theatre, and was now transferring to a larger London home. Gielgud not only starred in the piece by Gordon Daviot (Josephine Tey) but also directed it, hence the meeting referred to in the diary. Whatever animosity had existed between the two at the Vic was now temporarily set aside, possibly because Wolfit was the best replacement that could be found at such short notice. In any event, the play opened on 2 February 1933:

> First night of 'Richard of B.' a big success . . .
> Every[body] predicts a run including Albery.
> Should get seven weeks out of it at least.

His, and everyone else's, prediction fell far short of the mark. The play ran fourteen months, the longest Wolfit ever performed in one play. He received £20 per week; by Christmas he had earned £963.13.6. and saved £656. Poor part or not, it was serving his purpose.

IV

He had time to walk with Susan in the London parks, to row, to play golf, to read, to enjoy the luxury of secure employment in a fashionable success. Agate acclaimed Gielgud a great actor in the *Sunday Times*; the *Tatler* and the *Sketch* printed caricatures of the actors and John Pollock in *The Saturday Review* praised Wolfit for 'a deep and polished performance'. He had time, too, to visit old friends.

In the summer, on occasional weekends, he journeyed to Stevington in Bedfordshire, to see his companion from the Alexander Marsh company, Frank Milray and his wife. Their son John, who later took Mayes as his stage-name, was then twelve; he provided valuable glimpses of Wolfit away from the theatre, illuminating the lighter, warmer side of Wolfit's character:

I had not been doing very well in my school work, and my father probably asked Wolfit's advice, because he knew Wolfit had been a schoolmaster (although but briefly!). I was sitting reading in my bedroom under the eaves of the cottage one afternoon and Wolfit came clambering up the steps to sit on the floor beside me and asked me about school. He had a gentle charming manner, and seemed so young and vital—not middle-aged and nervy like my father—and I took to him enormously. I remember he was wearing a tweed jacket, had a wide, clear brow, long thick hair brushed back from it, and a manner that was youthful, *not* avuncular. He told me how he had found it difficult to pass exams at school, and that I was not to worry about such things, but just try and do my best. I didn't think of him as an actor at all—just an extraordinarily youthful and comradely adult the like of which I had never met before! . . . My father had a Victorian-Edwardian enthusiasm for a cold 'dip' and often took me swimming with him in the river Ouse which flowed a mile or so away from our cottage. . . . Wolfit accompanied us down to the river one evening to swim too. I remember him swimming, in spite of my father's warning, across a deep pool in the river that we thought dangerous. He swam confidently, his superbly muscled arms and shoulders rising out of the water. He had the figure of an athlete, trim-waisted, and I thought the clothes he wore rather 'way out' compared with my father's. A kind of silk jersey-knit sports shirt with just one button at the collar made him a thoroughly modern young man of the 1930s to me!
The second visit I remember him paying to the cottage he came down in a car, which I think was a bull-nosed Morris or some such. I think it had a 'dicky' seat at the back. He brought his daughter Margaret with him, who was some years my junior I think. My mother has since told me that Wolfit was particularly unhappy at that time because of the breakup of his first marriage, or because of circumstances that were preventing his second. . . . She said she remembered Wolfit giving his little daughter a bath at the cot-

tage. There was no bathroom, and we heated water in saucepans and preserving pans and used a galvanised iron bath in a bedroom. She said Wolfit enjoyed having his daughter with him tremendously, and she was touched by his happiness, and always re-remembered it afterwards.

I remember him driving away with Margaret in that car, returning to London. The fact that he was a motorist I took quite as a matter of course. Someone as healthy and friendly and gifted as he seemed would surely be a motorist too!

. . . Mother told me that during his visits to Stevington Wolfit would talk into the early hours of the morning with them of his plans for the future: of doing plays by Ben Jonson and other of Shakespeare's contemporaries. He talked much of Ibsen then, too, and Mother remembered him enthusing about classical music and telling of how much the work of great composers meant to him.

No matter how wild Wolfit's dreams may have seemed in those years, he knew very well that he would have to increase his reputation if he was ever to become an actor-manager. When Sir Philip Ben Greet presented him with the chance of playing *Hamlet*, albeit the 1603 First Quarto version, in honour of Shakespeare's birthday, Wolfit snatched at it greedily. Because the undemanding part of Mowbray finished in the second act, Wolfit had a good deal of time and energy to work for Sunday productions or special matinées. He secured Bronson Albery's permission and played *Hamlet* for the first time at the end of April 1933.

Philip Ben Greet was chiefly distinguished for his work of bringing Shakespeare to schoolchildren in the 1920s and 1930s. As has been noted, he was an important figure at the Old Vic, and his company rivalled Benson's as a training-ground for young actors. He believed that the First Quarto version of *Hamlet* was Shakespeare's first draft, and did not subscribe to the fashionable view that it was a pirated edition, taken down by the actors from their parts and sold to the printer. Wolfit, who had an uncanny instinct about what Shakespeare wrote or did not write, agreed with him. He theorised:

> In brief, I believe that Shakespeare grew in stature as a dramatist and poet and that this edition represents the first version of the play which found great favour with audiences. Accordingly, it was played at the Universities, as the title-page clearly states, and was no doubt taken on the tours which the Lord Chamberlain's Company undertook annually, and in time of plague when the London playhouses were closed. Shakespeare probably decided the time was ripe for a new version and had almost prepared it at the time of Elizabeth's death. At that time the playhouses would be closed;

and no one knew whether James on his accession would countenance the players or not. Money would undoubtedly be short and the new fashion of printing plays was coming into vogue. What more natural than this early version, which had been played so frequently, should be sold to the printer for a useful sum when Shakespeare had the new version all ready for performance? The full Second Quarto followed the first to the printer in 1604.

The First Quarto contains at least two startling differences from the later editions, both of which, from the actor's viewpoint, are of paramount importance. First, the soliloquy on death, 'To be or not to be', occurs immediately after Hamlet's encounter with his father's ghost, not five scenes further on—a most difficult bridge for any Hamlet to span in thought. Secondly, Gertrude actually says to Hamlet in her chamber: 'I never knew of this most horrid murder'. In both these instances I consider Shakespeare showed superior craftsmanship in the First Quarto than in the later editions.

The playing of the earlier version was to be a useful training for the real thing which was yet to come.

A fine actress from the Old Vic, Dorothy Green, played the Queen, and Thea Holme was Ofelia; Greet played Corambis (later Polonius) and John Clements was Laertes. Accoutred in H. B. Irving's black tunic, lent by Tom Heslewood, Wolfit gave a fine, athletic reading. From the *Daily Telegraph*:

> Mr. Donald Wolfit definitely wins his spurs with his performance of Hamlet.

The actor was encouraged more than ever 'to think in terms of actor-management. . . . One great obstacle to this ambition, however, was the lack of the sinews of war: I had no wealthy friends.' He did, however, have an unfailing sense of seizing his chance.

Richard of Bordeaux finished its run early in 1934; Wolfit, sniffing around for opportunity, now decided he must create an opening in order to have a 'trial run' in management. What better than to propose a Festival, and where more fitting than in his home-town? In a long article, in the *Newark Advertiser*, headlined NEWARK AND THE DRAMA—FESTIVAL WEEK SUGGESTED, Wolfit planted the seeds in the minds of the worthy citizens of Newark. The article contains a formulation of one or two beliefs which its author was to repeat with increasing vehemence over the years:

> the film industry is . . . a *substitute* for the *real drama* . . . the effect of seeing a great play nobly produced and finely acted

is profoundly moving and has the highest educational value.

And, on a more practical note:

> Providing suitable accommodation can be found and a suitable
> guarantee forthcoming—enough to cover expenses and no more—
> I should be delighted to bring a small company of London artists,
> etc. etc.

To suggest a cultural deficiency, and then to offer oneself as a remedy
may, as a piece of political manoeuvring, lack subtlety or finesse; as a
theatrical gambit it was highly successful. In April 1934, at the Palace
Theatre, Newark, with the guarantee he required, Wolfit presented
for one week his first company in *Arms and the Man*, *The Master
Builder* and *Twelfth Night*; his own parts were Bluntschli, Solness and
Malvolio. The company was not without distinction and included a
future Dame and another future Knight: Margaret Webster, Margaret
Rutherford, John Clements, Elspeth March and his old friend, Frank
Milray, whom he regarded as the best Sir Andrew Aguecheek he had
ever seen. The experience thrilled Wolfit, and he thirsted for more.

It was, of course, also to be the first occasion on which Wolfit gave
a curtain-speech on behalf of himself and his company. It is preserved
in full in the columns of the local newspaper, and was a pattern for
things to come:

> Well, ladies and gentlemen, the time has come to say 'Au revoir'!
> The Newark Drama Week, which has meant so much planning,
> and which we have all of us looked forward to with such excitement
> is over. Now that I have dived through these curtains for the last
> time, in response to your applause and appreciation, I do not know
> where or how to begin my thanks.

There followed an endless list of people to be acknowledged, a traditional part of all curtain-speeches: the Working Committee, the stage
staff, the company, Mr. Cann 'the courteous and genial manager', and
then, perhaps for the first and last time:

> There is also a great factor which we cannot ignore—a factor which
> has been essential to the success of this venture—or indeed of any
> venture today. I mean the Press. (Applause).

Having waxed fulsome over their contribution, he came to his
peroration:

Ladies and gentlemen, I fear I am a dreamer, but I am a dreamer who likes his dreams to come true. I wanted to present, in this theatre, some plays by the foremost dramatists of the world, played by a company of artists who put the right interpretation of these dramatists before every other consideration, so that their meaning and their message should get across these footlights to you with the full inspiration of the author. It is for you to say whether we have succeeded or not. I think your reception of us during the week has answered that question and made us very happy. I hope we have planted the seeds of the desire for a future Week of Drama in Newark. I can only conclude by quoting from *Othello*:

'These are the inhabitants of the island,
I have found great love amongst them.'
(Applause).

On the company's return to London, *The Master Builder* was presented at the Westminster Theatre and two weeks later at the Embassy for a short run. Margaret Webster had another engagement and Beatrix Lehmann replaced her. The company was well received, and the performance was described as 'Ibsen without Boredom at Swiss Cottage'. Managerially, Wolfit had the bit between his teeth.

It was a brighter time all round, for his domestic life was about to become more settled. The previous September, Chris had seen her solicitors to sue for divorce. In October 1933, Wolfit recorded in his diary:

To Lewis at 11.30 where I was served with the petition on behalf of C. by Wingfields. The damn fools dragged her in for identification.

By the late summer of 1934, the way was clear for him to marry Susan. On 15 September, at Chelsea Registry Office, the State recognised their union, and three days later the Reverend H. Gorse, his former Headmaster, blessed the marriage at St. Luke's, Chelsea, on behalf of the Church.

The couple moved to Bywater Street, S.W.3.; as Susan had abandoned her half-hearted acting career, she was able to provide Wolfit with the stable background for which he so longed. His second marriage had other advantages over his first, principally that his work, in the early years, kept him mostly in London so that they were not subject to long separations. But both partners were possessed of great individuality and stormy episodes were not unusual.

Nine months and some days after their marriage, on 30 June 1935, Susan gave birth to a girl, Harriet. During the labour, mother wanted father out of the way; understandably, his intensity was not of the most helpful kind at a time like that. Somehow, Susan managed to get a message to their neighbours, Monica and Richard Scott, asking them to lure the expectant father out of the house. The Scotts invited Wolfit to sit with them; he declined. 'You see,' he said in a confidential whisper, 'if I'm not there, Susan doesn't try.'

V

Ever since *Richard of Bordeaux*, Wolfit had discovered one certain way of increasing his capital, and that was by appearing in films. He managed to obtain employment in five British productions, the most notable being as Thomas Doughty in *Drake of England*, with Matheson Lang. The film industry did not welcome him with open arms until many, many years later. In the 1930s the division between stage and film actors was acute, and Wolfit was rightly regarded as belonging firmly to the theatre.

Shortly after his return from the Newark Drama Week in April 1934, Wolfit was summoned by Sir Philip Ben Greet to play Claudius the very next day for Shakespeare's Birthday Festival at Sadler's Wells. He accepted the challenge. He tore round London with Susan hearing his lines as they went: to the Old Vic where the Wardrobe Master, Orlando Whitehead, produced the same costume he had worn six years before in Gielgud's Hamlet; it fitted. Then to Mrs. Newman who found him a wig, and at last to the theatre at 1.30 p.m. for the performance of the tragedy in its entirety.

It was a star-studded cast with one of the foremost Hamlets of the day, Ernest Milton; Sybil Thorndike was the Queen, Marie Ney Ophelia, and Ben Greet himself the First Gravedigger. The smaller parts were played by Basil Dignam, Mark Dignam, William Fox, Tom Heslewood, Ambrosine Phillpotts, Ronald Adam, E. Martin Browne, Esmond Knight, Guy Verney, John Laurie, Torin Thatcher, Nicholas Phipps, Leslie French, and the musicians were Carl and Natalie Dolmetsch.

At the curtain call Ben Greet, rather ungraciously, took the first call before Milton; Wolfit never forgot the incident.*

After the hectic preparation, Wolfit suffered a collapse; he had travelled backwards in time six years and could not come round into the present. For two days he lay prostrate on his bed, and this confused mental state is an indication of the intensity of his imagination.

Of his progress at that time, he recorded:

> . . . emotionally I was unstable and unsatisfied, the victim of my own precipitation and unwisdom. I clutched at every part or acti-

* See pages 271–2.

vity that came into my hands, and plunged into short runs and several failures.

The most outstanding failure was a play called *Josephine* by Hermann Bahr, which Robert Atkins produced at His Majesty's Theatre. Alexander Korda had financed the venture, in the hope that it would make a film. A superb cast was assembled: Frank Vosper as Napoleon, with Lady Tree, Lyn Harding, George Grossmith, Mary Ellis and Emlyn Williams. They rehearsed for six weeks and ran for five nights. Mountainous sets and a cat that leapt into the stalls on the first night to cries from the gallery of 'Tally-ho' could not have helped.

These fretful years left their mark on Wolfit, and appear to have consolidated his resolve to strike out on his own.

The Wolfits lived simply; every penny he could spare was finding its way to the Stock Exchange, but his wife knew nothing of his financial affairs; he always pleaded poverty. To her request for a new dress, he would reply, 'Nonsense. You're the best-dressed woman I know.'

What he needed most was a boost to give him confidence to launch himself in the great classic roles upon which he had set his heart. The boost came from Stein Bugge, a Norwegian author and producer, who had come to England with his own play *Too Famous for Words* and Ibsen's first verse-drama, *Catiline*. The two men met and 'liked each other's enthusiasm'. Wolfit introduced Bugge to Baxter Somerville who had developed the Greyhound Theatre at Croydon into a fully-fledged repertory company. Somerville agreed to present both plays with Wolfit in the leading parts.

Ibsen, not surprisingly, was more successful than Bugge. Anmer Hall saw *Catiline* and decided to transfer it for a short season to the Royalty Theatre in Soho. For the first time Wolfit was actually starred in a London theatre; and it was his first major success, but, as he wrote:

... more important still the newly appointed director of the Stratford Memorial Theatre, B. Iden Payne, came to see the play and invited me to consider a season at Stratford.

The usual bargaining for roles ensued—Wolfit wanting a better line of parts than the ones offered—but eventually all was settled: Cassius, Tranio in *The Taming of the Shrew*, Don Pedro in *Much Ado About Nothing* ('although I longed for Benedick'), Gratiano in *The Merchant of Venice*, Kent in *King Lear*, Ulysses in *Troilus and Cressida* and Orsino in *Twelfth Night*.

Wolfit sensed that a vitally important moment in his life had arrived:

As soon as I had signed the contract I felt as if a ton weight had been lifted from me. It was not that the engagement offered security for six months in pleasant surroundings and congenial company. I knew in my heart that my deep and abiding love for the works of Shakespeare had been stifled for too long and that I was returning to put myself once again at the service of the master dramatist. I was fully cognisant of the difficulties of the Stratford Theatre, and of the barrage of criticism which, in those days, could descend on an actor who failed to measure up to the standards of Shakespeare's birthplace. I sought advice from Ben Greet who advised me strongly to go on and prosper. William Poel, alas, who could have advised me best of all was dead, but my own judgment did not prove wrong in this instance. So with my house on my back I moved to the banks of the Avon.

CHAPTER EIGHT

Donning the Purple

Your heart's desires be with you
—As You Like It

I

THE first attempt to turn Stratford-upon-Avon into a theatre occurred in 1769, when David Garrick inaugurated the famous jubilee. More than a century later, in 1879, Charles Flower, a brewer, presented the town with a memorial theatre to William Shakespeare; the first production was *Much Ado About Nothing*, Benedick being played by a rough, shrewd, pock-marked Irishman, Barry Sullivan, a great hero of provincial audiences. So delighted was he with his success that he returned the following year to another triumph. Through his endeavours, Edward Compton took command of the theatre for annual spring and summer performances, thus establishing the festival tradition. In 1886, Frank Benson, then aged twenty-eight, arrived, and stayed for thirty years. He transformed the theatre—'A beautiful building, one of the loveliest erected in England for many years' according to Oscar Wilde—into the nearest approach to a National Theatre in England. He persuaded almost all the leading players of those three decades to perform in honour of Shakespeare's birthday: Johnston Forbes-Robertson, Constance Collier, Henry Ainley, Matheson Lang, Louis Calvert, Lewis Waller, Herbert Beerbohm Tree, John Martin-Harvey, Violet Vanbrugh, Robert Loraine, Ellen Terry (Portia to her husband James Carew's Shylock), Madge Titheradge, H. B. Irving, Edith Evans—the list is incomplete—all fell under the charm of the theatre on the banks of the Avon.

W. B. Yeats, after a visit in the spring of 1901, reflected:

All day, one does not hear or see an incongruous thing . . . one need talk of nothing but the play in the inn parlour, under oak beams blackened by time, and showing the mark of the adze that shaped them.

The romantic idyll of the Festival appealed more, in those days, to the actors and those involved, than to the nation as a whole. J. C. Trewin wrote:

> It is well to recollect these Festivals now [1951] in a year when so many are discovering a suddenly fashionable Stratford-upon-Avon for the first time, and there is surprise that London's first players are ready to appear at the Memorial Theatre. Frank Benson would have smiled tolerantly.

Benson reverenced Stratford as a place where, he told a last-night audience, 'it is your privilege and mine to help to reawaken the sleeping soul of England'. Pre-war Stratford was uncommercialised and all who came were caressed by its spell in spring and summer; all, said Benson, 'sang for the joy of singing'—and, being Benson, played cricket and tennis and swam in the Avon. He created an atmosphere of athletic conviviality that still pervades the Warwickshire air.

He was justly rewarded in 1916. Returning from France, he took part in the Birthday Celebrations to mark Shakespeare's Tercentenary at Drury Lane, in the presence of King George V and Queen Mary. After the performance of *Julius Caesar* and a pageant of Shakespeare's characters, the King sent for Benson, who came into an anteroom to the Royal Box still wearing the blood-stained robes and ashen make-up of Caesar's ghost. Taking a sword from Arthur Collins, manager of Drury Lane, the King invited Benson to kneel and then bestowed upon him the accolade of knighthood. J. C. Trewin reflected:

> The occasion must have been dear to Benson's romantic heart; knighthood on the day of Shakespeare's Tercentenary, in a historic theatre, and at the heart of his profession, with many of the actors he had trained.

When he returned to Stratford it seemed as if the whole town was at the station to greet him; in triumph they dragged his carriage, horse-less, through the streets.

W. Bridges-Adams succeeded Benson in 1919. Seven years later the theatre burned down; this time another Flower, Sir Archibald, campaigned for funds. In 1932, the new theatre was opened by the Prince of Wales. Bridges-Adams retired in 1934 and was succeeded by Ben Iden Payne, an admirer of Poel's, Miss Horniman's director at the Gaiety Theatre, Manchester, and a shrewd judge of actors.

II

Iden Payne assembled a fine array of talent for the seasons of 1936 and 1937. Besides Wolfit, there was Baliol Holloway and a young

Trevor Howard. Norman Wooland, Michael Goodliffe, Pamela Brown, Barbara Couper, Rosamund John, Clare Harris, Valerie Tudor were all to increase their reputations over the years. A young woman whom Wolfit had first met ten years before in the Arts League of Service, Rosalind Patrick, was also a member of the company; she was the director's daughter and had reverted to her original name; she was now known as Rosalind Iden.

Perhaps the most remarkable member of the company was the leading man, Randle Ayrton, one of the strangest, most fascinating figures in the theatre of the 1930s. Originally Benson's authoritarian stage-manager, he had become an actor when well into his middle years. In 1936 he was sixty-six years old, crochety and aloof, but the purveyor of compelling dramatic power. He disdained London, but he gave, principally in Stratford, a series of performances which Iden Payne, and many of his fellow-actors, judged to be among the finest of the period. In those days, few of the London critics made the pilgrimage to Stratford, but it is doubtful, having regard to Ayrton's bias against the capital, that even if they had acclaimed him the greatest actor since Irving (as was the critics' wont) it would have lured him to the metropolis. Ayrton preferred to play in Stratford, to toil in his market-garden. He was, by his own inclination, a curiously isolated figure and, to the London sophisticates, more or less unknown. It was, as will be seen, Wolfit's good fortune, in one important respect, to play with Ayrton, and Wolfit never omitted to acknowledge the debt.

Wolfit was, if it is possible, more of a romantic than even Frank Benson. Either could have written:

> There is surely no place on earth more inspiring to the young actor than Stratford-upon-Avon in the early spring. The first half of the long rehearsals in London are accomplished, there are weeks of study and preparation and dress-rehearsals ahead, and if he is keen on his craft the very stones of the old buildings cry out a welcome that makes him feel a tiny speck in the long procession of Thespians who have brought themselves to the bankside since the first festival organised by David Garrick in honour of Shakespeare.

With his wife and new-born daughter Harriet ensconced at No. 46 Shipston Road, Wolfit walked by the Avon, a small Temple edition of the current play in his hand, the parts bursting in his head. At the age of thirty-four he stood, as he well knew, on the brink of success; Stratford was the biggest chance of his career, for it had been decided to add one more play to the repertoire with Wolfit in the leading role: *Hamlet*; it was now or never.

Wolfit's powers as an actor had never really been given full rein; he had not yet essayed a major role in one of Shakespeare's tragedies, for the Hamlet he had played previously did not require the technical and emotional pyrotechnics that are demanded by the Folio version. No actor could have been better prepared by a long, often frustrating, training than Wolfit; no actor better equipped by nature to endure the physical strain of the great Shakespearean roles. He was enormously strong, his figure athletic and muscular; from photographs of the Stratford season, he appears rather dashing—the inevitable black Homburg at a rakish angle—every inch a leading man. The serious-ness with which he approached his art had begun to show itself in a kind of determined earnestness, and a sense of deeper purpose, inextricably woven in his mind with the works of Shakespeare, was now provided by the season at Stratford. In private, he was often preoccupied, not answering when people talked to him, lost, no doubt, in his plans, his ambitions, his roles. If anything, he became even more fiercely impassioned about the thoughts of his future, which added to his natural intensity. His wife Susan recalled that it took him a week to get into a temper, and three weeks to get over it.

As he strode along the banks of the Avon when, as he was to write, 'the daffodils are blowing in the keen cold air, or even when rain has swelled the river until it swirls high under Clopton bridge and floods the meadows beyond', his mind was filled with Tranio and Cassius, with Gratiano and Ulysses, with Don Pedro and Kent, and with the most exciting prospect of all, Hamlet.

Iden Payne found him an easy actor to direct, except for a manner-ism with his right hand, forward and slightly away from his body, which he could not get the actor to stop; Iden Payne did admit, how-ever, that he was not the best type of actor for him to work with, as he was not 'light' enough.

No sooner had the season opened in the second week of April, than Peter Glenville, according to the press, asked to be relieved of Petru-chio because of the great strain he was under from other leading parts; Wolfit replaced him and thus played his first Shakespearean leading role, but his first acknowledged success at Stratford was as Ulysses in *Troilus and Cressida* ('a collector's performance,' said Trewin): 'the beauty and profundity of his speeches on Degree and the Ingratitude of time,' the actor wrote, 'called up all the reserves in me which I had learned from Poel and earned me golden opinions.' The sentence encapsulated Wolfit's preparedness and the confidence he had in his own powers; 'all the reserves in me' so accurately describes what sixteen years in the ranks had given him. The inner resources he possessed had been nourished by practice, by force of circumstance restrained; it was now to be allowed to come to the boil, and while bubbling away, Wolfit would be able to absorb, at close quarters, a role upon which his ultimate fame would depend.

Randle Ayrton had played *King Lear* many times before. At sixty-six he perforce conformed to Agate's notion 'that Lear is not, and never can be, a young man's part'. Ayrton certainly had *'fougue* and physique' which were the critic's other conditions for playing the part. But Iden Payne had the idea that to set off this performance and reveal it as a truly important interpretation, Ayrton needed a producer of exceptional skill and theatrical daring; he engaged Theodore Komisarjevsky to produce.

It was the first time that Wolfit, as Kent, had played in a production of *King Lear*, and he was deeply affected and later influenced by Ayrton's portrayal. The influence of one actor over another is very often not the kind that audiences or dramatic critics can detect, for it does not mean that one actor copies another's make-up, or delivers the lines with precisely the same inflections. Influences of a proper nature are far more subtle. What the older actor did for Wolfit was to provide insights and clues, even, perhaps, false clues, for he was a drier actor than Wolfit, lacking the younger man's volatility. Ayrton was a 'god-like tyrant' in the part, noble and patriarchal. When Wolfit would come to act *King Lear* he would begin where Ayrton had ended after years of study, and then blaze his own trail, enlarging the concept, grappling god, tyrant, noble patriarch to his interpretation and developing it further, performance by performance, into an ancient, barbaric chieftain. Ayrton was a magnificent Lear; Wolfit would become a great one.

Wolfit's Kent, according to J. C. Trewin, was as fine a performance as he ever gave, 'a fellow of plain and uncoined constancy'. Wolfit's gifts were, indeed, bubbling; the real test was now to come.

III

To the fashionable, in later years, Wolfit as Hamlet epitomised all that they considered vulgar, ridiculous and laughable. How could an actor with his robust temperament, his physique, play the most aesthetic of Princes? It was not to be thought about.

Wolfit's error was not that he played Hamlet, but that he played him for too long. Certain it is, if critics are to be believed, that his performance at Stratford in 1936 was an exciting, brilliant theatrical event. Agate wrote of Wolfit in 1944: 'I feel that he plays Hamlet only because no leading actor can afford to bypass the Dane.' There is an element of truth in that statement and this was no doubt so when Wolfit first played the part. Yet, there were aspects of Hamlet with which Wolfit, like all actors who lay claim to the role, could identify. Consider *The Times* review:

The spectacle offered us is that of a man of genius caught with all the contradictions and imperfections of his nature in a rush of events which shape his end, rough-hew it how he will.

Or the *Morning Post*:

He is, among other things, a Hamlet who makes no secret of pretending to be mad . . . or of reaching the verge of real distraction with the great scene with Ophelia. . . . It is not a Hamlet of imposed or exotic personality, but a Hamlet of passion, power, intense and lively humanity—and this, as we know, was Burbage's way.

It is no surprise to learn that on the first night, before the curtain rose, Ayrton put his head round Wolfit's dressing-room door and advised the actor to 'Give them a bit of the old!'

The Irving tradition of Hamlet in which Benson, Forbes-Robertson, Milton and Gielgud followed was a comparatively recent one. Garrick or Kean were certainly not in that mould; nor was Richard Burbage, as the critic of the *Morning Post* makes clear. If Wolfit seemed at times anachronistic to his own generation, it was because his gifts, his style were drawn from a cruder past, and thus appeared irrelevant to a pseudo-refined present. Pseudo, because refinement in no way reflected the reality of the times; on the contrary, it was Wolfit's generation that was the product of the most horrendous war in human affairs, and was soon to plunge into the midst of a yet more terrible holocaust. But the theatrical preference of the time was for aestheticism, for purity, for unsullied, virginal Hamlets. John Masefield, with the rugged eye of a poet, defined most accurately Wolfit's performance:

I was impressed by your Hamlet which seemed to me to catch in every line a vital point which no actor save yourself seems to have seen, that is, that Hamlet was, and knew that he was, in deadly danger at every turn.

With the influence of Poel, of Iden Payne, Wolfit acted what he believed to be the heart of the play, the guts of it, discarding the Victorian ideal and striving to interpret the role as he supposed the playwright first intended. And so, with James Agate, a balance sheet of Wolfit's Hamlet may be drawn:

On the one side is the lack of physical grace. There is very little suggestion of weakness, and Hamlet's reluctance to put paid to his stepfather's account is almost inexplicable as it would be in the case of a heavy-weight boxer or Woolwich Arsenal centreforward. One feels that this Hamlet turns the verse into what Coleridge called good working poetry, and that the flight of angels who must sing him to his rest are not volunteers but have been detailed for the job. There is no aloofness and little suggestion of the princely; this is a bourgeois Hamlet. On the other side of the account one must put a complete grasp of character mapped as a general maps out a battlefield, enormous virtuosity of expression, and depth of genuine, as opposed to manufactured, passion. I have seen many Hamlets of greater elegance and charm, and I agree that to those who rate the Prince of Denmark according to his pettableness, Mr. Wolfit must come very low. But this is to take the lap-dog view of Shakespeare's character, and to regard the play enshrining him in the light of that pagoda in which David Copperfield's Dora housed her yapping, snapping Jip. And Shakespeare's play is not a pagoda. It is, as Montague pointed out, 'a monstrous Gothic castle of a poem full of baffled half-lights and glooms'. If I must choose a caretaker to show me round I think it would be Wolfit, who puts me back into Shakespeare's day and time even if the character presented is not Hamlet but some elder, stronger-minded brother. But then I am all for Shakespeare acted in a vein half-way between Gielgud and Tod Slaughter.

As with all Hamlets, Wolfit was at his most vulnerable in the part. In Lear or Othello the actor can hide behind age or colour, but in Hamlet, the nerve-endings of his own personality are exposed for all to see. It is, therefore, understandable that when Wolfit came to analyse his interpretation of the part, he should write, unknowingly, about himself:

> It is necessary to have a comprehensive variety of light quick indications of his courtesy and savagery, his frenzy and tranquillity, his irresolution and impulsiveness, his timidity and courage, his self-pity and his power to reflect in his own disillusionment a spiritual world of contending forces.

The performance of Hamlet elevated Wolfit to the ranks of leading players. But, as must be remembered, it occurred outside London, without the attendant fanfares of national publicity. W. A. Darlington in the *Daily Telegraph* affirmed that it was 'one of the best individual performances I have ever seen at Stratford'. The critics were unanimously in favour of his portrayal. Wolfit, as a leading Shakespearean actor, had arrived. T. C. Kemp in the *Birmingham Post* proclaimed:

> Mr. Wolfit has crowned his season's work with a distinguished performance not unworthy of comparison with the great Hamlets of the English stage.

IV

Long before the 1936 season ended, Wolfit had been engaged to
return the following year. Komisarjevsky had been favourably
impressed by his Kent and offered him the part of Antony in his
forthcoming production of *Antony and Cleopatra* at the New Theatre,
London with the famous Russian actress Eugenie Leontovich as
Egypt's queen. She had recently scored a success in a light comedy,
Tovarich, but why this should have been thought to be a qualification
for playing Cleopatra was not stated. The two Russians, especially
the director, 'went mad with the text and achieved his ultimate disregard of Shakespeare as a dramatist'. It was a vastly over-decorated
production, except, perhaps, as far as the leading lady was concerned
who was 'clad in the scantiest draperies surmounted by a fireman's
helmet, adorned with large white plumes'. The cast was distinguished:
Margaret Rawlings and Rosalind Iden as Charmian and Iras, Leon
Quartermaine as Enobarbus, Ion Swinley as Pompey; the result was
another matter. In the words of *The Times*, 'Seldom has a play been so
tormented and twisted and stifled or a work of genius been so casually
scorned.' It was the same critic, Charles Morgan, who, with an
expertise worthy of Leo Rosten, produced a phonetic reproduction
of Leontovich speaking England's greatest poet, who had written:

> O, wither'd is the garland of the war,
> The soldier's pole is fall'n: young boys and girls
> Are level now with men.

But Leontovich seemed to prefer:

> O weederdee degarlano devar
> Desolderspo lees falln: yong boisenguls
> Alefelnow wimen.

James Agate, in a famous, devastating review, headlined ANTON
AND CLEOPATROVA: A TRAGEDY BY KOMISPEARE, did
nearly as well:

> When you sued staying
> Then was the time for words

in Leontovich's mouth became

> Wen you suet staying
> Den was the time for Wurst.

Wolfit fared somewhat better and received, for the most part,
sympathetic notices for what was clearly a valiant effort against
insuperable odds. There was, however, a warning note from Agate:

Antony is a lean wolf, bloated, out of training, with a middle-aged spread; a lean Wolfit, who is chubbier than he was, is not the same thing.

It is interesting that, in the time immediately following his first success, Wolfit should begin to put on weight; it was as if his physique mirrored an inner contentment he was now experiencing, aided by the knowledge that he was in demand, and well known.

Before the new season at Stratford, he played over Christmas, 1936, at the Q Theatre. It was a sentimental journey, for the part was Sir Percy Blakeney in *The Scarlet Pimpernel*. A perceptive critic in the *Morning Post* observed that Wolfit acted Fred Terry, rather than the part. His leading lady was Phyllis Neilson-Terry, Fred's daughter, and both were doubtless influenced by her illustrious parents.

At Stratford, in 1937, Wolfit added a roguish Autolycus in *The Winter's Tale*, an oily Iachiamo in *Cymbeline*, a glittering Chorus in *Henry V*, an intelligent Ford in *The Merry Wives of Windsor* and Captain Bobadil in *Everyman and his Humour* to his repertoire; he repeated his Touchstone (from the Old Vic) and, of course, his Hamlet, now the subject of a pictorial essay in *The Bystander* under the title 'Hamlet Impetuous'.

But the time had come for the great decision to be made: 'I must back myself or not be backed at all,' he wrote. '. . . I was seized with the overwhelming desire to undertake at least one tour of the plays of Shakespeare under my own management.' He had saved enough; he was just well known enough; his star was rising. All his life, this ambition had been constant. From bitter experience, he must have realised how little he conformed to the fashionable ideal of leading man; he was, by nature, too impatient to wait to be asked to play the great roles which he longed to encompass. And to mitigate, as it were, his personal aspirations, there was the inbred belief in service to the community which was as much a nagging impulse as any. He declared:

> I felt convinced that there were larger audiences in the British Isles than those which could be contained at Stratford, the Old Vic . . . and in Regent's Park. . . . Apart from these ventures there were only spasmodic tours in the country. Surely, I argued, there was room for fresh blood and a new policy which might embrace the country as a whole.

During the course of the season, he made his decision to become an actor-manager. Ayrton, who was to retire that year, strode into Wolfit's dressing-room.

'Well, Donald,' he said. 'I hear you're going to don the purple.'
Wolfit asked what that meant.

'That's what we used to call going into management in the good old days. Well, bloody good luck to you, my boy, and here's my Lear whip for you as a keepsake to use as Petruchio. It belonged to Oscar Asche as well so take care of it!'

Armed with that talisman, and with the extraordinary energy and vast talents of its leading man, the Donald Wolfit Shakespeare Company came into being. Its principal player would be the recipient of high praise; the company, of repeated critical savagery. They would become the butt of West End wags, of second-rate revues and third-rate comedians; actors, good or bad, would heap the company with scorn; even drama students would smirk in a superior way at the thought of them, for indeed anyone who wanted a quick and easy laugh would only have to mention the company's name. No matter if they trudged from one end of Britain to the other, or played in London with the bombs falling about their heads, or aboard troopships in the Mediterranean or across the vast North American Continent, they would be regarded as theatrical outcasts. Almost from its very inception, the Donald Wolfit Shakespeare Company became The Unfashionable Theatre.

Part Three

MR. WOLFIT

1937–1957

CHAPTER NINE

The Manager

'Tis best to give way; he leads himself
—King Lear

I

WOLFIT was an actor-manager for nearly a quarter of a century; as a manager he behaved like a general at the head of a beleaguered army, fighting five major campaigns. The first was against an unseen foe, the Theatrical Establishment, sometimes imagining enemies where there were none; the second—and by far the most damaging to him—was the persistent sniping at his soldiers and their equipment by the press, against which he had little defence; the third was a major pitched battle, his enemy, the State, represented by a wily Headquarters Staff known as the Council for Encouragement of Music and the Arts, and by the foreign propaganda arm, the British Council; the fourth was the annual skirmishes he himself conducted in an effort to conquer the capital city, London; the final campaign was one of which the General was quite unaware, but it was by far the most important and the most difficult: against himself. For, as has already been stated, his talent as an actor stood above the battle; his gifts for portraying the major roles in the classic English drama were almost without equal; that he chose to encrust those gifts in rusted armour and outdated strategy need not detract from his genius; despite the handicaps that he himself imposed, Wolfit, the actor, triumphed over Wolfit, the manager. The separation of his two functions is essential if one is to understand the contribution he made to his art; few were able to do so during his lifetime, but he was fortunate that the leading dramatic critic of his day, and a highly respected critic at that, James Agate, had not only the inclination but also the good-will to make that division. Agate's judgment is an important factor in the events that follow, and one that may be relied on, for Wolfit was not the only actor with cause to be grateful to the critic: the careers of Olivier, Richardson and Gielgud were also enhanced by his writings.

Yet, whatever Wolfit's faults as a manager, and they were numerous, he possessed one outstanding, golden virtue: a sense of service to the community. Norman Marshall wrote:

> Had it not been for his courage and enterprise, a whole generation of young theatregoers would have grown up during the war without having seen a Shakespeare play on the stage.

What could not be denied, even by his most entrenched detractors, was that Wolfit, year after year, sometimes under the most appalling conditions, brought not only plays by Shakespeare to the playgoers of Britain, but also plays by Jonson, Ford, Ibsen, Molière, Massinger, Sophocles, Rostand and Sheridan—and diminished his reputation as an actor by doing so.

The history of Wolfit, the manager, began on 11 October 1937 in Malvern.

DONALD WOLFIT

with his

SHAKESPEAREAN COMPANY

and

PHYLLIS NEILSON-TERRY

in

MONDAY EVG	HAMLET
TUESDAY EVG	MERCHANT OF VENICE
WEDNESDAY EVG	MACBETH
THURSDAY EVG	MERCHANT OF VENICE
FRIDAY EVG	MACBETH
SAT MAT	HAMLET
SATURDAY EVG	THE TAMING OF THE SHREW

The plays produced by ANDREW LEIGH

The company played to £503; Wolfit's share of the takings was £301.19.3.; his expenses were £293.15.5., having paid himself a token salary of twenty pounds; the profit, therefore, was £8.13.10. His worst fears had been confounded: he had made a profit in his first week in management. 'The heavenly trumpets blew in my ears,' he wrote. 'I walked up the Malvern Hill to my hotel on winged feet . . . everyone was paid and the world was mine.'

The conquering hero's progress had begun some months before in Stratford. With that same knack he had displayed as a child, he sniffed out the people who would best assist his ambitions. The Clerk to the Stratford Theatre Governors, Henry Tossell, recommended a business manager, Percival Selby, whom Wolfit infected with his enthusiasm and determination and, in time, turned him into an astonished crusader:

> I do not think for a moment that Percival Selby thought of himself as a crusader. He was only concerned to book a tour with a first-class company headed by Phyllis Neilson-Terry and myself. He found it a difficult problem. Weeks passed, and slowly the tour grew from three weeks into five weeks and eventually, after great persuasion from my new-found friend, there were nine consecutive weeks contracted: Malvern, Brighton, Wimbledon, Hammersmith, Southsea, Cardiff, Manchester, Birmingham, and Cheltenham.

Next on the list of *aides de combat* was Andrew Leigh, a man of puckish stature and a gentle nature who had some years before been Director of the Old Vic, where he was known as Merry Andrew. Wolfit had engaged him to produce and play some of the character parts for the first autumn tour. Together, Leigh and Wolfit journeyed to London to visit Miss Rosabel Watson, a musician, who had served for twelve years at Stratford, and was then employed by Robert Atkins at the Regents Park Open Air Theatre. Rosabel Watson, 'a little lady with bright piercing eyes and a ready smile', agreed to join him. In the years to come, she proved to be a loyal and sympathetic friend.

The finance for the tour came from Wolfit's own pocket; he did not ask for a penny from anyone. He had saved, according to his diary, £1218. He now used half the sum to launch himself; the other half was, presumably, to be kept in securities in case of disaster, which mirrored the twin spurs that had motivated his ruthless husbandry.

All was in readiness. Phyllis Neilson-Terry was to be leading lady because, in Wolfit's opinion, 'she had a useful name in the Provinces and was something of a draw in her own right'. The rest of the company was recruited from Stratford: Rosalind Iden to play Ophelia, Maria, Jessica (in a dark wig and nose putty), the Gentlewoman and Fleance—'and a very good Fleance, too'—in *Macbeth*; Clement McCallin, the juveniles; Eric Maxon and Stanley Howlett, the leading character roles; Andrew Leigh and Kenneth Wicksteed, the clowns; other parts to be played by Donald Layne Smith, Emrys Jones, Michael Goodliffe 'and a strong tail that could and did wag. In all I was responsible for twenty-eight salaries.' And he paid all of them, from the first week in Malvern and every succeeding week. When the accounts of his first autumn tour were balanced, Wolfit had lost just under eighty pounds, which by any reckoning could be regarded as a resounding success.

Wolfit was full of zest for his new-found life. He revelled in the responsibility, the all-embracing interest that management provided. In the first week, Wolfit, the manager, had added two major roles to the repertoire of Wolfit, the actor: Macbeth and Shylock. No waiting now for the Old Vic or Stratford to invite him; he was directing his own career as he saw fit. And the added weight of responsibility seemed to lend a charge to his fervour, for Wolfit was consumed by an almost indecent lust for acting and for matters theatrical.

With the tour over, he joined a fine cast at the Westminster Theatre, London, to play, for the first time, *Volpone* by Ben Jonson. Rachel Kempson was Celia and Alan Wheatley, Mosca. The performance was moderately well-received, but as far as the leading actor was concerned, it was a mere foretaste of what he was to achieve in the role.

During the run of this production Wolfit's father, William, was taken ill and died. He travelled to Newark to pay his last respects to the man whose approval he had so often sought, but with whom he had never enjoyed an easy, affectionate relationship. The *Newark Herald* headed its three-column obituary, 'A beloved Townsman, Passing of Mr. W. P. Woolfitt, Devout Churchman and Distinguished Freemason'; dutifully his actor son and daughter-in-law Susan laid a wreath, inscribed: ' "He was a man; take him for all in all, I shall not look upon his like again." God rest you, Father dear—Donald and Susan.' That same afternoon, as he had done after his mother's funeral, Wolfit returned to London and to the theatre. Later, he remembered:

> . . . never had I found a performance more distasteful or a greater strain. . . . This was the break-up of our family home at Newark. The house was sold, my brothers* and sisters being away or married, and the simple effects divided between the four of us. Little did my father realise that my share of his small savings would prevent me from going bankrupt.

The legacy he dropped into his coffers to broaden his repertoire and mounted *Cyrano de Bergerac* for the spring of 1938; both as a performance and a managerial venture it was a disaster.

> It [*Cyrano*] required a large company of nearly fifty people, and the title was apparently so obscure that I had to follow the classic example of Ellen Terry when she went on tour with *Madame Sans Gêne* and stick large bills across the posters: IN ENGLISH.

The play left Wolfit with fifteen shillings. In his diary he noted briefly, but doubtless to the point:

---

* An error: he had one brother alive, Albert.

27 MARCH SUNDAY—4th in Lent
End of 'Cyrano' Tour. Dead loss.

And on his balance sheet:

> Prince Littler cancelled Manchester and the tour ended here
> [Cardiff]. All salaries paid. Printing unpaid also some hire of
> scenery and my salary.

Nothing daunted, Wolfit began preparing for the autumn tour of
1938; he had sets and costumes; Selby managed to book a tour with
minimum guarantees at each theatre, so that Wolfit was able to
budget to an assured income. But he had to make a living through the
summer; there would be some months before the tour was due to
commence. To fill in the time, he accepted an invitation from Sir
Barry Jackson to appear in two Shaw plays: The Dutch Judge in
Geneva and Warwick in *St. Joan*, and as *Alexander* by Lord Dunsany.
In all three roles he was highly praised, especially for a spectacular
death fall down a flight of steps in *Alexander*.

While playing at Malvern he was planning for the future, thinking
deeply about his place in the theatrical scene. As if realising that actor-
management was even then being considered *passé* by the critics and
his fellow players, Wolfit, as would become his custom, formulated a
policy that seemed to be about the theatre in general, but was in fact
about himself in particular: he pleaded for *the actors' theatre*. He
made speeches and wrote to the press. Detecting an ally in St. John
Ervine, he wrote to him too, and received an encouraging reply:

> Broadly speaking, I share your views and have, on several occa-
> sions, in the *Observer*, advocated the actors' theatre. The defect of
> it is that the actor wants every play to be about him, but that defect
> is almost a virtue when we think of a theatre in which the play is
> about no one and nothing. It will not astonish me if you turn out to
> be the saviour of the theatre. You have spirit and quality—your
> Judge in *Geneva* was a grand performance—and you have a mind;
> and you're not afraid of yourself. I like to see manly actors on the
> stage. You're one. The next great crusade will be to purge the
> theatre of its pansies; but I can't get an article on the subject into
> print. Editors go all a-trembling at the very idea, yet everybody is
> *talking* about it.

Drawing comfort from the fact that a leading critic agreed with his
policy, Wolfit was even more delighted to read that Ervine shared his
views about homosexuals, so that when he came to rehearse for his
second Shakespeare tour, the company reflected an enriched policy:
the virile actors' theatre! Adding *Othello*, *Much Ado About Nothing*
and *As You Like It* to his existing repertoire, Wolfit was now in a

position to present a different production each evening of the week. Rosalinde Fuller was his new leading lady; Andrew Leigh again produced.

He began, at this time, to visualise a complete scheme of operations:

> It was apparent that I could not continue playing the great, leading roles of Shakespeare for more than a certain number of weeks in any one year. I was adopting the principle of repertoire and never playing a heavy tragic role for more than two consecutive performances. So by a judicious arrangement of any week's programme I could use Touchstone, Malvolio, Benedick and Petruchio to give me a little respite between Hamlet, Othello and Macbeth. Nonetheless the strain remained very considerable and I considered that some kind of Christmas play, and in the Spring season either a new play or a lighter classic revival, would serve my turn.

And so he hoped it would continue as far into the future as he could see. But it was September and it was 1938; he had not reckoned on the Chancellor of Nazi Germany with whom he had but one thing in common: a birthday, 20 April.

II

On the night of 30 September, Neville Chamberlain, having just returned from Munich, waved a piece of paper from the windows of 10 Downing Street and announced to the enthusiastic crowd below, 'This is the second time in our history that there has come back from Germany to Downing Street peace with honour. I believe it is peace for our time.'

The statement could not have been received with more relief than in the Wolfit household, for Susan was pregnant. A friend, on hearing the declaration, said, 'Good. Now Mrs. Wolfit can have her baby in peace.' Some days later, on 10 October, she gave birth to a son, Adam. The father received the news during a performance of *Othello* at the People's Palace, Mile End Road, in the East End of London. He continued to tour that autumn, produced as his Christmas play *Alice in Wonderland*, playing the Mad Hatter, added *Romeo and Juliet* in the spring of 1939—'. . . a part I never returned to and count it one of my failures'—presented a season in Dublin and Belfast during the last summer of peace, popped over to Caerphilly Castle to play *Macbeth* before the Princess Royal, and returned to Dublin to close his season with *The Scarlet Pimpernel*. He was heady with occupation.

At Caerphilly Castle he was befriended by the Marquis and Marchioness of Bute—the Marquis was the Lord of the Castle—and was given a suite of rooms in the Barbican Tower ('the best rooms I have ever had in Cardiff'); the Earl and Countess of Plymouth became devoted fans; Wolfit lived in a state of professional exaltation.

On 17 April 1939, ten days before conscription was debated in the House of Commons, at a time when both the Liberal and Labour parties combined to oppose the measure ('ill-conceived' said Mr. Attlee in the House), when men and women from all walks of life sincerely believed that a lasting peace had been won at Munich, Donald Wolfit, actor-manager, announced loudly and clearly that there would be war. Furthermore, he instructed his wife and children to depart for the safety of the countryside at once. Susan argued, but he could not be moved; he did not trust Hitler. 'I know something's brewing up,' he said. 'I always know when that man's going to do something. You forget we were born on the same day!'

On 20 April—Wolfit's thirty-seventh and Hitler's fiftieth birthday—the Wolfit family moved to Frensham, Surrey, and thus were comfortably ensconced when war was finally declared on 3 September; those who were less in tune with the Führer's intentions found it difficult to secure accommodation in the country, as the sirens began to wail over London.

Wolfit started to rehearse for his autumn tour on 1 September, 1939, two days before England declared war. The prospects were riddled with uncertainty. London was in the grip of 'the phoney war' and the populace feared bombardment from the air. Despite the Labour and Liberal parties' opposition to conscription that April, the measure had been passed in the House of Commons by 380 to 143 votes. Wolfit faced a company of young men on the immediate call-up list. His leading lady, Rosalinde Fuller, was in America; his business manager had packed a suitcase, grabbed a gas mask, announced his intention of leaving for Devon and joined the queue of many thousands at Paddington Station. But Wolfit announced to his company that he would proceed with the tour, come what might. Catherine Lacey agreed to rehearse in case Miss Fuller could not get back from New York.

But his problems were far from being solved. 'One or two actors deserted,' recalled the General, 'and had to be replaced, one or two were called up at once.' The next bombshell was delivered by the provincial theatre managements who considered that a tour of Shakespeare was inadvisable under conditions then prevailing, and in any event, the Government had indicated that all theatres might be closed for the duration: they tried to cancel the contracts.

Wolfit was besieged on all sides. Then, his attention was drawn to a letter from Bernard Shaw to *The Times* on the subject of keeping the theatres open. Wolfit wrote to the playwright, informing him of the provincial situation and received the following reply, from Ayot St. Lawrence:

> I started in The Times a correspondence on the subject which has been taken up all over the Press. All the follies that were committed in the first blue funk are already relaxing, and will soon be dropped.
>
> G. Bernard Shaw

Wolfit returned the completed contracts to the theatres, informing them that he fully intended to proceed with the tour, and that he considered it his duty to present the plays of 'our National Poet' to the people of Britain at that time. Once the concept of duty had entered Wolfit's strategic thinking, it was worth at least three armoured divisions: he pushed forward, unstoppable.

Once on the march, he re-negotiated his arrangements with the company: each actor would receive a basic salary and a percentage of the box office receipts. His tireless persistence was further rewarded by the return of his business manager—Devon under evacuee conditions was not to his liking—and Wolfit was now convinced that he had turned the tide in favour of his Shakespearean tour, but he was still without his regular leading lady.

Rosalinde Fuller was quite as intrepid as her leading man. When many on the other side of the Atlantic were convinced that England's destruction was imminent, Miss Fuller made three attempts to return. Twice the liner put back into port; on the third attempt she succeeded in reaching England in time to open the tour at Brighton. It was, in Wolfit's words, 'a brave deed', all the more so, when one considers that on 4 September the liner *Athenia* was sunk by U-boats, and that on 4 October the steamer *Clement* met a similar fate in the South Atlantic.

On 9 October 1939, Wolfit wrote:

> . . . we launched our first black-out tour of the war. Our repertoire consisted of *Hamlet, Othello, The Merchant of Venice, Twelfth Night, The Taming of the Shrew* and a new production of *Julius Caesar* with striking coloured togas and clever armour designed by Paul Gibson.

Wolfit played Marc Antony.

The tour ended in the first week of December in Norwich. He recorded in his account book: 'Black-out city and warnings all week. THE worst week we have ever played so far.'

The takings were £161.2.6.; the company's share £88.11.0.; the preceding weeks had not been much better. His business manager, presumably seeing no future with the company, left him once more— this time for good. Wolfit returned to London having taken another financial caning. But he was soon at work again, re-staging his production of *Alice in Wonderland* for the first Christmas of war; he was tired, but not dispirited.

Wolfit was fortunate to secure the services of Charles Landstone, a friend and a man of great experience in the theatre, as General Manager. Landstone wrote:

> . . . we were supposed to do a week in Dublin [with *Alice in Wonderland*], three times daily, to be followed by a fortnight in Limerick. But the theatre owners got so frightened by the first day's reaction, that they cut the performance down to one daily matinée in Dublin and cancelled the fortnight in Limerick, paying up in full, rather than have their theatres torn down by an irate Irish public, that expected a full-scale old-time pantomime.

'*On nous a donné l'oiseau*,' Landstone informed his mother by postcard. 'Get back to England' the Dubliners had cried, and Joseph Chelton's line as the Cheshire Cat, 'You're mad, I'm mad, we're all mad here!' was greeted by a howl of derision which drowned the actors for the rest of the performance. 'On the Saturday night,' Wolfit remembered, 'we retired gracefully to England with our minimum guarantee.'

They returned to a London transformed by the dread anticipation of bombing; nightly, the black-out was strictly enforced; the wearing of gas masks was compulsory; instruction was being given in air raid and fire precautions; deep shelters were being constructed. Wolfit wrote:

> . . . mankind was reverting to holes in the ground for safety. How could the theatre withstand this attack on civilisation?

III

On the journey back from Dublin, Landstone and Wolfit discussed the possibility of a London season of Shakespeare. For two days they visited manager after manager but were met with nothing but refusals. Late on the second day, they met Herbert Jay, proprietor of the Kingsway Theatre. A man of great charm, he confided to Landstone, in private, that he 'hated to see Wolfit on a certain loser', but would consider the proposition. The following day, while the three men inspected the stage, Jay quoted an entire speech from *Henry V*, endeared himself to Wolfit, and agreed to let him have the theatre, rental sixty pounds per week, Wolfit to pay all overheads.

At about this time, Wolfit formed Advance Players' Association, a non-profit-making company, which meant that any surplus had to be

re-invested in the company. In collaboration with Jay, Wolfit printed
playbills that asked

Have you ever

seen a play

by

WILLIAM SHAKESPEARE

OUR

NATIONAL

POET

?

The Kingsway season lasted a month and lost four hundred
pounds, but the actors received a fine press. The *Daily Herald*, in a
headline, advised YOU SHOULD SEE MR. WOLFIT, and all the
serious critics treated him with considerable respect. The *Daily
Worker* was alone in damning the venture: SHAKESPEARE? it
asked; Wolfit in his press book, wrote by the side of the notice:

> Let this be a warning. My business manager regretted that he
> could not increase expenditure further and declined to take adver-
> tising space in this paper. D.W.

It was Wolfit's first London season as an actor-manager and he
presented himself as Othello, Hamlet, Malvolio, Benedick and
Shylock. Although he lost money, he earned golden opinions from
the critics and from those members of the public brave enough to
venture forth in the blackout. Two such were John Maynard Keynes,
the economist who revolutionised economic theory, and his wife
Lydia Lopokova. Keynes was Bursar of King's College, Cambridge,
and founder of the Arts Theatre in that city. He invited Wolfit to present four plays in Cambridge for a limited season but which might be
the nucleus of a repertoire for a later tour. Wolfit sent Keynes a copy
of John Ford's tragedy *'Tis Pity She's a Whore*, which had not been
performed in England for over three hundred years. The economist
replied:

> It is a wonderfully strong piece of work, which needs doing with
> gusto and in the Italian manner. But I had not realised that the
> theme was so exclusively incest without mitigation or remorse.
> Clearly it is strong meat for the general public. On the other hand,
> the title, fortunately perhaps, is calculated to warn away the
> squeamish.

After discussing the practical arrangements and the amount of performances, Keynes, who was shortly to become adviser to the Trea-

sury on war finance, concluded: 'I am asking Higgins to let you have a float of £30 at once, as suggested by Mr. Selby.'

Understandably, considering the passionate conflict at the heart of the play, Wolfit awaited a reply from the Lord Chamberlain with some trepidation. In due course, he was informed that the Lord Chamberlain had no jurisdiction over the work as it was classed as an 'old play', having been first performed prior to the Theatres Act, 1843.

While preparing for the Cambridge season which he knew, at best, could only be of very limited duration, Wolfit was determined to find a way of making a contribution to the war effort. Entertainments National Service Association—ENSA—had been formed under the control of Sir Seymour Hicks with headquarters at the Theatre Royal, Drury Lane. Wolfit wrote to Hicks placing his services at ENSA's disposal, to play Shakespeare to the troops. Hicks replied enthusiastically. 'It is a splendid suggestion,' he wrote, and promised to take up the matter with Basil Dean who was the Association's Executive Director, and Director of Entertainments for the NAAFI Hicks wrote again two days later:

28 March 1940

My dear Mr. Donald Wolfit,

At a general meeting today at Drury Lane, no definite decision could be arrived at as there was a great divergence of opinion that Shakespeare would be the right form of entertainment to give the troops and therefore much as I should personally like to see Shakespeare presented, the matter had to be held over for the time being and I understand Mr. Basil Dean has written to you on the subject.

For the time being Wolfit's offer was placed in cold storage, and in May, he presented *'Tis Pity She's a Whore* in Cambridge.

Wolfit played Giovanni, and Rosalind Iden Anabella, his sister. A distinguished audience, which included Desmond McCarthy the critic, gave the company a rapturous reception. In the *New Statesman and Nation*, McCarthy observed:

It is a play of amazing vitality, with passages of dramatic poetry both vigorous and delicate, notably the love scene between Giovanni and Anabella, when brother and sister, kneeling before each other, declare their desires . . . movingly acted and spoken by Mr. Wolfit and Miss Rosalind Iden.
. . . The manner in which Mr. Wolfit sustained the morbid, frenzied and tender intensities of Giovanni's part was remarkable.

During that May, Winston Churchill was summoned to Bucking-

ham Palace, accepted the King's commission and formed a National
Government. By the end of the month, the British Expeditionary
Force commenced the retreat from the beaches of Dunkirk. On 13
June, the schoolchildren of Greater London began to be evacuated.
The following day Paris fell. On the 18th, Churchill informed the
House of Commons there were 'greater reasons for vigilance and
exertion, but none whatever for panic and fear,' and, later in the same
speech, forecast the Battle of Britain. He ended with his famous
exhortation to the nation: 'Let us therefore brace ourselves to our
duties, and so bear ourselves that, if the British Empire and its
Commonwealth last for a thousand years, men will still say: "This
was their finest hour." '

The summer of 1940 found Wolfit in the Home Guard in Frensham
where he was commanded by an old army officer to 'bring me the first
dead German. That's what I want to see, the first dead German
caught in this village.' Dutifully inspired, Wolfit recorded

> . . . I marched and countermarched in an ill-fitting uniform and
> camped out five nights a week on the common. I learned to read the
> stars again and to watch the course of the planets and waited for
> the church bells to ring and announce the invasion of Great
> Britain.

Like many others, he must have thought the time had come on 7
September: six hundred and twenty-five bombers of the Luftwaffe
meted out on London what William L. Shirer described as 'the most
devastating attack from the air ever delivered up to that date on a
city'. In due course, the London theatres were ordered to close down.
But the provincial theatres were not. Wolfit summoned all his energies and tried to organise an autumn tour. He failed:

> Communications became strained and telephone calls impossible
> except for Government work. I would cross London to find my
> scene store closed and the proprietor away from London. To gather
> transport was a nightmare. The actors came to rehearsals after
> sleepless nights ignorant of their parts. . . . Reluctantly I was
> compelled to cancel the autumn tour. . . . It seemed the end of my
> managerial activities and yet I was loath to give in without a
> struggle.

The strain of these weeks told heavily on Wolfit; he was close to a
breakdown and his wife, Susan, described him as wandering about in
a state of shock, 'like a zombie'. Because of his distrust of drugs, she
had to employ surreptitious methods to help him. While he sat in a
chair, staring into space, she conspired with her neighbour, the local

doctor's wife, to take some action. The doctor's wife procured a pill, 'a depth-charge', which she passed through the fence to Susan who managed to conceal it in her husband's food. He slept for forty-eight hours, woke utterly refreshed and with an idea burning in his brain: to present a short programme of excerpts from Shakespeare, if a suitable London theatre could be found to house it. His energies restored, Wolfit approached Miss Salmon, secretary to Lionel Falck, lessee of the Strand Theatre, darkened when the aptly named comedy *Aren't Men Beasts!* had been suspended. Falck was in Devon; Wolfit sent a telegram, making a 'crazy offer' for the Strand at a rental of ten pounds per week and payment of wages to five heads of departments. That same afternoon he received a reply from Falck: CRAZY OFFER ACCEPTED. The Donald Wolfit Shakespeare Company was about to embark upon its finest hour:

. . . between one and two, we would present in costume excerpts from the plays, songs, sonnets and prologues. We would call it Lunch Time Shakespeare. Only the stalls of the theatre would be used, and sandwiches and coffee were to be provided in the stalls bar. The valiant Rosabel Watson came to my rescue with three musicians, token salaries were accepted by everyone, and a borrowed and rather tattered Union Jack covered the big sign *Aren't Men Beasts* over the front of the theatre. We managed to find a printer who would paste up our titles outside. Cathleen Nesbitt came to do scenes from *Macbeth* with me; Rosalind Iden did the Chorus from *Henry IV*, Part II (the famous Rumour Chorus) that seemed so appropriate; Frank Drew sang groups of songs. My wardrobe I managed to retrieve from store and, by a miracle of foresight, placed the baskets under the electrician's board.

And, when necessary, Susan hand-printed the change of programmes for display outside the theatre.

The cultural life of London during the most dangerous hours in its long history was supported, in those last terrible months of 1940, by Myra Hess, who gave recitals at the National Gallery, by an hour-long programme of ballet at the Arts Theatre and, of course, non-stop revue at the Windmill. 'We never closed' could have been Wolfit's motto, too.

In between Home Guard duties, Wolfit travelled up to London three times a week to rehearse changes to the programme. Sixty-one people attended the first performance (admission one shilling per head) on 13 October. The next day, the theatre was hit by an enemy bomb. Wolfit noted in his accounts book:

Dressing room destroyed. Co. dressed on stage. No water. No heat.

Stalls only used. Coffee and sandwiches served in stalls bar.

He gloried in the discomfort; he rejoiced in the danger, for this was the theatre put to a use he understood, and which inspired him. He was serving the community in an hour of great national emergency, and in the only way he knew: by acting, and by acting Shakespeare. It was the Arts League of Service, the Sheffield Repertory company all over again, but now with a manifest purpose for all to appreciate. Never could Wolfit's definition of the theatre's true function be more clearly demonstrated: he was in the capital, refreshing a bomb-weary population, at the very heart of the peril. If enemy bombers were approaching, Mary Pitcher, dressed as an Elizabethan page, announced cheerfully: 'The warning has just gone. We shall proceed. Will those who wish to leave do so as quietly as possible.' Everything was improvised from cubby holes for dressing rooms to the remains of double swing-doors for Ophelia's bier.

To continue the season, Wolfit appealed for funds. The Marchioness of Bute sent one hundred pounds; Mrs. Bernard, a friend of Rosabel Watson, gave two hundred and fifty pounds; the newly created Council for the Encouragement of Music and the Arts helped with fifty pounds and Wolfit dropped four hundred pounds of his own into the pot.

He introduced a shortened version of *The Merry Wives of Windsor* with Irene and Violet Vanbrugh, then in their seventies, who like everyone else received three guineas a week and no more. During the run, Irene was created a Dame of the British Empire. Later, the company embarked on a full performance of *Hamlet*; returning after lunch to make up, Wolfit was amazed to see the Strand Theatre encircled by queues. An old flower-seller sidled up to him and said, 'Look at them, guv'nor, does your bloody heart good, don't it?' There was one performance of *Othello*, two of John Ford's tragedy, 'though a land mine exploded outside the theatre and ruined the first performance entirely'.

In the midst of the season, Wolfit learned that the Stratford Memorial Theatre had visited the army camps with a programme of Shakespeare. Once more, he communicated with Basil Dean, more or less demanding that his company be allowed to undertake a similar tour. From Drury Lane, he received the following reply:

2 November 1940

Dear Mr. Wolfit,

I am glad to have your letter and to know that your season at the Strand Theatre has been so successful. I am sorry to say that the visit of the Stratford Memorial Theatre to the camps, whilst much appreciated for the quality of the performances, has not proved to the liking of a large majority of troops. Therefore, I regret that at the moment it is not possible for us to extend the experiment by arranging dates for your company.

With many regrets,
Yours sincerely,
Basil Dean.
Director of Entertainments

Wolfit's hackles rose; doubtless, he inhaled noisily, for the letter seemed to offend everything in which he believed. In a passion he scribbled a draft reply on the back of Dean's letter:

Dear Mr. Dean,

Your letter of the 2nd to hand and your decision with very real regret.

I am no diplomatist and fully realise that you occupy a powerful position but I disagree so absolutely with your contention that the majority taste must rule that I wish to state my opposition to your view quite bluntly and frankly and I would rather state it to you openly than to continue to express my view in every quarter possible without communicating my point of view to you personally.

I believe so fundamentally in the value of our classic drama that I am continuing to work at the same expenses salary as my artists at the Strand and losing my personal savings on the venture and ready to do so.

You have a great trust committed to you in your position in ENSA and to pander to popular taste in the matter of our national drama is unworthy of your early record in the theatre which did so much for the best in the theatre. To present the classics should never have been an experiment but an essential basis of your entertainment for the forces. Before you destroy this letter do me the honour of reading it through again.

Wolfit had now stated, with absolute sincerity, his position and he never wavered from it. Whatever allegations of megalomania were to be levelled at his management, the very core of his purpose was his belief that the drama, on the highest plane, made an immeasurable contribution to the quality of human life, and no one should be denied the opportunity of thus benefiting, whether they liked it or not. As far as the armed services were concerned, it would be some years before Wolfit would be proved triumphantly right. For the moment, he continued to make his contribution from one o'clock until two at the Strand Theatre.

On Saturday 1 February 1941 the season ended with a full performance of *The Merry Wives of Windsor* in aid of the Lord Mayor's Distress Fund.

Wolfit had become a national figure. The *Daily Record and Mail*, giving voice to a dozen articles published the length and breadth of the land, roared: SHAKESPEARE BEATS HITLER! and in *Theatre World* a long article appeared under the title 'Donald Wolfit's Great Achievement in War-time'.

He had lost all his sets and costumes when his store room had been bombed, and saved only those few in use at the Strand. He had sunk the last of his capital into the venture, and had lived on a pittance. But he had won the hearts of many by what was undoubtedly a remarkable season. He had been acknowledged as a courageous manager; his recognition as an actor had not yet been fully realised.

IV

Wolfit's public life had taken an exhilarating turn; his private life, once more, was the cause of great personal anxiety. He was in love for the third time in his life, intensely and passionately in love with a member of his company: Rosalind Iden.

Rosalind came from a thoroughly theatrical background. Her father was Ben Iden Payne, who had persuaded Miss Horniman, the tea heiress and, in his words, 'a woman of the greatest integrity', to lease the Gaiety Theatre, Manchester, so that he could institute the first repertory company in England there. His wife, Mona Limerick, was leading lady and she, in later years, used to become infuriated when Miss Horniman received all the credit for the success of the Gaiety season. During their time in Manchester, in 1911, Rosalind was born; she was their second daughter. The date of her birth would be the cause of great amusement to her future husband: 29 July, the same as Benito Mussolini.

Iden Payne belonged, on his own admission, to the 'theatre underground', and took his place in the *avant-garde* of his day. Mona Limerick was an actress of considerable talent, much admired by Bernard Shaw, who had been enchanted by her performance as Anne Whitfield on a tour of *Man and Superman* with Esmé Percy. Her career, however, was dogged by illness. When playing at the Coronet Theatre, Notting Hill Gate, she had been offered a contract by Herbert Beerbohm Tree at His Majesty's, but she suffered a breakdown in health and could not fulfill it. Instead, Lillah McCarthy was engaged.

For two years after the Gaiety season, husband and wife toured with their own repertory company and organised seasons at Sheffield, Leeds, Glasgow and Edinburgh. But the marriage did not last; Iden Payne went to the United States where he was appointed director of the Little Theatre, Philadelphia. Mona Limerick remained in England with her two daughters, Sara and Rosalind.

As a child, Rosalind exhibited as much eagerness to perform as her future husband had in his youth, but she preferred to dance, to interpret the music *à la* Isadora Duncan. Soon she found herself being taken to auditions by her mother who, having heard that the Everyman Theatre, Hampstead, was looking for a child to play a Cockney in Galsworthy's *Foundations* put up both her daughters for the role. Rosalind, possessing the classic pallor of a London sparrow, was engaged and spent one whole night being taught by her mother to speak in a true Cockney accent.

Other engagements followed; most distinguished of them was as Toby in *Through the Crack* by Algernon Blackwood, presented by Edith Craig. It was distinguished because the prologue was spoken by an old lady who could barely see, Ellen Terry. Later, for Shakespeare's birthday, Ellen Terry appeared as Portia in the trial scene from *The Merchant of Venice*. Edith Craig allowed Rosalind to appear as a Page, so that she could always say she played with the great actress in one of her most famous roles. While sitting in the green room, Ellen patted the page on the head and said, 'You're a nice little boy, aren't you?'

Rosalind's more formal education was supervised by Margaret Morris; it was thought that she would become a dancer and she was engaged in that capacity by Eleanor Elder for two years, and met Wolfit then for the first time. When she left the Arts League, she studied for three years under Ninette de Valois. Some time towards the end of the 1920s de Valois was approached by Lilian Baylis and asked to supply someone who would refurbish the opera ballets, and dance solo parts; de Valois recommended Rosalind, who became ballet mistress at the Old Vic while Wolfit was finding his Shakespearean feet in the same building, though they hardly met.

Lilian Baylis took a maternal interest in Rosalind, and was extremely fond of her, for the young ballet mistress was talented and conscientious. In 1931, Lilian Baylis offered her young protégée the chance of creating the Sadlers Wells Ballet Company, but she shied away from the opportunity, doubting her own ability to organise and to administer so potentially large an enterprise. Ninette de Valois herself undertook the task and created not only Sadlers Wells, but also British ballet.

Rosalind went on to study with Tamara Karsavina; again she received enormous kindness, the great ballerina soon realising that her new pupil was extremely poor; Karsavina never took payment from her, but, instead, provided Rosalind with the opportunity to give demonstrations, lectures, private lessons for which she was paid; in this way, Rosalind was able to live. When she was engaged to dance the Fairy Godmother in a pantomime she was expected, as was the practice then, to provide her own costume and orchestra parts. Karsavina not only provided the necessary music, but also arranged the dance.

The necessity of earning a more substantial living took Rosalind away from Karsavina's care, and thrust her into the centre of 'The Other Theatre', in Norman Marshall's revues at the Festival Theatre, Cambridge, which later transferred to the Gate Theatre, London. At about the same time, Iden Payne returned from America to take up his appointment as director of the Stratford Memorial Theatre; he had not seen his younger daughter from the time she was seven years old. After witnessing her antics in a Gate Revue, he said, 'You should be an actress,' and to support his belief, engaged her for his forthcoming season.

The relationship between Rosalind and Wolfit, which it would seem the Fates had been trying to arrange without success for a number of years, was founded on a profound and passionate love. In Rosalind, Wolfit had at last found a woman who worshipped him as a man and, furthermore, reverenced his talent as an actor. In return, he found the combination of femininity and vulnerability in her irresistible.

In the early years of their romance, at least until 1943, their love was subject to the severest strains. Both partners suffered from having to make the most agonising personal decisions. Wolfit, as has already been seen, took responsibility seriously; his second marriage to Susan had produced two children, Harriet and Adam; Susan had been a loyal wife. At times, the turmoil, fanned by feelings of guilt, was overwhelming. On one occasion, Rosalind left him, then returned. On another, she suffered a complete collapse. In the end, their decision to marry was made for them by the realisation that they could not live apart from each other. From 1940, Rosalind shared in Wolfit's life, in his struggles and in his triumphs; she played the leading women's roles in all his productions and, because she was for ever seen beside an actor of his ability and power, was constantly underrated; she served him and the theatre selflessly. As an actress she had a surprising power of her own, an exquisite voice and a diction, learned from her mother, of extraordinary beauty.

By 1941, Wolfit had elevated Rosalind to the leading roles; Portia, Celia in *Volpone* and Mistress Quickly. Their service to the community did not end with the Lunch Time Shakespeare at the Strand. For the next three years they toured the British Isles, adding *A Midsummer Night's Dream* (Wolfit as Bottom, Rosalind as Titania) and *The Scarlet Pimpernel* to their already comprehensive repertoire.

They played the principal provincial cities, often under attack from the air; they made further forays into London. The continuance of the company, however, was dependent not just on Wolfit's tenacity as a manager, but more importantly on his skill as an actor, for the power-house that drove the company onwards was his talent; all his courage, persistence and determination was harnessed in its service.

CHAPTER TEN

The Actor

The mightier man, the mightier is the thing
That makes him honour'd, or begets him hate;
For greatest scandal waits on greatest state
—The Rape of Lucrece

I

FROM 1938–43, Wolfit had realised his ambition to play all but one of the major Shakespearean roles under his own management: Hamlet, Macbeth, Othello, Shylock, Petruchio, Benedick, Richard III, Falstaff (in the *Merry Wives of Windsor*), Malvolio and Touchstone; he had also played Volpone by Ben Jonson.

His Hamlet, first presented at Stratford, had already been considered, and favourably, as we have seen, by the leading critics; they were not as unanimous about his Macbeth and Othello.

When Miss Caryl Brahms, the author and critic, wrote, 'In the theatre of my mind's eye I see Donald Wolfit perpetually bestriding the stage in some twopence coloured Victorian play-print,' she, perhaps, had Macbeth most vividly in her imagination. Macbeth was a part in which Wolfit made no discoveries: he played it four-square in the Victorian tradition, which does not mean that he failed to bring his considerable theatrical imagination to the role; if anything, he brought too much imagination. Wolfit played the bloody side of Macbeth to the hilts of both the daggers with which he murdered Duncan and, as a result, was able to display some incisive dramatic effects: a masterful demonstration of physical danger as he mounted the steps before the murder; the change of wig from raven-red for the first part of the play to ghostly white for the second. 'Macbeth shall sleep no more,' prophesy the witches, which was the key to his interpretation of the final movement of the drama: the sleeplessness of an exhausted lion with barely enough strength to toss its whitened mane. In all Wolfit performances there was at least one startling vocal effect. 'I have lived long enough' was the desperate cry of a trapped animal, evoking horror, rather than pity.

Agate, who had urged Wolfit to present the play in London, regretted when he saw it that,

> Mr. Wolfit's Macbeth fails because the character does not lie in the actor's personality. Because no actor can be Macbeth who deprives him of his poetry, introspection, vacillation, remorse. 'Be bloody, bold and resolute,' enjoins the Apparition. But then Mr. Wolfit is already bloody, bold and resolute, and has been so from the beginning.
>
> The character goes wrong from the start. From the words 'Duncan comes here tonight,' followed by Lady Macbeth's 'And when goes hence?' This is the first in a long time ('What beast was't *then*,' etc.) that murder has been mentioned between them, and now the impetus comes from the lady, who in her immediately preceding speech has already settled the business in her own mind. ('Father is in the study praying for guidance; mother is upstairs packing.') Murder is as yet only at the back of Macbeth's mind ('My thought, whose murder yet is but fantastical'), which means that there should be no more than the glimmer of a possibility behind the words, 'Tomorrow, as *he purposes*'. But this is not our Macbeth's notion. At his wife's question he disengages himself, steps back a pace, goes through prodigies of winking and nodding which would stagger the blindest horse, and incidentally ruins Lady Macbeth's 'O never shall sun that morrow see!'. . . In short Mr. Wolfit turns the whole play into a ranting, roaring, Saturday night melodrama, full of sound and fury but signifying nothing of the play's pity and melancholy.

Not all the critics shared Agate's view. Trewin, writing in the *Observer*, considered that 'Mr. Wolfit sustains a performance unwavering in its excitement and its hold upon the mighty line'.

It was undoubtedly a part in which Wolfit was able to demonstrate his extraordinary vocal technique, both its range and strength. His voice was, for example, not in the least strained for 'Arm, arm and out!' in Act V; the exhortation to battle was delivered with as much rumbling fury as anything that had gone before. But despite Stephen Williams' claim, in the *Evening News*, that the performance was 'a splendid monument crumbling to a ruin', the complete vision of the part was at times obscured by Wolfit's ability to play superb moments, even complete scenes, which unbalanced the grand sweep of the tragedy.

Yet, to lovers of virtuoso acting, it was those very moments that made a visit to *Macbeth* worth while. One such theatregoer wrote from Renishaw Hall:

My dear Mr. Wolfit,

I always hoped one day to see a great actor, and last night I certainly did so. I shall never forget your going up, and coming down the stairs, from Duncan's chamber. . . . I only write this, because I think one should feed the artist's self-esteem. I know it's a necessity for a writer.

Apart from Chaliapine, and young Grasso, who was drained when he was only 23 or 4, I have never seen great acting. Your performance is as different to others, as a lion is from a tamed cat.

Yours gratefully,
Osbert Sitwell.

Incidentally, how good the whole performance is. May you and all your undertakings prosper. You can be certain that when my sister and I are in reach, either here or in London, we shall be in your audience.

And from his sister:

Dear Mr. Wolfit,

The greatness of your heart-shaking Macbeth will remain with us all our lives. We shall carry with us the memory of that leonine grandeur and terror, the doom implicit in every movement, each tone of voice in that scale of anguish, the feline ascent of the steps, and the unutterably broken descent, all moved one to an unbearable pity. I thought I knew how great the play is. I did, but there was the embodiment still to come. Fuseli should have seen that embodiment. We should then have drawings of your Macbeth, as transcendental as those of Mrs. Siddons as Lady Macbeth.

. . . I can only say that we would go to any distance to know again an experience so great as that we knew in witnessing your Macbeth.

Believe me,
Yours sincerely,
Edith Sitwell.

The two opposing views of Wolfit's Macbeth, on the one side Agate and many leading critics, on the other the Sitwells and their allies, dramatise the problem that casts a shadow over the assessment of any performance by an actor of extraordinary gifts, for the truth is that only *virtuosi* can be indescribably bad one night, and indescribably magnificent on another. In Wolfit's career this was certainly true and because he seemed to attack roles with such violence, his approach to Macbeth may have pleased a particular playgoer who shuddered at a similar approach to Hamlet. It is a problem impossible to resolve satisfactorily, but it is because of the conflict that the mystique surrounding the interpretations of the great classic roles persists from one generation to another.

Certain it was that Wolfit's public loved him as Macbeth. To his followers, who flocked to see him in the role year after year—financially it was always his most successful play—the performance embodied all that was expected of the actor-manager. He played it more than two hundred times and he himself reflected in a letter to one of his actors, Joseph Chelton, 'and dear God the hair and gum I must have used—and the dragons blood!!!'

Othello Wolfit conceived on a personal theory that there was not time for the Moor to consummate his marriage to Desdemona; Othello's jealousy, erupting out of so slight a pretext as a missing handkerchief, was more understandable in a man consumed with frustrated desire. But however convincing the inner motivation, English critics, brushing aside the diminutive Edmund Kean, have always judged the externals of Othello to be more important. They have demanded that the Moor be of towering physique and of noble visage. Agate:

> Here again I have to consider the nature of the player's physique, and I am reluctantly forced to say that Mr. Wolfit is not among the very small number of actors who can black their faces and retain their dignity. His first act the other night only wanted a banjo to suggest Margate, and his last act, through the same disability, was lacking in grandeur. Against this I do not remember ever having seen the hurt and perplexed animal of the play's middle acts given with greater power or with a more natural pathos.

Once more there were 'great moments' to sear the memory: the dreadful menace of 'Look you, prove my love a whore', the barbaric compulsion of Desdemona's murder.

Shylock he played as a villain full of venom and hatred, spitting on the Christians at the end of the trial scene. He conceived him as a young patriarch in keeping with the requirements of Talmudic law that enjoins Jews to marry young. Malvolio was a superb creation of pompous superiority, though he may have been guilty of playing for too much sympathy at the end. Wolfit omitted the scene where Malvolio is imprisoned and visited by Feste pretending to be Sir Topas. The actor contended that the scene was the work of another pen. 'I cannot learn it,' he declared, 'and if I cannot learn it, Shakespeare did not write it!'

Petruchio and Benedick were a fine, lusty pair. Indeed it was said that one expected Wolfit's Benedick to claim his marital rights the moment the curtain fell. His Falstaff in *The Merry Wives of Windsor* was rich, juicy and broad in effect. But his finest comic display, and by common consent one of his most magnificent creations, was Volpone, the Fox. It was a luxurious performance. No actor then alive could portray a character's relish in his own evil better than Wolfit. When Volpone laughed it was, as Joseph Chelton described it, 'gloriously diabolical, right down from the bowels of Hell and up into Jupiter's anteroom'. Sensuality took on a religious significance in Volpone's bedchamber; when Wolfit's Fox touched silks or fingered a jewel, or sipped a heady wine, it was in the nature of an unholy communion. John Mayes:

> It was a part that showed Wolfit at his finest in comedy, and also in playing some of the finest verse passages from 17th-century drama. His scene alone with Rosalind Iden in which he makes himself known as a vigorous, lustful Croesus with the imagination of a poet and the proclivities of a satyr, showed Wolfit's marvellous range and command of vocal technique. His hypnotic, chuckling laugh as he faced his Celia, was an extraordinarily powerful moment, and an audience waited, completely controlled, not knowing which way the fox would jump, and then came his frightening, slow, pacing walk towards his victim followed by another soaring speech of verse splendours.

Volpone was the first part which Wolfit stamped as his. Actors essaying the role in future would suffer by comparison; even one of Wolfit's own daring effects had been passed on, during his lifetime, as if it were traditional business: the blood-curdling howl after receiving the sentence of the court, followed by the line, 'This is called the mortifying of the Fox!' and the holding on to the final hissing sibilant.

In 1943, Wolfit played *Richard III* for the first time. Where, perhaps, he erred as Macbeth, he triumphed absolutely as the hunchback King; for the melodrama of Richard does not require the subtlety demanded by the Scots tragedy. 'Richard's Himself Again' wrote Agate. 'His Richard is conceived in the back-of-the-pub Saturday night vein demanded by this roaring melodrama.' Wolfit gloried in Richard Crookback:

> I revelled in the hunchbacked toad, his ruthless progression to the throne of England, his hypocritical wooing of Lady Anne and his final agonising cry: 'A horse, a horse, my kingdom for a horse.'

the cry which Agate described as 'agony made vocal':

> The spectator, no longer concerned whether Richard is a good King or a bad, is appalled at this cry of a man about to die on his feet. Baffled enjoyment of his well-laid schemes, vengeance on Rich-

mond, the fury of a trapped animal—all these are merged in the hoarse scream which still rings in my ears.

But Agate had one further thing to say about Wolfit, and it was the first inkling the critic had of what was to come: '. . . there is on view a fine, and in some respects a great, actor'. The critic had perceived in the actor those attributes necessary for encompassing the major classical roles: his intense, passionate imagination, his enormously strong physique, and the most potent asset of all: his voice. It was blessed with an astonishing range, capable of preserving resonance in all registers, without strain, from a bass growl to a nasal falsetto. Because of vast reserves of breath, and because he knew how, by practice and experience, to control the letting out of that breath, Wolfit was able to sustain long passages of lyrical beauty, or descend, without apparent preparation, to brutal anger. It was his to command: it could soar, swoop or whisper; and his bright blue eyes exactly reflected each nuance.

He had proved his power, his vitality, his insatiable appetite for acting. His versatility was unquestioned, for he was able, as it were, not only to change make-ups, but also to change hearts. Of his range, Caryl Brahms observed that not one of his creations was 'even first cousin to another . . . creatures compounded of passion and pity, gusto and grandeur'. But let it be remembered that even after the Kingsway season at the outbreak of war, or the Lunch Time Shakespeare, even after the glowing praise of half-a-dozen critics, Wolfit was still regarded as an old-fashioned, anachronistic barn-stormer by the fashionable, wincing *côterie*. His hissing detractors affected to admire him in his lesser roles, which was their way of diminishing him. Wolfit knew only too well that if he was to enlarge Agate's view of him, he would have to take the establishment by storm; this he now set about doing and, being Wolfit, did so, as it were, literally.

II

In the late summer of 1942, on 24 August, Wolfit played King Lear for the first time; it was not a successful performance:

> I was disappointed and knew I had failed. The magnitude of the task and the unnerving cosmic quality of the tragedy became apparent to me as the performance went on. I seemed to myself to resemble a small boy who, wading into a rough sea, sees a big wave coming, jumps in the air to avoid being overwhelmed, and is flung on to the shore. Physically I was exhausted, but not mentally or spiritually. I spent the night in study.

Wolfit worked at Lear for two years, playing it forty-two times before he was seen in it in London; but of his first attempt, that night in Cardiff, he wrote to David Maitland, an amateur actor who had asked for advice:

> You have to tear your heart out and it won't come at first—mine resisted for at least twelve performances and after that it became unbearable until I had to stop.

He had decided to include *King Lear* in his repertoire earlier that year. A few months previously he had been visited by Ernest Stern, an Austrian refugee from Hitler, who had designed *The Miracle* for Max Reinhardt. He was one of those indefatigable Europeans who can sustain *joi de vivre* in spite of the most dire oppression: he had escaped from the Nazis, been interned by the English and, undeterred, had popped up in Wolfit's dressing room with models and designs, 'simple sets ideal for touring'. He and Wolfit worked closely together for the next ten years. Having made the decision to attempt Lear, Wolfit discussed the problems with Stern who, on hearing Wolfit's intentions, replied:

> 'Quite right,' he said, 'I did it with Reinhardt; we had a hundred knights. Magnificent!'
> 'Yes,' said I, 'but I shall have to do it with six.' 'Very good,' replied the indomitable Stern, 'I did it first of all with Reinhardt with six knights and it was much much better. You do it with six.' Stonehenge was the set I envisaged. 'Very good, that is what you shall have; but with some little devices, cunning devices, I will show you in three days,' said Stern, and left the house in an air-raid.

Nugent Monck from the Maddermarket Theatre was engaged to co-produce with Wolfit. Following Granville Barker's advice in his *Preface*, they decided to have just one interval, after the blinding of Gloucester, but the major contribution Wolfit made to the text was in Act I, Scene iv, when the King, returning from hunting, is subjected to the insolence of Oswald, the first of a series of carefully planned indignities by his eldest daughter, and with the demand that he reduce in number his train of one hundred knights.

In the Folio version, Lear, after cursing Goneril, makes an exit, only to return four lines later to deliver a second curse. Wolfit's instinct told him that something was at fault: 'Shakespeare seldom reduces his dramatic tension with a feeble exit and a return in such a short space of time,' he wrote in an introduction to the tragedy published by the Folio Society. He felt so strongly that he made cuts, rearranged the order of speeches, so that 'Hark, Nature, hear, dear goddess!' follows rather than precedes 'Life and death! I am asham'd that thou hast power to shake my manhood thus . . .' He also omitted Lear's line on his re-entrance 'What, fifty of my followers at a clap, Within a fortnight?' because, to him, it had

> . . . no ring of truth about it and I believe was added in performance by the actor to bridge the gap and thus came to be included in the Folio.

The result of his doctoring was that he achieved a more coherent, dramatic shape to the scene:

> . . . the cumulative effect . . . has been heightened beyond any words I can find to express. The greater curse of Lear upon Goneril now succeeds the lesser, which my instinct tells me was Shakespeare's dramatic intention.

Rosabel Watson suggested that the only musical accompaniment should be the sound of a trumpet and 'a few solemn chords'. The costumes Stern painted himself by hand; 'swords and shields from Forbes-Robertson's *Macbeth*' wrote Wolfit, and with these preparations under way, and 'carrying in my memory the great Lear of Randle Ayrton. . . . I began to study.'

Despite the fact that a real thunderstorm assisted Wolfit's stage-management on the first night in Cardiff, Wolfit felt himself beaten. 'I could not encompass the task,' he admitted, and 'fell back on sheer technique to carry me through to the end.'

But he continued to persevere, never playing the part more than twice in any one week. He showed the performance to London in a season at the St. James's Theatre in the winter of 1943, was politely received, but no more than that. By the spring of 1944, he felt himself to be ready once more.

III

The night of Wednesday 12 April 1944 was misty and damp and chill. London was again under attack, but the weather was shortly to improve and the raids slackened.

Wolfit had taken the Scala Theatre for a thirteen-week season which had begun in February; after nine weeks, he decided to try *King Lear* once more.

He arrived at the theatre with Rosalind at five, dressed in a voluminous brown teddy-bear coat acquired in Canada while touring with Barry Jackson. Black homburg on head, shoulders stooped, the actor advanced towards the stage-door, paused and glanced at nearby bomb damage, appeared to nod gravely as if he understood some symbolic message contained in the ruins, and marched into the theatre.

It being the first performance of the play that season, he went on to the stage, lit by the naked bulbs of working lights, to make sure all was in order. He surveyed the grey set, something like Stonehenge, gazed up at the position of the spotlights, nodded once more, and retired to his dressing room; it was noticed that he was unusually preoccupied.

He undressed and, wrapped in a pink towelling dressing gown, began to make up, painting in the heavy lines on his forehead and about the eyes, whitening his thick bushy eyebrows, high-lighting his nose with a broad line. Next came the white beard, then the wig, stuck down with white-hard varnish. As the make-up took form, as wig and beard were fixed in place, and the joins disappeared under the thick grease-paint, so his hands began to tremble, his eyes to narrow and appear rheumy, his head to shake. At last he powdered—Brown and Polson's cornflour—and brushed it off, once more to reveal the aged face of the King. Last, he lined his hands, to age them, too.

With forty-five minutes to go to curtain-up, he called for his dresser. In silence, the clothes were handed to him until at last the heavy cloak sat upon the bent shoulders; the triple coronet was offered and he fixed it securely on his head, nodding and shaking as if with palsy.

When the assistant stage-manager called five minutes to the rise of the curtain, Wolfit slowly descended to the stage, his dresser in attendance, carrying a silver salver upon which stood a moist chamois leather, a glass of Guinness and—rare in war-time—some peeled grapes. Actors who happened to be waiting in the corridors stood aside to allow the little procession to pass; Wolfit nodded to them with an expression of infinite weariness. The silence backstage was oppressive.

He waited in the wings, doing his best not to concern himself with the bustle of activity that precedes the performance; this, in itself, was unusual, for in other plays, no matter how large or wearying the part, he would be hissing last-minute instructions to the stage management, electricians and actors. But not this night; he stood perfectly still, with Rosalind, ready as Cordelia, beside him, occasionally glancing at her with a look that seemed to want to make sure that she understood the weight of all the world was upon his shoulders. He talked to no one; members of the company gave him a wide berth if they had to pass. He did not even enquire about the size of the audience; he might be expected to gaze through the peep-hole, but he did not; the house, in fact, was painfully thin, less than half-full.

His stage-director ordered the actors to stand by. The house lights dimmed. Rosabel Watson received her cue, and the trumpet sounded. The curtain rose slowly.

Kent and Gloucester begin. In the wings, Wolfit fidgets with his
cloak, sceptre and crown, pulling at his beard, relaxing his neck
muscles. Now comes his cue: Eric Maxon, as Gloucester, says, 'He
hath been out nine years, and away he shall be again.' The trumpet
sounds once more. 'The King is coming'.

Lear enters from the extreme down-stage position, and crossing to
centre, orders 'Attend the lords of France and Burgundy, Gloucester.'
It is a sombre voice, accustomed to command. The King reaches
centre and turns his back on the audience, pauses, his head shaking
almost imperceptibly, and then advances towards his throne; once
seated, he commences the division of his kingdom, which the actor
believes to be the first step in the betrayal of Kingship upon which the
tragedy is built.

How gentle but firm he is with Goneril, as if making himself more
affectionate than is his wont; and so with Regan, more indulgent perhaps, yet no less certain of his authority. To Cordelia, he invites her
honesty by a slight descent into sentimentality. Her reply halts him.
'Nothing will come of nothing' is uttered with a contempt for her
sincerity. Her banishment is delivered as if Lear pronounces on behalf
of some primeval, barbaric power. The King is set on his path,
obstinate, angry, unreasonable.

It is a gentle Lear who toys with the disguised Kent, an indulgent
King who is amused by the Fool, played by Richard Goolden almost
as old as his master. At the first insult delivered by Oswald, Lear is
incredulous.

> LEAR: My lady's father? my lord's knave, you whoreson dog, you
> slave, you cur!
> OSWALD: I am none of this, my lord, I beseech you pardon me.
> LEAR: Do you bandy looks with me, you rascal?

And with sudden savagery, the King reveals his whip—Ayrton's
whip—and flays the insolent steward, punishing him out of a savage,
determined impulse. But in the scene that follows with the Fool,
Lear's mood reflects his concern for his own frail position, preoccupied with the unexpected hardening of his eldest daughter's
affections. His temper is unpredictable; the whip dangles by his side,
twitching dangerously from time to time. His tongue lashes round
'No lad, teach me'; 'Dost call me fool, boy?' is puzzled, but not without venom; the relationship between King and Fool is founded on
love and compassion, which deepens as the scene proceeds, as if the
King, sensing his alienation, admits the wise clown to Cordelia's
place in his heart.

The King's fury with Goneril is at first a show of paternal wrath,
but as the scene gains momentum, so the actor's reshaping of the text

begins to work to his advantage, for he has built slowly and carefully to the hideous curse upon Goneril:

> Into her womb convey sterility,
> Dry up in her organs of increase,
> And from her derogate body never spring
> A babe to honour her! If she must teem,
> Create her child of spleen, that it may live
> And be a thwart disfeatur'd torment to her,
> Let it stamp wrinkles in her brow of youth,
> With cadent tears fret channels in her cheeks,
> Turn all her mother's pains and benefits
> To laughter and contempt, that she may feel
> How sharper than a serpent's tooth it is
> To have a thankless child!

And from the air, arms upstretched, Lear clutches the physical parcel, as it were, of his savage imprecation, pulls it down and then, to be rid of it, hurls it at his ingrate daughter.

When the King next appears it is with the Fool and Kent, and he cannot keep from his voice a growing, agonising hurt, the pain of rejection. 'O let me not be mad, not mad, sweet heaven! Keep me in temper. I would not be mad!' It is spoken like the first distant echo of the wind; it is a vocal intimation of the storm; the thunder breaks from him on seeing Kent in the stocks. 'By Jupiter, I swear no,' is not idly spoken; it rumbles. Now the passion, the fury, the pain increase. In the scene with Regan, the old man is consumed with emotion, bordering on self-pity. 'I can scarce speak to thee,' he utters crying; tears are on the actor's cheeks. But the mood changes. Regan begins to advise her father on how he should behave; his response, 'Say, how is that?' contains danger, which quickly turns to incredulity at his daughter's persistence, then to irony, from irony once more to fury. It is an incredible display of shifting mood and emotion. 'How came my man i' the stocks?' he demands in a pathetic attempt to regain authority. The actor has laid the seeds of the King's madness in the instability of the old man's passions. The appeal to the gods, 'If you do love old men' is an appeal for sanity.

But Lear is more than a father spurned by ungrateful and ambitious children, more than a man whose reason is endangered. 'I gave you all,' he cries, and the actor speaks the line as though aware for the first time of the enormity of his own self-betrayal: it is the King, stripped bare of power and authority. His strength is drained in the argument concerning the number of his retinue, and again he is no more than man, aged, helpless. He turns his back on the audience, crouching low, sobbing into his hands. Regan asks, 'What need one?'

Now cries the wind: 'O reason not the need' it pleads, and the actor's voice is burdened with piercing, whining overtones, then is entrapped in despair, '. . . let not women's weapons, water-drops, Stain my man's cheeks!' The vocal thunder cracks. 'No, you unnatural hags' is accompanied by an electrifying effect: Lear's cloak, a wide full circle, swirls in a petrified arc as the King turns upon his daughters, and the actor embarks on the major climax of Lear's mounting crisis.

> I will have such revenges on you both
> That all the world shall—I will do such things,—
> What they are, yet I know not, but they shall be
> The terrors of the earth. You think I'll weep;
> No, I'll not weep: I have full cause of weeping.
> But this heart shall break into a hundred thousand flaws,
> Or ere I'll weep. O fool, I shall go mad!

The 'terrors of the earth', delivered in the nasal register, harsh and grating, is echoed by a thunderclap which seems to arrest the King's anger, for it is the gentle, pitiful frailty of 'O fool, I shall go mad' that finally takes him out onto the heath.

The storm that night was not, nor on any subsequent night would ever be, loud enough to drown the actor's voice which soars above wind and thunder and rain. 'Blow, winds, and crack your cheeks! rage! blow!' he commands, daring the elements, taunting them to overwhelm him. The actor has ascended into the cosmos. He obeys Granville Barker's injunction, 'Lear *is* the storm'. With Kent and Fool crouching at his feet, he stands against a tall obelisk, bathed in white light, the tempest in his mind communing with the outraged elements:

> Let the great gods,
> That keep this dreadful pother o'er our heads,
> Find out their enemies now.

cracks like a mighty lightning flash and the power is spent; tones of child-like simplicity enter the actor's voice, so bereft of reason and majesty; all that remains is naked man, a tormented soul, sheltering in the hovel. 'Wilt break my heart?' asks Lear, before entering; it is not a king's question in the actor's reading, but man's, base and brought low, humiliated, humbled. For the actor is playing, too, for the scene that is to come with blind Gloucester. 'Ay, every inch a king,' jogs Lear's ancient memory of some glorious past. 'I am a king, my masters, you know that,' has a forlorn, hollow dignity, as the actor pulls the two knights with whom he plays the scene, to their knees, demanding of them meaningless obeisance. The more pitiful still the exit: 'Nay, if you get it, you shall get it with running. Sa, sa, sa, sa,' comes like an infantile game, devoid of reason, begging compassion.

The actor achieves sublime peace in his waking after the storm; an untroubled calm pervades his person. For one terrible moment he leads all to believe he may have regained his sanity as he recognises his Cordelia, but the hope passes.

The physical test of the actor is still to come and, incredibly, he has voice to rend the air. 'Howl! Howl! Howl!' catches yet again the wind, but it is the final terror. He carries Cordelia, the rope hanging from her neck; he places her on the ground, touches her face with infinite gentleness, distractedly tugs at the rope, and strokes her hair.

> And my poor fool is hang'd! No, no life!
> Why should a dog, a horse, a rat, have life,
> And thou no breath at all? O thou wilt come
> No more; never, never, never, never, never.

The actor treats the finality as if seeing a dark, awesome vision of eternity. The tragedy of King Lear has come almost to its end:

> The oldest hath borne most; we that are young
> Shall never see so much, nor live so long.

The solemn chords of the dead march are heard; the curtain falls.

The atmosphere back-stage had, all through the performance, been infected with auspicious excitement. Wolfit, when not on stage, behaved with strange, unaccustomed remoteness. Even during his change of cloak, which was always performed by Rosalind, he said nothing to her, but she could feel an unfamiliar tension in every muscle of his back.

The few in the audience that night bellowed their acclaim loud enough for twice their number. The shouts of 'bravo', the cheers, were an acknowledgment of a momentous performance. As Wolfit stood waiting for his turn to bow, he dabbed at his face with the moist chamois leather, downed the last drop of Guinness—he had drunk and sweated out eight bottles that evening. At last, his turn came: as was his custom, he pounded the curtain with his fist ('let 'em know you're coming' he used to say) and stepped out through the opening, into the light, clutching the curtain for support. The volume of acclaim washed over him; the actor who had not surrendered to the storm, surrendered now to his public. Wearily, he raised a hand for silence—it came at once. In a spent voice he offered his thanks for the way they had received 'the greatest tragedy in our language'. Exhausted, he withdrew, the sound of renewed cheering still ringing in his ears.

In the privacy of his dressing room, he undressed, unstuck beard and wig and, holding on to the back of a chair, instructed his dresser to sprinkle surgical spirit over his back and to rub hard with a towel. That night the actor slept well.

IV

The critics the next day were mixed. *The Times*:

> Mr. Wolfit would not seem quite the man for a being symbolical of the tempests that break on his head.

W. A. Darlington observed that he 'had yet to see the play greatly acted'. Herbert Farjeon, in the *Sunday Graphic*, noted that Wolfit 'was big enough for Lear, but not deep enough'. It was, however, of little importance, for that same Sunday, James Agate, by far the most influential critic of his generation, wrote:

EVERY INCH KING LEAR

... While Macbeth may be the most difficult character in Shakespeare to interpret, Lear is the most difficult to act. The difference is that between the slow bowler and the fast. Brains will make the one; *fougue* and physique, which are natural gifts and not intellectual attainments, are necessary for the other. To begin with, Lear is not, and never can be, a young man's part. It is not in the nature of things that a young actor, whatever his brains, should be able to body forth the gigantic figure of a Colossus of heathen antiquity. Mr. Wolfit has the minimum number of years necessary for the accomplishment of the most tremendous task that can ever confront the player. Let me say straight away that he has enormously improved since he was last seen in the part some fifteen months ago. Of his performance at the St. James's I remember saying that he did nothing we could not explain, and that his playing, while it never failed or flopped, never lit on the floor of magic. Let me now reverse that judgment. On Wednesday evening Mr. Wolfit did nothing which one could explain. As for the floor, he opened abysses before our feet. Indeed, I am not sure there was not occasional question of 'amazed and sudden surrender to some stroke of passionate genius'. It is certain that the audience surrendered to the stroke of something without quite knowing what. It left the theatre conscious of having been swept off its feet and not bothering to wonder why.

It is the business of the critic not to wonder but to expound. What are the things that we demand from any Lear? First, majesty. Second, the quality Blake would have recognised as moral grandeur. Third, mind. Fourth, he must be a man, and what is more, a king, in ruins. There must be enough voice to dominate the thunder, and yet it must be a spent voice. Lear must have all of Prospero's 'beating mind', but a mind enfeebled like his pulse. The actor must make us feel in the heath and hovel scenes that we are in the presence—*pace* Mr. Shaw—of a flaming torch beside which Michael Angelo and Bach are but tapers. The impression may not be correct, but he is not a great actor who does not create it. Mr. Wolfit had and was all the things we demand, and created the impression Lear calls for. I say deliberately that his performance on Wednesday was the greatest piece of Shakespearean acting I have seen since I have been privileged to write for the *Sunday Times*.

The critic continued by perceiving a new motivation that Wolfit had revealed for Lear's vehement preoccupation with the sins of the flesh: an unbearable half-thought that his daughters were not lawfully begotten. He concluded:

If I were the Government I should let any bricks-and-mortar National Theatre stew in its own juice, and send Mr. Wolfit round the country with a sufficient subsidy to enable him to make first-rate additions to his company, and a posse of dramatic critics to see that he did so.

Agate, with that notice, burst the dam of resistance; the flood of praise followed after him. Wolfit wrote that Agate's review formed a garland

which I am as proud to wear as any champion returning from the games in the Roman theatre. It is only in words that the actor may record his steps; he cannot show his painting or sculpture; his music cannot be put on record so that posterity may judge its worth. Only from the tongues and pens of contemporaries can a record come.

He had more cause for pride in the days that followed. C. B. Cochran wrote a letter to the *Daily Telegraph* in which he affirmed:

In Donald Wolfit a new 'giant' has arisen. . . . It is my decided opinion that there has been no actor on our stage since Irving's great days comparable to Wolfit in the great roles of the drama. State aid for the theatre is in the air. Why not start by giving Wolfit his own theatre?

Wolfit, at his first performance of Lear at the Scala, had played to £96.19.0. When he next gave the part it had risen to £273, and by the end of the week to £334. Fashionable London had, with Agate's assistance, discovered a new theatrical giant.

Charles Morgan, the critic and playwright, wrote to the actor:

I am glad to think that when we are all gone and he [Morgan's son] is an old man in the chimney-corner, he will tell people not yet born how, when he was twenty, he saw Wolfit play Lear.

Not only the famous and the fashionable wrote, but also he was deluged with letters from ordinary theatre lovers, faithful followers from as far back as his days at the Old Vic; he kept them all, remembrances of his triumph. But one letter in particular, from Renishaw Hall, held pride of place:

Dear Mr. Wolfit,

The cosmic grandeur of your 'King Lear' left us unable to speak. My brother Osbert and I had hoped to come round and shake you by the hand, but we realised it would be impossible, for two reasons— that it would have been an intrusion, after such a work of revelation, and because, as I say, we could not speak.

Surely this stupendous revelation of the redemption of a soul (to see only one aspect of the play) is one of the greatest *religious* works ever born from the heart of man. And equally surely, even when Shakespeare himself was there to advise and to fire, there can have been no greater performance. All imaginable fires of agony and all the light of redemption are there.

Believe me,
Yrs sincerely,
Edith Sitwell.

V

Where was Wolfit's place in the long, magnificent tradition of English acting? Agate, shortly before his death, told Robert Speaight that Wolfit was undoubtedly the greatest actor he had seen since Irving. Cochran's assessment was similar, the two men having seen both actors. To those who are not old enough, there are only contemporary reports, portraits and photographs to act as guides; all sources would seem to confirm that although Wolfit may have given the greatest performance *since* Irving, he was certainly nothing like Irving either in style or physique. Agate himself confessed that he would not dream of casting Wolfit in any part that demanded 'physical grace and conspicuous elegance', yet Irving epitomised both qualities and, in repose, had about him the look of mischievous aesthete. In any event, Irving was an innovator; Wolfit was not. Irving created a style of acting in which Forbes-Robertson and Benson followed, a purer, more lyrical approach to the art, which was very recent in historical terms.

Irving was, of course, a far superior manager to Wolfit. Not that he was any great respecter of the text; not that his productions, despite the use of talented painters, skilful costumiers and gorgeous materials, served the plays any better, but his presentations, as has been observed, were in harmony with contemporary taste, which made the actor's performances all the more acceptable.

Wolfit's talent was of another kind, and much cruder in its application. His interpretive gift was for what he instinctively judged to be the heart of the play. He could not act according to an intellectual, scholarly theory; he could not suit his performance to a director's private conception of the play; he could not invent for the sake of inventing, or be novel for the sake of being novel. To Wolfit, a play called *Hamlet* was *about* Hamlet—if not, then Shakespeare would have called it something else—and being about Hamlet, he saw his actor's duty as fleshing out the role with all the gifts and insights he could demand.

It is interesting to note that, on more than one occasion, Agate placed Wolfit in an Elizabethan context. In his review of the actor's Hamlet, he admits that Wolfit 'puts me back into Shakespeare's day and time'; of *Volpone*: 'he speaks the verse as an actor of Jonson's day must have spoken it.' R. B. Marriott, who knew Wolfit well, observed, 'I have never known anyone talk so well and so intimately of Shakespeare and Marlowe. It was as if he had known them in life as fellow men of the theatre. One could easily imagine that he had just left Kit Marlowe somewhere near Tower Hill.' T. C. Kemp was put in mind of Burbage upon witnessing Wolfit's Hamlet, and Edith Sitwell experienced a similar sense of the past after the actor's Lear. Wolfit, it seemed, recalled not Victorian Gothic, but something far older and far more profound.

Agate, again, at his most perverse:

> Look at this actor's mask from any angle—except that it has no angles where Irving's had nothing else—and we see at once that it is the mask of a comedian. . . . Here is an actor who can summon up all the expressions there are except the tragic one, the lack of which *in a tragic actor* must be a short-coming.

If portraits are anything to go by, then Richard Burbage must have suffered the same handicap. Yet, as G. B. Harrison reports, Burbage was, by 1568, 'already making a name for himself as a tragic actor'. Agate exempts Richard III from the rule of facial angles; well he might. Harrison:

> Burbage made his name in Richard III, and his acting in the final scene when Richard dies, furious and despairing, on Bosworth

Field, was much admired. Indeed there was a story current a generation or two later that when a Bosworth inn-keeper used to show visitors over the battlefield, he would point out to them the place where Burbage cried: 'A horse! A horse! My kingdom for a horse!'

But there is, of course, more to it than mere physique. Shakespeare must have accounted it of secondary importance in the man who created his Hamlet, Lear and Othello.

The effect Wolfit had on those susceptible to, or trained in, historical hypotheses sprang, not from his appearance, but from his emotional power; Wolfit, capturing the imagination and transporting it to sixteenth-century Shoreditch, did so because he possessed, and had nurtured, an intense vitality that perceptive men and women of his age associated with the uncontrollable surge of renaissance man.

But many of Wolfit's other contemporaries, suffering from the influence of the Victorian age, which was grotesquely over-decorated, were more preoccupied with externals. They placed undue importance, as their fathers had done, on outward show, on form, on style, rather than essential content. By the 1960s this standard of judgment had reached fever-pitch in regard to the classic drama; the ancient soul of a play had, it seemed, to be concealed in modern theory to make it acceptable to a modern audience, no matter what distortions to the theme resulted. Perversely, the more contemporary significance that could be *imposed* on a classic play, the more successful the interpretation. Wolfit, both instinctively and by virtue of his training with Poel, opposed this view and, because he coincided with the beginning of the trend, seemed anachronistic, an impression he aided and abetted by shabby productions.

To those who assessed his theatrical ancestors, however, superficial values were of less importance than inner content. Audiences of the past, too, it would appear, cared little for appearances. What mattered to them, and what they demanded of the actor, was an ability to aim as near to the heart of a character as his gifts made possible, and to display passions without embarrassment; they came to see the actor, not the play.

Wolfit was the latest in a long line of English actors who conformed to a similar pattern: men whose dramatic power was contained in a graceless physique; men whose style of acting was often questioned by their contemporaries but who overcame those reservations by the immensity of their projected passions.

Burbage died in 1619, and after the Cromwellian gloom had lifted, was succeeded by Thomas Betterton as the first of players and, in Betterton, the tradition of the large, powerful actor was reborn, the tradition of torrential emotion housed in an unlikely mould. In *Curiosities of Literature*, Isaac D'Israeli wrote:

> Betterton, although his countenance was ruddy and sanguine, when he performed *Hamlet*, through the sudden and violent emotion of amazement and horror of his father's spectre, instantly turned as white as his neckcloth. . . .

or, from Anthony Aston's *Brief Supplement*:

> Mr. Betterton, although a superlative good actor, laboured under an ill figure, being clumsily made, having a great head, short, thick neck, stooped in the shoulders, and had fat short arms which he rarely lifted higher than his stomach. . . . He had little eyes and a broad face, a little pock-bitten, a corpulent body, with thick legs and large feet. He was better to meet than to follow, for his aspect was serious, venerable and majestic—in his latter time a little paralytic. His voice was low and grumbling; yet he could time it by an artful climax which enforced universal attention even from the fops and orange-girls.

Despite the 'ill figure', Pepys was able to record on 28 May 1663:

> . . . And so to the Duke's house; and there saw Hamlet done, giving us fresh reason never to think enough of Mr. Betterton.

Betterton reigned for fifty years until his death in 1710. David Garrick, another round-faced actor of power, was born in 1717. According to his biographer, Murphy, Garrick's Lear was among the actor's finest creations. Yet, the portraits agree he was not very tall, not very slim, and to his contemporaries was known, affectionately it is hoped, as 'Little Davy'. Murphy affirms that 'it was in Lear's madness that Garrick's genius was remarkably distinguished'. And Garrick was not, as a man, without his faults, as if, like Wolfit, his theatrical passion spilled over into his private life: a fiery temper, vanity, snobbishness and an undeserved reputation for meanness were grist to the mill of Samuel Foote, the actor's bitterest critic. And how Garrick's productions would have been disparaged by today's standards: costumed in the dress of the time, in versions of the plays shamelessly edited and re-written; *King Lear* was played with a happy ending.

There are many others of the same mould who did not attain Garrick's mastery of his art, but James Quin, his contemporary, was thought superior by Walpole. Quin, robust and vital, 'born to play Falstaff', said of Garrick, 'If the young fellow is right, I and the rest of the players have been all wrong.'

Then, there is the strange case of Edmund Kean, the 'little ill-looking vagabond' of whom Coleridge declared, 'To see Kean was to read Shakespeare by flashes of lightning.' Leigh Hunt, comparing Kemble and Kean, admits that his taste favours the classicality of Kemble, the noble Roman, but

> Kean knows the real thing, which is the height of the *passion*, manner following it as a matter of course, *and grace being developed from it in proportion to the truth of the sensation.*

But Kean's passion, his power, were not the spontaneous out-pourings of uncontrolled genius as is commonly supposed. His own words, to Garrick's widow, the eternal cry of the actor:

> The people don't understand their business; they give the credit where I don't deserve it, and pass over passages where I have bestowed the utmost care and attention. Because my style is easy and natural they think I don't study, and talk about the 'sudden impulse of genius'. There is no such thing as impulsive acting. All is premeditated and studied beforehand. A man may act better or worse on a particular night, from particular circumstances, but although the execution may not be so brilliant, the conception is the same.

Hazlitt faulted Kean for 'an over-display of the resources of his art', and of his Othello: 'Mr. Kean is in general all passion, all energy, all relentless will.' The tradition of the power-generator contained in un-likely architecture dominates the English theatrical landscape. The men who have borne that shape have been at the very centre of what is best in acting, which is not to say that they are the only shape or form which house power, passion, will and energy. Kemble, Macready and Irving represent another. Wolfit belongs unquestionably to the Burbage mould, which is not an attempt to secure for him a place in theatrical history that only posterity can bestow, nor to elevate him above his contemporaries, but to set him down beside them, and to show that Wolfit's kind have existed before, and will, doubtless, exist again. If they and their colleagues were musicians they would be known as *virtuosi* or *maestri*; in the theatre, for want of a better phrase, they are known as 'great actors'.

VI

For four weeks after Agate's notice of Lear appeared, Donald Wolfit was fashionable. It was reflected in every way, but especially by the box office receipts, which doubled; it was difficult to obtain seats, especially for performances of *King Lear* which had, in a short space of time, become something of a theatrical event. Agate's review, as has been noted, increased the takings each time Wolfit played the aged king, but the critic's power is easily discernible in the receipts for the other plays in the repertoire.

The two weeks previous to the notice appearing, the company played to £871.1.3. and £783.3.9. (a lost performance for Good Friday accounts for the fall). The week of King Lear, receipts rose to £1373.5.3. which may be attributed to the press in general; on the Sunday, came the Agate review: the following four weeks' returns were:

10th Week: £1626.0.0.
11th Week: £1489.1.8.
12th Week: £1369.0.0. (no performance on Monday)
13th Week: £1545.16.6.

Wolfit's triumph reopened the debate on the National Theatre. Cochran's letter to the *Daily Telegraph* bluntly suggested that the State give Wolfit his own theatre; *News Review* took up the suggestion in a long article entitled 'Donald Wolfit—Greatest Actor since Henry Irving'; in Newark, a proud citizen, Labour Councillor O. Essame, suggested a municipal theatre be built out of ratepayers' money to be called 'The Wolfit Theatre'. James Agate devoted two columns in the *Sunday Times* to 'The National Theatre' in which he came to the conclusion that Englishmen did not want one; he posed the question: 'The point is how far the State is entitled to spend public money on something the public doesn't want.' He noted with interest that, in his diary for 1942, on 22 January, during a Wolfit season in London:

Donald Wolfit's manager telephoned to say that at every performance Czechs, Poles, Norwegians, Belgians and French have accounted for 50 per cent. of the audience and sometimes 75 per cent. The rest have been Jews; had we relied on the Christians we should have played to empty benches.

There was more to it than just the Europeans' love of theatre which attracted them to Wolfit: their enthusiasm was inextricably woven in to Wolfit's style as an actor, his emotionalism, his size, his ability to project passion. As in 1942, so in 1944, the large population of exiles from Europe flocked to the Scala Theatre. Leo Pavia, Agate's secretary, a German Jew, and 'a walking literary as well as musical reference library' according to his employer, wrote to the actor: 'May I, as one of your very great admirers, say how much I hope you will find a theatre and give us a delight not equalled by any other leading actor?'

And from another European, temporarily resident in Britain:

Dear Mr. Wolfit

May I, as a foreigner in this country, express my greatest admiration and deepest gratitude for the unforgettable experience my many visits to the Scala during your exceptional Shakespeare Season had been.

I thought till then that the greatest playwright had been forgotten in this country, judging by the lip-service generally paid to art. I do not know much about the standard of taste in the past, for instance in the Victorian theatre, but judging by what I read about the period of Garrick I believe that the sober-minded who at that period ruled the world with coal and steam, must have felt themselves far too superior to their bear-baiting ancestors than to pay true homage to the sovereign of the stage.

Now, when by sheer luck during the raids I saw your Shakespeare on the icy evenings in the Scala Theatre, I watched a stray auditory gradually changing into a devoted community of people whose minds you had freed from the nonsensical grip of the mechanical world of the present. I saw you perform a miracle enabling us for longer than the few hours we listened to you, to shake off the universal frustration of man's present life. Your acting made us soar in the delirious spiritual atmosphere as if we had been coming to Shoreditch to see Shakespeare himself where his genius had created a 'spiritual' Empire of English Culture, when he had been banned by the Gentlemen of the City for the sake of morality.

I was well astonished when the critics now, at the end of your season, finally discovered you, and, maybe, even 'leading society' in time will be tempted to discover for themselves the difference between the message you are bringing them and the trivial murder-plot of the average commercialised theatre.

Very grateful for the great work you are doing and very sincerely yours,

Oskar Kokoschka

Wolfit lived in a state of daily elation. He was forty-two years old, resident in a theatre in London, playing Shakespeare, acclaimed from all quarters. Where could this not lead? The idea of a National Theatre with himself at the head could not have been far from his thoughts. He fully intended to convert the Scala into his London base and then, perhaps, establish a claim, as great as the Old Vic's, to becoming the State's theatre. But events overtook him: the British were fighting a desperate war; in two months they, with their allies, would launch the invasion of Europe; London filled with American soldiers; the War Office requisitioned the Scala Theatre for the use of the American Army. Wolfit recorded in his accounts book:

> Our season was forced to end as the American Army took over the theatre and forced us out of it. High authorities even to the P.M. were approached but we had to move. So ended our biggest season of the war.

Cochran did all he could to help: 'I have been in touch with Abrahams [proprietor of the Scala]. . . .' he wrote, 'and he has given me the exact position. I have also spoken to some friends who would I think be happy to help financially if you could secure a theatre permanently on possible terms.' Questions were asked in the House of Commons, letters of protest appeared in the press, but to no avail. Wolfit, having found a footing, lost it.

When the season came to its enforced close, Wolfit and company wearily packed their costumes, dismantled the scenery, and set off on a four-week tour of the Garrison Theatres with *Much Ado About Nothing*. ENSA, evidently, had reversed its former judgment and, the invasion of Europe imminent, now thought that Shakespeare was the stuff to give the boys. With the onset of autumn, Wolfit began his annual tour of the provinces, presenting his usual repertoire and a new production of *Macbeth*—a great grey stone castle—designed by Stern and which had cost in excess of two thousand pounds. A memorandum appended to his accounts book records that, at the King's Theatre, Hammersmith, on 26 September, 1944:

> Doodle bug at its worst. One came over during the Hamlet soliloquy ['To be or not to be']. I continued in dead silence except for its noise and it cut out over the theatre and landed 50 yards behind and blew in the dock door—we continued.

The tour of seventeen weeks was undoubtedly Wolfit's most successful financially since he had become a manager. Few weeks were recorded where a surplus of less than two hundred and fifty pounds was not realised; in Nottingham, it was as much as four hundred pounds, and in Scotland, he was clearing, after expenses, between eight and nine hundred pounds. He was able to pay off a large number of debts, including his production costs of *Macbeth*.

But however triumphant Wolfit's return to the provinces after his acclaim in London, he was suffering torments in his private life: Rosalind was taken seriously ill.

His second marriage to Susan had reached crisis point; his relationship with Rosalind had endured the agonies of recriminations and doubts, but the tempest had passed; their decision to share each others' lives had been made, and between them there now existed a profound tenderness. In Rosalind, Wolfit had, apart from the year in Sheffield, found a partner who was able to partake in his public and private life. They were serenely happy together, enjoying common interests outside the theatre: their taste for literature, for humour, for friends, was remarkably similar. Rosalind supported and encouraged him; above all, she provided much needed calm and tranquillity. Now she was ill. Wolfit, ever an alarmist in matters of health, fretted and feared the worst. In large capitals he recorded:

ROSALIND VERY ILL AND INTO WESTMINSTER
HOSPITAL WHILST DOODLE BUGS FELL ON LONDON

Having urged the surgeon, George McNab, and Sister Ann Proctor, to take good care of her, he declared, 'You see, she is the moon to my sun!'

He rehearsed for the tour by day and, by night, spent every available minute with Rosalind. There were urgent arrangements to be made, for he had to find replacements for Rosalind's roles. At short notice, he did amazingly well: Joan Greenwood agreed to play Ophelia and Celia in *Volpone*; Mary Kerridge played Portia. Four weeks later, in Cheltenham, he wrote with love and with relief:

Rosalind rejoined me for good. She did not play but rehearsed gently and recovered her strength—the gods were propitious and we prospered, and our work went well.

CHAPTER ELEVEN

The Company and the Critics

O, it is excellent
To have a giant's strength; but it is tyrannous
To use it like a giant.
—Measure for Measure

I

No company ever worked harder for less reward of any kind, for from 1941 onwards they were to receive every sort of discouragement for their labours. The first hint of what was to happen came from Ivor Brown, writing in the *Observer* in 1941. He mentioned 'the varying qualities' of the company; it was a gentle reproof. By 1944–5, the critics unanimously condemned Wolfit's supporting players with the exception of Rosalind Iden whom Agate, Brown and Trewin all praised unreservedly for her Ophelia, Portia, Viola and, more especially, for her Rosalind in *As You Like It*, which had gaiety, wit and sincerity. And, in time, when she came to play Lady Macbeth, she surprised a good many critics with what Alan Dent called 'a steely show of power'; for the rest, the attacks were savage and unrelenting.

Were they really bad actors? or was there another explanation? Many of them went on to make names for themselves in other companies, many were already well known when working for Wolfit. The reasons, therefore, for their apparent inadequacy lay in Wolfit himself.

The charge most often levelled at Wolfit was that he was afraid to play with actors of equal standing, that he deliberately undercast the rest of his company in order to stand out more vividly. These accusations, repeated often enough, became difficult to refute, for the evidence to support them was apparent each time the company took the stage. Furthermore, the accusations served to fan the theory of a megalomaniac actor-manager, and it was a theory greatly to the taste of the fashionable and the gossip-writers. The truth, however, though it may serve to endorse the same theory, was that Wolfit feared no other actor alive or dead, and did not undercast *deliberately*. He simply saw no necessity to organise the company any other way and for two reasons: the first was that Wolfit was acclaimed as a great actor despite the poor standards of his supporting players, and the second was a virtue, not a fault, of this particular actor-manager: loyalty.

His first company was a fine all-round team, many of whom came direct from Stratford-upon-Avon. When war was declared, however, the demands on manpower forced Wolfit, as they did everyone else, to cast either older men or those who, for one reason or another, were exempt from military service. The critics dutifully made allowances, but even so, Wolfit received a worse scathing than other managers. Initially, the fault lay in Wolfit's productions. They were ruthlessly centred round him, not because he was afraid of not shining in a more balanced presentation, but because that was the tradition of actor-management, the tradition in which he had grown up. Then, too, with constant touring the sets became shabby. Because he financed himself, he was fiendishly careful of 'wasting' money, so that he often neglected to renew productions until they were past renewing.

But the company suffered from Wolfit's penny-pinching most of all when it came to costumes. Good or bad actors will always seem better actors when decently accoutred. Wolfit's actors wore darned tights, patched doublets, frayed tunics, and wigs by Madame Gustave of Long Acre, who insisted upon supplying them in three kinds: "'alf-flow, Elizabethian and barbaric'. Wolfit himself preferred these wigs with their joins made of a broad band of material, requiring thick layers of make-up to hide it, instead of a light, transparent gauze that was the accepted method of most other wig-makers.

Wolfit had very fixed notions about the costuming of characters: 'good' characters should wear blue and be blonde: 'evil' characters should wear black and be raven-haired. The sets were, at first, adequate. But Stern's designs were very muted in colour—greys and browns predominant—and after being shunted from theatre to theatre looked more grim than was perhaps originally intended. But this rationale apart, the truth was that Wolfit had little visual sense and although Rosalind, herself an accomplished painter, tried privately to persuade him that he was guilty of some terrible lapses of taste, he could never see it. She offered a theory for this deficiency: that his powerful theatrical imagination was like a child's which is capable of seeing shapes and colours not visible to others, which is capable of transforming a plain wooden box into a chariot; Wolfit, Rosalind ventured, never outgrew the belief that the red fringe of his mother's rug was Tom Foy's hair.

Because the productions were built round him, Wolfit shamelessly

neglected the smaller parts. He was only a good director if he himself
was not in the play. Peter Copley, a member of the company in 1939
and again in 1943, recalled that during the season in Dublin, Wolfit

> had arranged to play Macbeth opposite some Duchess on her castle
> walls in Wales—very snobby we all thought; so he directed us all in
> Dorothy Massingham's 'The Lake' which we played while he was
> away. I played a part well beyond me opposite Rosalind Iden: by a
> mixture of insistent explanation, a sort of authoritarian kindness
> and occasional demonstration, he got a performance out of me and
> taught me a hell of a lot.

But that was in a non-Shakespearean play in which the actor-
manager did not appear. It was a different tale when the company
worked in more usual circumstances.

Rehearsals began at ten, Wolfit having arrived half an hour earlier
to deal with letters and business matters. As the hour struck he would
stride onto the ill-lit stage or into the cold rehearsal room, seat himself
in one of his stage thrones, and commence four hours of uninterrupted
labour. He generated an atmosphere of oppression, insisting on
clarity of diction, accuracy of text—for he knew the plays down to the
last indefinite article. More often than not, he would have chosen a
'whipping-boy', some poor unfortunate young man who would never,
in Wolfit's eyes, be able to do anything right. The manner in which he
addressed the men of the company was a good indication of his feelings towards them: a friend would be called by his Christian name;
a senior actor or a newcomer would earn the prefix 'Mr.'; an actor
out of favour would be summoned by his surname alone.

To Wolfit, rehearsals were the means of getting the externals right;
his own interpretation was conceived in private, and developed by
playing the part repeatedly. He therefore mumbled his speeches in
order to give time to the other characters; this method had grave
drawbacks. When breaking-in, for example, a new Edgar in *King
Lear*, Wolfit would recite the King's part *sotto voce e molto prestis-
simo*, cut to cue perhaps, so that when the new actor was confronted
on the opening night with a Lear of the first magnitude, poor Tom,
inadequately rehearsed by any standards, would flounder and falter
through the complexities of the character.

Wolfit ignored the subtler nuances of the supporting parts. Direction was given in general terms ('you must be more evil' or 'more
noble' or 'less sympathetic') so that the particular traits of character
were lost.

There were occasions when he did take trouble. From Peter Copley:

> . . . at rehearsal he was getting impatient with the Kent (we were

all, of course, the only available cheap war-time actors!) and suddenly [Wolfit] leapt on the stage and played the scene for him with
a wit, warmth, lightness and truth that were electrifying.

And John Mayes:

> . . . during a Lear rehearsal Wolfit showed Cornwall and Albany,
> Goneril and Regan, the dissolution of order, the grasping of the
> crown for themselves that was beginning as the King had abdi-
> cated his power. He made great grasping gestures that clutched
> down, down, sawing the air. It was superb to see an actor *acting*
> an idea to fire others to act the scene. It was not often, however,
> that he could find the time or energy to show his own acting great-
> ness in rehearsal.

Wolfit's chief direction to his company was contained in one word
that he had learned in his youth: 'PACE!' 'Pace, pace, pace!' he
would bellow, which was his way, as it was so many actor-managers'
before him, of getting the company to speak at unnatural speed, so
that he could speak more slowly. He could be brutal and bullying to
those who did not obey, or who asked the fatal question 'Why?'
Rehearsals revealed the darkest side of Wolfit's nature, and the worst
lessons he had learned in his youth were the ones he remembered best.
It was not that Wolfit's actors were bad; it was that they were never
given any help to be good.

As the war proceeded so Wolfit's own powers increased. When he
was acclaimed as a great actor at the Scala, he doubtless felt it unnecessary to alter the level of his casting because he had been personally successful without the help of what he chose to call 'all-star
casts'. And, concealed beneath his innate shortcomings, was a virtue:
loyalty. Wolfit possessed that quality in abundance, to those, let it
be said, who were in turn loyal to him. If an actor had served a tour,
Wolfit could not bear to dismiss the man. 'I shall have something for
you in the autumn,' he liked to say to the old faithfuls. For his war-
time company he had recruited, by necessity, old or infirm men; he
was loyal to them until they were too old, too tired, or too ill to act.
If he heard that an old actor he had known was in need of work, he
would do his utmost to help. Charles Doran, Baliol Holloway,
Andrew Leigh and many others benefited from this trait.

There was yet another contributory cause to Wolfit's low standards
that was accepted at the time without question: his meanness. But on
examination that, too, does not stand up without some qualification.
When business was bad, he and Rosalind took token payments of
twenty-five pounds a week; if good, they received their full salaries of
seventy-five pounds. If a week proved truly disastrous, Wolfit took

nothing. Because he was footing the bill himself, he paid his company as little as he could. 'What's your lowest?' he would ask when engaging an actor; but quality in the theatre, unlike other places of human enterprise, does not necessarily require a high price. Good actors, longing to play the classic drama, would have worked for sums far below their commercial values. John Mayes offered an explanation:

> . . . allowance should also be made for a blindness to mannerism, an inability to see the performance as it really came over from the front. Once one is inside a company, working only with the artists on stage, or seeing them in rehearsal at close range from a throne set in the floats, it is possible to develop a quite extraordinary deafness and blindness to their faults—and one can also be in the position of developing a personal fondness for friends which makes for uncritical loyalty in seeing their work at close range. . . . Allowance must be made for Wolfit, therefore, who employed many of the older actors in his companies because he wanted to help them. They may have been cheap to employ, but I am sure that a much more important thing to Wolfit was that he could give them a job.

Wolfit's help did not end with giving them a job; many an aged ex-member of the company received a small pension from him, secretly given, known only to himself and his business manager, who had to write out the cheques.

During performance, the demon in Wolfit was never far below the surface, though it depended on what character he was portraying. As Touchstone, or one of the other comedy parts, he could be friendly and gay. As Macbeth, the demon took command. His eyes, like steel rapiers, would search out and stab deficiencies. A light or an actor out of position, and Wolfit would hiss a reprimand from behind his beard. A throne wrongly angled would produce a terrifying glare at the prompt corner, and a surreptitious moving of the offending piece of furniture (and sometimes even of an offending actor) with his upstage knee.

Above all, inside the theatre, Wolfit created an atmosphere of terror which any dictator would have envied. In later years, ex-war heroes, men who had braved the Nazi onslaught in North Africa or France, former prisoners-of-war, men who had suffered torture at the hands of the Japanese, would dart into dressing rooms or cower in the shadows rather than meet him in the corridor after a scene that had not gone to his liking. It was not a threat of dismissal that produced fear; it was the very intensity of Wolfit's personality when enraged.

Wolfit's company had to contend then, not only with the stupefying task of playing eight major plays, week after week, tour after tour, in less than adequate costumes, for less than adequate remuneration, but also with the ruthless energy of Wolfit himself in all his unpredictable moods. For, as John Mayes has written: 'It was the *variety* of the Wolfit persona that was so baffling.'

But, as has been observed, the satanic side of Wolfit appeared only in rehearsals or during performance, in either case when he was physically inside a theatre; outside he was quite different. Away from the daily pressures, the enormous labour of eight leading roles a week, he displayed a sincere and loving interest in his employees. An actor had only to be ill for Wolfit to summon a doctor, more often than not at his own expense. A marital disaster elicited understanding, sympathy and advice. Like many a Victorian papa, Wolfit was a great giver of advice, as shall be seen in a later chapter.

John Mayes provides a glimpse of Wolfit away from the theatre, while on tour:

At Cardiff on the Wednesday Wolfit invited me to have lunch with him and Rosalind Iden at their digs. . . . It was the first time that I had experienced their kindness as host and hostess, and it was a quite overwhelming experience. . . . It was an occasion when I experienced an aspect of Wolfit's personality that I had seen in full play in his friendship with my parents, but had almost forgot in the course of sweating it out under the stress of nervous anxiety, and embarrassment for others. . . . Donald and Rosalind treated me as though I were a VIP. I was able to *talk* to him. And he listened to me! . . . I was dismissed with smiling affection. . . . That evening Wolfit in the theatre was the same malevolent, devil-faced Macbeth off-stage as he had been all the year. If anything there seemed a hint of an *extra* glint of fury in his eye for me—as though I were not to make any secret, personal capital out of the fact that a few hours before he had been my genial host!

The light relief of company life occurred in Aberdeen, when the Wolfits acted as genial hosts to the entire company; there, at the Royal Caledonian Hotel, Wolfit gave a party. John Mayes:

The invitation notice said it was an old custom in Wolfit's companies that at Aberdeen, the point furthest north and therefore of the turnround in their progress back towards London, all should get together at a supper, after which each member would be expected to entertain the assembled guests in turn. Anyone unable, or unwilling, to do this would be 'ejected as an unworthy mummer!'

Wolfit did not exempt himself from the task of entertaining his guests. On each occasion, he wrote a poem with reference to some of the company. One survives written in his own hand and it captures the atmosphere of the touring company, the self-contained world in which they lived their lives:

Lines to the rhythm of a well-known poem

> Oh! the long and dreary touring
> Oh! rehearsals under Wolfit
> Oh! the packing and unpacking
> And the laundry calls on Monday
> Sigh the staff and sigh the actors
> Groan the worn-out wardrobe baskets
> Little baskets—worn with travel
> What another play this autumn
> Are there more plays still by Shakespeare
> Has he got a sleeve—what's up it
> Mighty tourer—ruddy nuisance!
> Then up spake old Brownlow comic.
> Skipping gaily up the staircase
> Throwing walking sticks from off him
> Come my children this is touring
> Railway journeys lie before us
> And there is great reservation
> Special coaches for the actors
> And kind foremen on the railways
> Who will see you miss connections
> Put your coaches in the sidings
> Where you'll sleep in great discomfort.

Each member of the company is mentioned in the parody. One example:

> Silent rapt in contemplation
> Michi Maxono the mighty
> He the player under Irving
> He the mighty man of grease paint
> And the teller of great stories
> Of the tribes that were real actors
> When the theatre was the theatre.

He concluded with some self-knowledge:

> On away awake ye mummers
> Hoist your tights and pack your greasepaints
> For the landladies are groaning
> There's no coal and no provisions
> And your combines will be cheerless

Hark a voice, it is the Goodyer
Crying loudly up the staircase
Daphne Daphne Daphne Daphne
Call the half be quick about it
Or the Wolfit mighty hunter
Will be howling in a bloodlust
It will be no Laughing Matter
On away awake ye mummers
And I thank you all for coming.

The company needed laughter as a respite not only from the pressures of work, but also to withstand the persistent critical onslaught which weekly was their expectation.

II

The critics produced a consistent reaction in Wolfit: if he received a good notice, then the critic had 'a great mind'; if a bad notice, the actor declared war. Wolfit crossed swords with all the major critics of his day, except Agate. The pattern was always the same: a notice either disparaging the actor or the company would appear; Wolfit would then write personally to the critic and receive a reply. One such from Harold Hobson is typical:

I am sorry that you have lost respect for me as a critic. I have certainly not lost interest in you as an actor. How could I? Memories of the superb performances which you gave in the 1920s at the Sheffield Repertory Theatre are still fresh in my mind.

. . . What can I possibly say to your long, interesting, vigorous and distressing letter? That I have deeply hurt you and your colleagues is obvious, and, though perhaps you may find this difficult to believe, giving pain is not a thing I enjoy. But it is the very essence of my job to speak the truth as I see it, and I don't think that your company is a good one. In saying this I am not advancing a daring paradox, or showing any individual perversity of opinion. Most of my colleagues have said the same thing, and my great predecessor, James Agate, who in many ways was one of your deepest admirers, said it very often.

I am impressed by all you say about your desire to help young actors, inexperienced players, etc. But surely as a critic I am not, and cannot be, concerned with the kindness of your motives in employing these young people. I am asked only to comment upon their performance, which is an entirely different matter. Your point about going to Peterborough and the other places where Shakespeare is unknown weighs on me heavily. I can see that in taking Shakespeare to the provinces, even if in some ways, in my opinion, unsatisfactorily, you are doing a valuable social work. Now when judging your production am I to think only of helping you to crack the tough British provincial nut, or to bear in mind what you once wrote James, that Garrick is your yardstick? Surely compliment to you is greater if I measure you up against Garrick rather than bring to your supporting players some more lenient standard of judgment.

With all good wishes,
Yours sincerely,
Harold Hobson.

Wolfit resorted to every gambit he could think of to counter adverse criticism. Invariably, he committed the disastrous mistake of writing to the editor which inevitably gave the offending critic the right of reply and, consequently, the last word. To Wolfit, that was not the end of the fight, simply the loss of a round. His next step was to ban the critic from the theatre, which has ever proved a futile step, for drama critics are at liberty to buy their seats and express their views publicly like anyone else. Often, the banned critic, having bought his ticket, would write a disarming notice, which, for some reason, only served to increase Wolfit's enmity. His fight with the press reached classic proportions, as shall be seen, with the advent of Kenneth Tynan.

At the heart of Wolfit's impassioned and aggressive reaction to the critics was the knowledge that they were very often right. His defence was threaded with unchanging themes, offered in mitigation: service to the community, the giving of work to actors, and the quoting of other more favourable reviews. But, as Hobson's reply illustrates, the critics' counterplea was their concern with maintaining high standards. Wolfit imagined, however, that they were either in the employ of some rival, or part of a deeper theatrical conspiracy to defeat him. What he would never believe was that most critics sincerely wanted him to succeed on every level; this is borne out by many pleas that Agate made in this respect, by Hobson's letter and later actions, and by the volume of well-intentioned criticism that was incorporated in books by Trewin and many others.

In the early part of the war, the press showered Wolfit with publicity of every kind and recognised his courage, his determination, his belief—which he demonstrated practically—in the higher purpose of his art. But, in the summer of 1944, the critics in London were treated to a dazzling series of revivals at the New Theatre, where the Old Vic company, unable to play in their bomb-damaged home in the Waterloo Road, were led to a famous, triumphant success by Laurence Olivier, Ralph Richardson and John Burrell. The plays were superbly cast, directed and mounted; if Wolfit had seemed to escape lightly with his touring productions, he now suffered dreadfully by comparison with the standards set by the Old Vic company at the New Theatre. His own position as a Great Actor, hotly disputed of course, was also to suffer by comparison to Olivier who seemed to conform exactly to Agate's predilection for Shakespeare being played in a vein half-way between John Gielgud and Tod Slaughter. Olivier's Oedipus, Mr. Puff in *The Critic*, Sergius Saranoff, Hotspur, The Button Moulder, were a gallery of magnificent portrayals seen in a setting to match his gifts, and supported by a host of talented men and women. And with his Richard III, Olivier assaulted the summit of Olympus, and planted his standard there. If Wolfit wanted to compete—and he did—then he would have to change his whole style of approach, renounce actor-management as he understood it, and place his fortunes in the hands of a director with authority. But, as has been seen, his allegiances were to the Victorian theatre; he had for too long tasted independence both of production and personal interpretation. The critics fought a losing battle; yet, it is much to their credit—to Agate in particular, later to Hobson—that they discerned Wolfit's unique qualities as an actor and strove to give the man a sense of the value of his own worth which, in their eyes, he debased by his methods.

His own performances were not free from attack either. The years of touring produced a staleness in his acting that required some unlooked-for stimulus to banish it. A London first night would suffice, but more usually an accident or mishap during a performance would extract a greater intensity to make the performance succeed as a whole, for he well knew that the assessment by an audience of a play was dependent on their surrender to his powers as an actor. Then, too, Wolfit required to be reviewed by the critics more often than any other leading actor. Each time he played in London he presented himself, with rare exceptions, in the same parts, in the same plays. It is interesting to note that the first time a critic saw Wolfit, say, as Othello, he would notice less of what was at fault either with the company or with the Moor. But because of the frequency of Wolfit's London seasons, the same critic was forced to assess Wolfit as Othello eight or nine times. It was difficult enough for them to find something new to say about the play, let alone the performance. As the familiar presentation began with Rosabel Watson, in the orchestra pit, leading four or five elderly women through some Elizabethan dirge, so the critic's eye roamed; if he succumbed to the actor's power on the first occasion, he was usually bristling with reaction by the last.

Yet, Wolfit took personal criticism marginally less violently than he did attacks upon his company, especially if they came from someone who had been formerly sympathetic. J. C. Trewin, reviewing *Othello*, wrote for the *Observer*:

> . . . He tends now to repeat his cadences and lose the great swell of the Othello music.

Two days later, Wolfit communicated with the critic:

Dear Mr. Trewin,

    This is a personal request and you may not feel disposed to answer it, but I do respect your judgment and taste so much in matters theatrical, that I should be very grateful if you could find time to explain precisely what you mean by my cadences being at fault. It may be a habit I have fallen into or acquired, it may be something in my vocal outfit, but it would be a very great assistance to me if you would explain your criticism so that I might be able to take myself to task on what you feel is a deficiency. After all the longer one is in the theatre the more one has to learn, and I am very ready to do so.

Yours very sincerely,
Donald Wolfit.

The critic replied:

Dear Mr. Wolfit,

    It was very good to hear from you, and I felt disarmed by your charming letter. What I meant was that, in your Othello, you were inclined (I hasten to say this is purely a personal view) to fall into certain vocal monotony. To my ear too many of the speeches had a pattern too uniform: you seemed (unusually for you) to be repeating your modulations and to be losing variety and expressiveness. Just as a prose writer is plagued by assonances (I can spot one in the first sentence of this letter), so last Wednesday it seemed to me that you were haunted—unconsciously—by one note, one modulation, and could not escape from the repetition. It may be that, having heard you so often and knowing the range of voice you can command—I have never forgotten your speaking of Ulysses in *Troilus* in '36 at Stratford—I'm unduly sensitive to any changes.

The actor responded:

Now that is very kind of you. I know exactly what you mean, and I realised it is something to watch. I think it attacks me towards the end of a long and tiring role, because I seem to remember the same criticism with regard to my Hamlet a year or two ago.

    I do appreciate your simple and lucid explanation. Very many thanks.

Wolfit's docility cannot just be attributed to his respect and liking for the critic; the actor was never singular in his motives. He may, at that moment, have wanted to present to the world the face of 'a humble artist' or of one 'who never tired of learning', but whatever the reason, the fact that, on Trewin's own admission he had been disarmed, meant that it made it more difficult for him to be as critical in the future.

All Wolfit's persecutory imaginings gushed to the surface when he felt the critic was motivated by malice; then he saw himself as the victim of a secret, vicious conspiracy. The best encounter of this kind occurred with the then critic of the *New Statesman*, Stephen Potter, who was later to add the word 'one-upmanship' to the English language. In a very long notice, Potter summed up all the criticisms that had been levelled at the actor-manager. On the whole, it was a very well reasoned, sympathetic review, ending on a note of gratitude to Wolfit for 'allowing us . . . the pleasure of wandering through the tender gloom of *Cymbeline*'. He did, however, venture to attack certain of the actor's idiosyncrasies: his acknowledgment of applause on a first entrance, the drowning of himself in light and the other actors in darkness, and of repeating an effect—'a caddish laugh' —three times as Iachimo. There is also a reference to Wolfit's curtain-call: 'He clutches the curtain for support, just as exhausted, we hasten to add, whether he had been laying himself out with King Lear or trotting through twenty minutes of Touchstone.'

Wolfit, it appears, wrote off in a fury. Unfortunately, his letter is not preserved, but Potter's reply is, and it gives some clue to the nature of the actor's attack. The critic is forced to regret wounding the actor; he counters a sinister accusation: 'I am not even writing for the mysterious "masters" which you mention.' But it is Potter's last paragraph that elicits, perhaps, the greatest interest:

> One sentence in your letter caused me great distress. It would seem I have quoted lightly a reference to what may be in fact a slight physical infirmity or natural weakness. If I have indeed been so boorish, will you please accept my humble apologies and complete retraction?

The only reference to any physical act is the one to Wolfit's curtain call. It would not have been past the actor's resources to plead a weakness in the lumbar region which forced him to hold on to the curtains 'to ease the pain'; it is tempting to speculate that this was the case. In any event, whatever the ploy, Wolfit certainly had the inventor of Lifemanship grovelling in the prescribed manner.

III

From time to time, the company were compensated for their hard labour. On 31 December 1944, as a direct result of Wolfit's persistence, they embarked at Newhaven and travelled to Paris, being one of the first theatrical companies to play to the forces in Belgium and France. Any doubts that may have been expressed as to the advisability of presenting Shakespeare to the troops were now convincingly dispelled. Both in Paris and Brussels the plays were enthusiastically received. Wolfit felt especially vindicated by the remark of one soldier, Field Marshal Montgomery, who attended a performance of *Hamlet* in the Belgian capital. After the final curtain, he strode across to the Prince of Denmark and said, 'We are old friends. I have seen you so often at Stratford-upon-Avon. This is what I have said the men have wanted for a long time.'

Montgomery's view was supported by an American soldier, then in Paris, Wayne C. Booth, now of the University of Chicago:

I was a GI in the European theater in World War II, and sometime in 1944 or '45. . . . I was lucky enough to see him and his troop do *Hamlet*. In the desert of my life then, it was a great moment of release, and his performance was so fine that although I do not ordinarily remember actors' names—especially nearly twenty-five years later—I have always remembered him and a surprising number of details of his performance.

The European tour concluded, Wolfit agreed to the suggestion that the company should journey to the Middle East, to play a season at the Cairo Opera House. In March, they set sail aboard the *Durban Castle* from Liverpool, with two thousand men en route for India. Wolfit remembered:

During a talk to one of the officers* on the first day out I was given to understand that the morale was not very high; the men were feeling that the war was drawing to a close in Europe and they were not there to see the end of it. On the third day out from the Clyde the O.C. Troops, Colonel Silver, sent for me. He had discovered, on looking through the list, that there were some actors on board, as well as a few Ensa replacements in the shape of dancing girls. Could we give any sort of entertainment, I was asked; my answer was that we could give a whole play by Shakespeare, in fact several if required. This was rather a facer for the poor Colonel, but after some consideration he said that he would like us to do a play the following evening for the officers.

Wolfit decided on *Much Ado About Nothing* because of its success in

* David Dodimead, the actor, then a Major and Ship's Entertainments Officer; after the War he joined Wolfit's company.

the garrison theatres. Robert Copping, one of the two Assistant Pursers aboard the ship, recalled the unusual voyage:

> After a few days at sea Donald Wolfit staged some Shakespearean plays for the troops, the cast playing in khaki ENSA uniforms; their costumes, having been stowed away, were inaccessible. The theatre was the dining saloon and in spite of a rolling ship and the stuffiness of black-out conditions the shows were a great success and played to audiences jammed tight.
>   . . . Many had to be disappointed. Normally seats were reserved for the Captain and officers of the ship when shows were given in troopers, but on this occasion a ballot system operated and I regret I had no luck.

Besides *Much Ado*, the company gave performances of *The Merchant of Venice* and *Hamlet*, in which Wolfit and Godfrey Kenton as Laertes, mimed their daggers and swords for the final duel. But the fact that all the men were not seeing the plays concerned Wolfit, who believed that Shakespeare was every man's birthright:

> Those who had seen the plays were describing them to others, and reading groups were being started, for there were a number of copies of his works on board. We were now sailing quietly through the Mediterranean and, having spied out the deck space available, I went to the Colonel and asked if we might be allowed to give *The Merchant of Venice* on the aft troop-deck to all men on board who had not seen one of the performances. He gave his consent. . . .
> The audience of eighteen hundred men squatted close-packed on the deck in their shirt-sleeves, hung on to the gantrys and even sat in the lifeboats. They cheered when Bassanio chose the right casket; they cheered again at the elopement and at the confusion of Shylock in the trial scene. That was an afternoon indeed!
>   After the performance I asked the audience how many of them had ever seen a play before. About one hundred hands went up. To my further question as to how many had seen a play by Shakespeare fewer than twenty hands showed. Thus did we treasure our literary and dramatic heritage in the year of grace nineteen hundred and forty-five!

Not everyone aboard welcomed the presence of the actors. The ship's adjutant, a soldier, according to Assistant Purser Copping, of 'ramrod discipline' was distinctly critical of their effect on the ship's morale. He was renowned on a previous voyage for exhorting American troops to 'Let's just pretend that we are real soldiers, shall we?' He found it more difficult to insult the actors, but finally settled for a reference to them over the ship's Tannoy system as 'men with hair like birds' nests'.

But Wolfit's enthusiasm was movingly rewarded. On arrival at Port Said, every member of his troupe was presented with a card, printed on the ship's press:

AN APPRECIATION
From all Ranks on Board to
DONALD WOLFIT
AND HIS COMPANY

For their hard work and unselfishness in giving them a unique opportunity to see a series of superbly acted Shakespeare plays

Much Ado About Nothing
The Merchant of Venice
Hamlet

AT SEA
MARCH, 1945

> 'The best actors in the world
> . . . these are the only men'

Copping described the parting:

> When Donald Wolfit and his company finally left us at Port Said they were given a great send-off with two thousand troops lining the ship's rails to wave and cheer, and with an improvised band playing 'For he's a jolly good fellow'.

'I must confess,' wrote Wolfit, 'that the tears were running freely down my cheeks in a most unsoldierly fashion.'

The season at the Cairo Opera House was no less triumphant. On the day booking opened, the theatre was sold out for the first week; soon, there were no seats available for any performances: 'there was a long line of khaki commencing at the box office and stretching right across the front of the theatre and out of sight round the corner,' Wolfit proudly recorded.

King Farouk attended a performance of *Much Ado*, and Wolfit, together with ten senior members of his company, were presented to him. Wolfit described the scene:

> He professed very great interest in Rosalind's performance as Beatrice and I suffered acute embarrassment when he beckoned me on one side and inquired whether the lady was as gay, volatile and amusing off the stage as she was on. To this I managed to reply that I thought it was impossible for anyone to emulate the matchless wit

of Shakespeare in his creation of Beatrice, which, I fear, was not the answer he hoped for, and after a short silence I managed to bow and withdraw. Quite a tricky moment, all things considered.

But Farouk was a King, and Wolfit believed in Kingship. The actor could not fail to add, 'He was, however, graciousness itself.'

During their stay in Cairo the British Ambassador Lord Killearn (formerly Sir Miles Lampson) entertained the visiting players. Later, at a luncheon party, Wolfit proposed the Ambassador's health, saying that he considered Lord Killearn a great improvement on his predecessor Sir Miles Lampson. The story, which Wolfit professed not to recall, was greatly appreciated in diplomatic circles.

The worth of the company's efforts was expressed by a member of the audience, Gordon Smith:

> The opportunity of seeing the Wolfit company was like a visit to a forgotten world of sanity, and I felt at the time that by his efforts he had given an amount of pleasure to his audiences that is rarely within the power of a performer to offer. I have often hoped that someone had the chance to tell him this.

From Cairo, the actors travelled to Alexandria, but the stay was brief because of severe illness in the company. However, the invalids had cause to be cheered by the news from Europe. On Monday 30 April 1945, ten days after his fifty-sixth birthday, Adolf Hitler shot himself in the mouth, and his body was committed to flames in the garden of his Chancellery in Berlin. The Third Reich survived him by seven days. At midnight on May 8–9, as Shirer has recorded, '. . . a strange but welcome silence settled over the Continent for the first time since September 1 1939'.

The Allies celebrated VE Day, and later VJ Day. Wolfit, the actor-manager, looked back over the past six years and summed up his feelings:

> I like to feel that these war years represent a victory, too, for Shakespeare. We had played his great plays all over the British Isles to civilians and servicemen alike; we had done hundreds of performances in bombed London, and had taken him to France, Belgium and Egypt. We had done our job.

CHAPTER TWELVE

Disappointment and Anger

. . . . and hear poor rogues
Talk of court news; and we'll talk with them too,
Who loses, and who wins; who's in, who's out;
                                            —King Lear

I

WOLFIT was not immediately rewarded for his war work. With some disappointment he read the Honours Lists in vain, and felt acutely neglected when, in 1947, Laurence Olivier and Ralph Richardson received knighthoods; Wolfit had not even been offered a lesser reward.

Honours for members of the theatrical profession have always been subject to dispute. The worthiness of this or that recipient seldom passes unquestioned. George Grossmith's telegram to Cedric Hardwicke on the occasion of the latter's knighthood may be said to be a general reaction to many others who have received a show of favour from the State: 'Amazed and delighted,' wired Grossmith.

To report Wolfit's disappointment at not being honoured for war service is not to denigrate the service itself. Wolfit's motives for almost everything he undertook were ever complex and, paradoxically, simple. He was driven by a sense of service, by a belief in Shakespeare as an educative force, by a desire to take the classic drama to the community at large; he was also driven by a passion for acting leading roles and by a need for recognition within the community he strove to serve. The boy from New Balderton hungered for acceptance and when, in 1942, he was elected to the Garrick Club, he cherished his membership as a sign of favour by the Establishment; but recognition on a national scale was to elude him for a little time yet.

The system whereby one actor is preferred over another for an Honour is enmeshed in the wheels of the bureaucratic machine. The methods of recommendation by official and semi-official bodies are necessarily kept secret; the influential are anonymous. But some indication of the lack of regard in which Wolfit was held in such circles may be gained by his activities in the first days of peace.

Wolfit had long cherished ambitions to possess a London theatre of his own. In the summer of 1945, an attractive proposition presented itself in the shape of a vacant theatre with historic associations—the Lyceum, the scene of Irving's great triumphs.

Wolfit had been balked at the Scala by the American Army; he had presented seasons at the Kingsway, which now lay in ruins, and at the Winter Garden, which was barn-like and out-of-the-way. The St. James's and The Strand had also housed the company, but their proprietors could not be expected to hand over their valuable commercial properties to a Shakespearean actor-manager as his permanent residence.

In midsummer of 1945, Wolfit heard with some excitement that the London County Council were proposing to dispose of the lease of the Lyceum. On 10 August he wrote to Maynard Keynes, who had recently been elevated to the peerage, in his capacity as Patron of Advance Players' Association.

Dear Lord Keynes,

I have today put in an application to the London County Council for a possible three years vacancy of the Lyceum Theatre, which I am given to understand they are prepared to let. It would be a matter of very great regret to me if this famous building ended its days as a store house.

It has been stripped of all fittings, and seats, and I fear could only be re-equipped if I had some help from the London County Council with the necessary orders for materials etc.

Your very great kindness to me in the past emboldens me to ask if I might have your support in this tremendous venture in the possibility of my application being considered. I believe with that help the building might be got ready at the beginning of next year.

Keynes, as Wolfit well knew, was also chairman of the newly-formed Arts Council, born out of the Council for the Encouragement of Music and the Arts, but he must have been shocked by what followed: Keynes handed his letter to Mary Glasgow, the Secretary General of the Council, and received a reply worded in a way best calculated to provide Wolfit with an excuse for deep inhalations:

Dear Mr. Wolfit,

Lord Keynes has asked me to answer your letter to him of August 10th on his behalf. He is leaving the country for a short time.

You ask about possible help to yourself to acquire a lease of the Lyceum Theatre. Much as the Arts Council would like to support your claim, they cannot very well do so in this case, because they contemplate taking a lease of the theatre themselves! I should be

grateful if you would keep this information to yourself for the present.
I do not know how the negotiations will go or whether, in fact, our
project will be realised. But it is only fair to tell you that we have this
in mind and that that is the reason we can offer no help to you. I
ought to add that, if the Arts Council does succeed in obtaining this
lease, they intend to use the Theatre as a Concert Hall in order to
make up, in some degree, for the present extreme lack of accommodation in London for orchestral performances.

Wolfit, his pen dipped in venom, retorted:

Dear Miss Glasgow,
     Your letter of the 24th to hand.
     Lord Keynes has been a patron of my Association for many years
and I would point out that as I wrote to him personally, I did not
envisage a reply from the Arts Council.
     Although it is kind of you to say how much the Arts Council
would like to support my scheme, I am wondering whether it has
been proposed to them that they should do so. In any case I find that
my scheme to restore the Lyceum Theatre London as a home for
Shakespeare is in opposition to your own scheme to reconstruct it as a
Concert Hall.
     . . . As London has lost ten theatres and only one Concert Hall, it
seems this was an opportune time for the Council to have dropped the
word 'encouragement' from their title.

Yours sincerely,
Donald Wolfit.

Wolfit was not easily diverted from a course upon which he had set
his heart—that was so all his life. He now turned his energies to
raising money in order to lay claim to Irving's former 'temple to the
drama'; to this end he wrote to all the most influential and well-to-
do people he could call to mind. One who was both influential and
well-to-do was George Bernard Shaw. The great Socialist replied from
4 Whitehall Court:

18th September 1945

Dear Donald Wolfit,
     My business and yours is to take money out of the theatre, not to
put money into it.
     The greatest actor of my early time was Barry Sullivan: Irving was
a dwarf beside him. Irving took the Lyceum in London and had the
utmost success attainable there, being finally knighted and established
as the unquestioned head of his profession. He was buried in Westminster Abbey. After 30 years of glory at the Lyceum he left it for the

provinces without a penny in his pocket. When he presently had to go to the seaside to recover from an illness his friends had to send round the hat. He died on tour for a living. The last time I went to the Lyceum to see him play, the booking clerk opened his eyes in undisguised amazement when I put down cash for my stall. The rest of the house must have been paper.

Barry Sullivan took a cheap theatre (the Holborn, now a boxing booth) and found, after a month or two, that he had lost £700. Irving often lost £7000. Sullivan's enormous dignity was outraged. Under other managements he had been declared by The Times the leading legitimate actor of the British stage. His Hamlet at the Haymarket with Helen Faucit had left all the other Hamlets nowhere. His salary was £80 a night. He shook the dust of London from his feet and took to the provinces, where he soon never left the Number One cities without £300 in his pocket every week. He died worth £100,000. He played Hamlet many thousand times. Like Irving he never got past the eighteenth century as to his repertory, and he acted in wings and flats all his life; but people went to see Barry Sullivan no matter what he played; and the house was always full.

I leave you to draw the moral. Is it to be Irving over again with you, or Barry Sullivan?

London is an actor's snare, unless he is goodlooking, dresses and speaks nicely, and does not act, mostly because he cannot.

Faithfully,

G. Bernard Shaw.

Wolfit despised Shaw for that letter. Whatever the actor's faults, his last consideration was to make money out of the theatre, as was clear from the nature of his entire career and his willingness to make financial sacrifices should the need arise. Deeply disappointed, he wrote to others but without success. He could not compete with the Arts Council and, in any event, whether or not they were serious in their intentions of converting the theatre into a Concert Hall, was never clear, for in due course the Lyceum became a *palais de danse*.

Wolfit scorned the idea of public subsidy and had been in conflict with CEMA since its inception in 1940. He had accepted their contribution towards his Lunch Time Shakespeare at the Strand, but further attempts to acquire state aid came to nothing, principally because of Wolfit's determination to remain independent of any control whatsoever. There was, however, an underlying attitude, contained in all the communications he received from official bodies, of disdain; the attitude became more overt in the actor's dealings with the British Council whose responsibility it is to make the life and thought of Britain more widely known abroad.

In September 1946, Wolfit decided that the time was ripe to venture across the Atlantic Ocean, to the Dominion of Canada. Realising that the cost of such an expedition would be prohibitive, he applied to the Drama Department of the British Council for assistance. The Director was Stephen Thomas, and he acted on the advice of his Advisory Committee, which included Ivor Brown, the critic, Lewis Casson and Bronson Albery, the theatre manager and proprietor; Lord Esher was Chairman of the Council.

Thomas replied to Wolfit's application for funds:

23rd September 1946

Dear Donald Wolfit,

You will remember that I said in my earlier letter that the funds at the disposal of the Drama Department were fully committed for the current financial year, but that I would place your request for the sponsorship of the British Council of your proposed Canadian Tour before the Drama Advisory Committee.

The Committee has now had an opportunity of considering the matter and I am to say though it appreciates the artistry of your own performances and indeed those of certain individuals of your Shakespearean Company, it cannot feel that the general standard of your productions is properly representative of the English Theatre at the present time. This decision of the Committee makes it impossible for your company to appear in the Dominion under the aegis of the British Council.

As I think you have been informed, my Council's assistance in the matter of priorities and travel facilities can only be extended to people travelling strictly upon the Council's business, so I regret to say that its Communications Department will be unable to intervene on your behalf in this case.

Yours sincerely,
Stephen Thomas,
Director, Drama Department.

Wolfit was shocked and pained by the words and tone of the letter; but pain quickly gave way to rage. He opened fire with letters to Thomas, Esher, Brown, Casson and Albery. In his letter to Thomas, he demonstrated the depths of both his hurt and his fury:

4th October 1946

Dear Stephen Thomas,

I am in receipt of your communication of 23rd September. As your meeting to my knowledge took place on the 19th September, your letter, dated 23rd September and posted on the 27th to be forwarded, in itself shows a leisured approach and no real appreciation of what such a delay may mean in matters theatrical.

The decision, of course, contains a studied insult to the work of the company and one which my Association will not tolerate, and copies of your letter have been forwarded to members of my Council. They will naturally require to know the constitution of the committee that reached this decision, and unless as a nation we are to fall still further under the methods so beloved by a certain section of bureaucracy, I think they will insist on an answer.

They may also, as the Director of the Drama Section of the British Council is known to have practised in the theatre as an inferior actor and an unsuccessful producer for many years, even question his ability to foster such a decision.

They may also enquire fully and at long last into the question of our visit to Cairo last year when the British Council used us to advertise their work, requested us to play extra matinées to English children in Egypt and had our full cooperation in the matter, and further why no recognition of this work was forthcoming either before we left or on our return. They may well enquire whether the sending of a young conscientious objector to head a repertoire of plays to war-scarred Europe is properly representative of the English theatre.

In short, I anticipate my Council will ask for the fullest enquiry into your decision, as to when a representative viewed the work of the company or reported on it in an unprejudiced manner, and if reports from our visits overseas were received and considered. Further, they may decide to ventilate the matter in the House. I hope they will do so.

Yours faithfully,
Donald Wolfit.

The personal attack on Thomas's qualifications for the position he held is typical of Wolfit's theatrical prejudices: he despised the idea of ex-professionals holding power over him; the identity of 'the young conscientious objector' is lost in the smoke of battle and is not important, for Wolfit was lashing out in furious agony.

Thomas remained silent, but other replies were quickly forthcoming. Bronson Albery began: 'I was away at Southwold when the British Council discussed giving assistance to your tour of Canada and to make my alibi complete I should add that my opinion was not asked about it nor did I contribute it.' The next day, Albery telephoned Percival Selby, Wolfit's General Manager, to say that he had just seen a copy of Thomas's letter and that he disassociated himself from it in every possible way and, in reporting the telephone call to Wolfit, Selby confirmed that Albery considered the letter 'indecent and improper in the highest degree and appreciates how hurt and shocked you are'. Selby further reported that Lord Esher had no knowledge of the letter either, and was about to conduct an investigation. Ivor Brown, too, disclaimed any knowledge of the terms Thomas's letter was couched in. In each case, it was the *wording* of the letter that was made the focal point of attack and defence, not the sentiment expressed. Wolfit threatened resignation from the Garrick Club; Brown and Albery begged him to reconsider, which he did. But the allegation the British Council had made was never refuted and was, in any case, an opinion generally held by many. The phrase 'not properly representative of the English theatre at the present time', however ill-considered in the setting down, doubtless reflected the views not only of the Drama Director but also of those who advised him; it stuck in Wolfit's throat; he neither forgot nor forgave. Instead, he determined to take his revenge and show the bureaucrats the stuff he was made of.

One of the Council of Management of his own Association, his friend from Terry days, Marguerite Steen, did her best in a long letter to calm him; he disregarded her advice that his 'sanest course would be *wholly to ignore* this piece of gratuitous insolence', and she continued, 'I agree with you that the decision *impugns* your status in the theatre; yes, my dear old thing, it impugns, but it cannot *alter* it. Your status is steady as a rock. . . . The One Thing That Matters is your getting to Canada. Let this be foremost in your mind and be lofty-minded!'

But Wolfit found it well-nigh impossible to be 'lofty-minded' in the sense that his loving friend desired; it was not part of his nature. He was a creature of basic human passion, good and bad. He bore grudges, nursed resentments, and allowed hatreds to smoulder. With these wasteful, but nevertheless, powerful emotions feeding his determination, Wolfit concentrated the next twelve months on building up the resources of his Association to enable him to take his company to Canada unaided by the British Council or anyone else; he would do it alone; it was, all things considered, the only way he knew.

CHAPTER THIRTEEN

Canada and Camden Town

The people are the city
—Coriolanus

I

WHEN in doubt: tour. From the autumn of 1946, the time of the British Council letter, until the winter of 1947, Wolfit conducted three campaigns in the provinces and threw in an assault on London for good measure. There were two tours of his Shakespearean repertoire sandwiching another of Tolstoy's *Redemption*. Wolfit and Shakespeare were good box office; Wolfit and Tolstoy were not. In February 1946, he took the Winter Garden Theatre for a nine-week season, notable for an extraordinary theatrical event: he presented *Othello*, but with a change of roles. Consumed as he was with resentment, it was not surprising that he should choose, for the first time, to play Iago; the Moor was powered by Frederick Valk, the refugee German actor, who had fled from the Nazis to become leading actor of the German Theatre in Prague, adopting Czech nationality, before having, once more, to seek refuge elsewhere. As an actor, Valk may have lacked flexibility; he lacked little in brute force and Teutonic might. He was possessed of a deep, growling voice, rich and resonant, a massive turret of a head and the body of an armoured tank. Steeped in the European tradition of unashamed passion, he was easily as intense as his Ancient. It was a rare occasion in the English theatre, bringing together as it did two actors of blinding emotional strength; the audience and most critics were flattened as dough before steamrollers. The youthful Kenneth Tynan:

. . . Some, I am told, boast of having seen the Chicago fire; others of having escaped the Queta earthquake by the merest pebble's breadth, and I have known men swell as they recall the tremendous and bloody exploits at Hiroshima. My vaunt is this: I have lived for two hours on the red brink of a volcano, and the crust of lava crumbles still from my feet. I have witnessed a performance of

Othello, in which Donald Wolfit played Iago, and Frederick Valk Othello. How hushed I was! How young and how chastened: so much so, that for days afterwards, long after I had sent my final, particular roar of 'bravo' coursing and resounding about the theatre, I could speak of little else but these twin giants and the authentic ring of their titles to greatness.

Agate saw the performance as a contest:

For the first eight rounds the fight was all the Nottingham boy's. Making rings round his heavier and apparently slower-thinking opponent he scored as and how he liked, seeming unable to choose between any of half-a-dozen ways of finishing him off. And then, in the ninth round, the fight underwent a complete change, the Czechoslovakian woke up, and from that point to the end there was only one man in it. . . . That Iago lost the fight to Othello, 'tis true: 'tis true 'tis pity, and pity 'tis 'tis true. The responsibility for this rests with the natural order of things. Wolfit won a magnificent fight relative to his audience, who were with him to the end.

Wolfit's Iago was rated by W. A. Darlington as the actor's best performance after Lear and Richard III. Elspeth Grant, writing in the *Daily Sketch*, described the interpretation accurately as 'sergeant-majorly': he fawned with ingratiating servility on his superiors and unleashed his coarse brutality on those beneath him, or those from whom he had nothing to gain. There was no mistaking Wolfit's Iago for anything but a villain: 'His eyes leer with villainy, his lips curl with villainy, his little beard bristles with villainy, his ear-rings quiver with villainy, and his nose is a villainous nose,' observed Alan Dent in the *News Chronicle*. The critics, without exception, rejoiced that Wolfit had at last invited a male actor of comparable stature to join his company. Dent concluded, '. . . it was a joy to see him hand in hand and face to face with his match'.

The two men had a suspicious respect for each other. Wolfit, having rehearsed with the new Othello, informed his stage management that Valk was exceedingly strong: a wooden chest, that the Moor must throw open during the action of the play, should be double-hinged; the instruction was obeyed. On the first night, Valk, in his passion, threw open the chest, and doubly unhinged the lid, which struck the backcloth. Wolfit kept his distance, though he did speak sharply to Valk for bruising Desdemona, on stage, in an uncontrolled fury. Rosalind, the Desdemona, admitted to feeling genuine terror when the Moor's hands closed round her neck, for Valk had little physical control when acting, and Desdemona is not the best role in which to find it out. J. C. Trewin detected her plight:

'I felt intense sympathy that night for a Desdemona trapped in a power-house'.

The season at the Winter Garden closed in April with a surplus. At the end of May, Wolfit and a company of forty opened in *Redemption*, directed by Harcourt Williams. Five weeks later, Wolfit recorded: 'Final week of a heavy losing tour. Without Manchester and Glasgow as promised we never had a chance to pull up.'

The tour of *Redemption* aggravated a problem that faced all touring managers: storage space, for the sets and costumes of the Shakespeare plays had to be stored while Tolstoy was being played. In the middle of June, Wolfit found an ideal store room opposite Holloway gaol: an eighteenth-century building that had once been a Temple of the Arts. Not only was there room to store, but also to rehearse. It was called the Athenaeum and housed Wolfit's company in rehearsals and his theatrical possessions for nearly seven years. It was to be his headquarters from which he directed the battle and, perhaps because of its name, was to provide a fitting setting for the Wolfit legend that was being born; the legend of the touring-manager, fierce and unpredictable, a megalomaniac, a barnstormer belonging to a bygone age, but an actor capable of greatness.

By the time he had embarked on his autumn tour of 1946, plans were already under way for the attack on Canada. Business was brisk; most weeks he was increasing the resources of the Association by five hundred pounds. December opened with an eleven-hundred-pound surplus from his week in Manchester, and confirmation that the company would sail on the *Aquitania* at the end of the month. Even then he was beset by difficulties. A key figure in the stage management was 'almost arrested by the police', Wolfit recorded. 'Cheque paid by APA to be refunded. Had him under contract for Canada alas—time showed him up.'

But Wolfit was used to such emergencies; he reorganised, and was fortunate to obtain the services of a new general manager, Graham 'Jimmy' Pockett, who had the necessary experience to administer the mighty undertaking. On 22 December 1946, the company, thirty-one strong, set sail. Wolfit had managed without help, and he was quickly to prove that Canadians at least did not share the British Council's views.

II

The Canadians could not show their appreciation of the English company more clearly than by besieging the box office. From the first week, in Ottawa, to the last, a month later, in Toronto, they provided Advance Players' Association with a surplus of twenty-five thousand dollars. So great was the company's success that the Schuberts, the New York theatre-owners and impresarios, invited the actor-manager to send his representative to negotiate a New York season, which they would guarantee against loss for three weeks.

Wolfit opened at the Century Theatre, New York, on 22 February 1947, with *King Lear*; he catalogued the state of affairs prior to curtain-up in his accounts book:

Anti-British feeling high.
Chorus girls picket the theatre owing to failure of musical. 'Tell Ham to Scram' on board.
Trouble over amplification in theatre orchestra and lighting.
Bevin attacked Truman.
Anger from Jews over M. of Venice and threats to close us up.

It was no more than he was used to, and when it came to the notices the next morning, it was like reading second-hand London newspapers. The New York critics attacked with self-indulgent savagery. 'O to be in England now that Wolfit's here' declaimed one. Brooks Atkinson, in the *New York Times*, was glib: 'It is hard to tell whether *Lear* is written in verse or in Billingsgate.' Lacking Agate's wit or style, the notice was brash and destructive. George Jean Nathan, the most respected of American critics, resorted to esoterica: his list of greater performances included Novelli, von Sonnenthal and Gemier. However, Stanley Kaufmann, formerly critic of the *New York Times*, wrote to the actor personally:

21 Feb., '47
Dear Mr. Wolfit,

Although I have no connection with the New York Times or any official capacity in the theatre, I should like to take upon myself the duty of apologising to you for Mr. Brooks Atkinson's review of your performance of 'Lear'. I saw the play the day the notice appeared, and I would believe that he was suffering from softening of the brain if I could first be convinced that he had a brain.

You are the first British-speaking actor I have ever seen with what I call innate power: the ability to command a stage and an audience easily and securely . . . and complete lack of cowardice about emotion. What a relief it is to see an actor who isn't afraid to act, who understands that the business of the theatre is not to see how little emotion one can get away with but how much one can stir . . . your performance had not a trace of modernity in it. You are the first Shakespearean actor I have seen in years who did not make me feel that he had just put down a cigarette and a cocktail glass in the wings.

But you see, Mr. Wolfit, you made a mistake as far as the New

York critics are concerned. Most of them know or care nothing about the things I have just mentioned. If you had come in with a production in which the sets were chromium with neon decor, if the costumes were of silver oilcloth and the lights came up out of the floor, if it were more difficult to distingush the male from the female members of your company and if one could understand only one word in six words—ah, then, what a success you might have had.

As it is, you will have to bear the scorn which our critics have for actors and directors who merely do plays, who don't do anything *to* plays. But, for whatever consolation it's worth, you have my admiration and gratitude.

Sincerely,
Stanley Kaufmann.

Wolfit had one further consolation: the box office. He played to seventy per cent capacity, was given a standing ovation for his Hamlet and Volpone, and was able to congratulate himself:

> Season ended in triumph. We over-rode the critical press and cleared expenses. Brought home over $32,000 for the Treasury.

He also had in his possession warm words of gratitude and admiration from Lord Alexander of Tunis, the Governor-General of Canada, and from MacKenzie King, the Prime Minister. But the New York critics had hurt him deeply; on his return the actor, at his most furtive and confidential, declared to a friend, 'You see, my boy, the theatre is controlled by an international cartel of poufferie!'

Bolstered by a pleasant reserve fund of nearly ten thousand pounds, Wolfit took the Savoy Theatre, London for an eight-week season and lost nearly every penny. It was a dismal, depressing time. The winter of 1947 was one of the worst in living memory; Wolfit, at forty-five and at his most rotund, bade farewell to Hamlet which he had played for more than two hundred performances over the past eleven years; the actor was dispirited and depressed.

In the autumn of that year, he was off on his provincial round again and, encouraged by memories of his enormous financial success in Canada, decided to visit the Dominion once more, but this time a more ambitious itinerary was arranged. In December 1947, Wolfit again crossed the Atlantic, in the *Empress of Canada*, and was met by the news that the tour had been cancelled while he was at sea. The booking manager who had to break the news had, perhaps, seen the actor as Macbeth; perhaps he remembered Wolfit's reaction to the 'cream-faced loon' who brings dread tidings; perhaps he had seen Lear convey sterility upon a daughter's womb; if he had not, he was to witness similar fury at very close quarters. Wolfit raged. He invoked the names of Lord Alexander and MacKenzie King, of James Agate and Charles Cochran, of Edith Sitwell and John Masefield. He cursed and stamped and swore until, flashing papers in the frightened man's face, he declared that they were letters from the Governor-General and the Prime Minister: he was no ordinary actor, he was here by command of the Government of the Dominion of Canada. The tour went ahead as planned.

From Halifax to London, Ontario, and then into territory where, the pioneer noted, 'the theatre has been dead for twenty years almost', to North Bay and Winnipeg, to Edmonton and Calgary, in the depths of the Canadian winter, and to Vancouver, where it was warmer. After three months of performing in cinemas and town halls, in blizzards and snowdrifts, the company embarked on the *Aquitania* for home. Wolfit wrote in his accounts book:

> The return was perhaps too soon and we were no longer the sensation. Canada watches New York for advice. Whole tour . . . showed a small loss of $2000.

On the return crossing, a gale swept the decks of the ship. Wolfit was thrown through a plate-glass window and severely cut his arm. He arrived in England, arm in a sling, looking, as ever, to the future. He had gained on the first tour, and lost on the second; up and down, success and failure, it was the pattern of his management.

III

On their return from Canada, Wolfit and Rosalind married, choosing his birthday as the date. The couple soon settled in Hampstead, in a small, attractive cottage—two up and two down—within easy reach of the Heath. It was their first real home together and, being touring actors, they treasured it. The style of their life was simple and unpretentious; the cottage was cosy and comfortable, the walls adorned with Spy cartoons of theatrical figures, with playbills and commemorative programmes, and with portraits of Wolfit himself. At home, the actor was mellow and calm, extremely domesticated and given to singing old music-hall songs while doing the washing-up. But he longed for space; when a new part presented itself he would learn it, walking on Hampstead Heath in all weathers, pausing now and then to gaze from on high over the roof tops of the city in which a theatrical home had, for so long, eluded him.

It was Wolfit's lot to secure those theatres in London which were not keenly sought after by others. In May 1948, he took the Westminster Theatre for yet another production of *The Master Builder*, but this time with a young director of growing reputation, an *enfant terrible*, Peter Cotes.

The reasons for Cotes as Wolfit's choice were, in some ways, devious, and they revealed how the actor's mind worked on a political level, in the sense that he was aware of having to develop tactics to refute the criticisms which were levelled at him; Valk as Othello was one such example; Cotes was another.

Cotes had been the object of critical attention both for his productions and for a book, *No Star Nonsense*, which despite its title, contained a eulogy of Wolfit's Lear. But the actor's mind went back four years earlier, to glowing personal notices he had read in *Queen* magazine by the same man, under the pseudonym Peter Northcote, of his performances in most of his other roles at the Scala. Wolfit assessed the situation: here was a director, much admired by the critics, who, in turn, much admired him as an actor; the combination could only work to his advantage.

At the start, the omens were encouraging: both had a passion for hard, intensive rehearsals and, apart from serious disagreements as to how the play should be lit, Wolfit benefited from working under the stern eye of a perceptive director. The conflict over lighting worsened during the dress-rehearsal period. Wolfit played the second act, the great duologue between Solness and Hilde, before a fire that he insisted should bathe him in a blazing red glow; Cotes insisted on a more realistic effect; once the director was out of the way, the fire glowed redder. Later, when Wolfit himself reproduced the play, the assault on the steeple was accompanied by Wagner's 'The Ride of The Valkyries'.

Wolfit's obsession with *The Master Builder* began in 1934, and continued until the end of his life. In the first instance, he would certainly have been attracted by the length and meat of the part, for that was what always drew Wolfit towards a play, but as time passed, something more profound, more deeply embedded in the content, fired his imagination. Superficially, the obvious ground is the Master Builder's fear of youth dispossessing him; but Wolfit was not afraid of youthful talent in that sense;* he could be cruel and bullying to the young men in his company, but that is not the same thing as holding them down for fear they would supplant him. His fascination for the play, the hold it exerted over him, was rooted in the mysticism of a character who could ask Hilde Wangel:

Don't you think, Hilde, that there are people singled out by Fate who have been endowed with grace and power to wish for some-

---

* He admired many younger actors, notably Paul Scofield, Tom Courtenay, John Wood, Richard Pascoe and Nicol Williamson.

thing, desire it so passionately, *will* it so inexorably that, ultimately, they must be granted it? Don't you think so?

Solness it is who admits to the troll in him, who declares, 'Oh, there are so many invisible demons in the world, Hilde. Good demons and evil demons. Fair demons and dark. If only one always knew whether it was the fair that had hold of one, or the dark!' For Solness's dilemma, the one that haunted Wolfit for more than thirty years, was of the fiercely practical earth-bound man, with the aspirations of the mystic, in whom fair and dark demons war. And in the symbolism of the final scene, when Solness climbs the church steeple only to fall when in reach of his goal, there was an element of prophesy pertinent to the actor's own psychology.

The critics were always divided over his interpretation. At the Westminster, with Rosalind as Hilde, a fine, brooding tension was achieved in their great scenes together. Cotes wrote '. . . he made Solness positively hum'. Certain it is that Wolfit possessed unique insights into the role that sprang from his own nature which, on the one hand, served the highest ideals and, on the other, faltered when in reach of them.

IV

The search for a London theatre continued, but the West End had shaken off war-time austerity and was once more flourishing. It was the era of H. M. Tennent, the London management who, under the control of Hugh 'Binkie' Beaumont, presented a spectacular series of successes with most of the leading actors of the day in works by play-wrights such as Noël Coward, Christopher Fry, Terence Rattigan, N. C. Hunter and Jean Anouilh while reviving Wilde, Lonsdale, Shaw and Sheridan in stylish productions, exquisitely dressed and set. Whatever the criticisms of the Beaumont regime, the standards of presentation were scrupulously maintained at the highest level, and the actors and directors were seldom less than first-rate. But, as with any large organisation, Tennent's influence and power appeared all-embracing; accusations that they were operating a monopoly were made against them, and questions were, in due course, asked in the House. A parody to the tune of *Bella Marguerita* was popular at the time:

> In September when the plays are casting,
> Binkie Beaumont said to Daphne Rye:*
> 'We must hold a very big audition!'

---

* Beaumont's casting director.

All the little boys were heard to cry:
'O bella Binkie Beaumont!
O, so beautiful to see!
We are hoping every meau-mont
Mister Beaumont
Has a part for me!'

The worlds of Wolfit and Beaumont did not revolve in the same cosmos; watching the current trends in the theatre, Wolfit felt more isolated than ever. As if to over-dramatise his situation, he looked north to Camden Town, chanced to see a vacant theatre, formerly a famous music-hall, called the Bedford, and there in February 1949, pitched his tents.

The *Daily Worker* caught the spirit of the venture:

LET'S HAVE A BASIN OF HAMLET

The Bedford, formerly a famous music hall, is to assume a new dignity next Monday when a season of Shakespeare opens there.

Donald Wolfit and his company are to open in the theatre—London's second oldest. . . . I saw a barrow boy park his bananas in a side street and make his way to the booking office. 'Never miss a week at the old Bedford, chum,' he said.

'Shakespeare? Why not. I'll take a basin of Hamlet any time.'

. . . Camden Town is not surprised by this latest arrival at its beloved old theatre.

Since the days when the brightest stars of the old-time music hall and variety trod its boards it has had a sad and varied history, becoming a repertory theatre, a touring date for travelling revues, a home for old-fashioned melodrama and even a centre for all-in wrestling matches.

The season at the Bedford was one of Wolfit's most famous assaults on the bastions of the establishment. He presented Shakespeare at popular prices—(6/– 4/6 3/6 2/– BOOKABLE)—and received unstinted praise for his courage. The company included Rosalind Iden, Bryan Johnson (a fine Fool in *King Lear*), Patricia Jessel and Joseph O'Conor. It was for O'Conor that Wolfit mounted a production of *Hamlet*, renouncing the royal role for himself, and playing the humbler Gravedigger. At the end of the play, O'Conor, as the Prince, was led through the curtains by the Gravedigger now dressed in morning clothes, looking like an undertaker.

The season was an unqualified success; the Bedford was full night after night. The company was playing to one thousand pounds per week (approximately seventy per cent capacity). MR. WOLFIT FINDS HIS PERFECT AUDIENCE, rejoiced the *Daily Worker*;

a photographic essay appeared in the *Sunday Graphic and Sunday News* with the caption 'SHAKESPEARE OUSTS SLAPSTICK'. There were photographs of 'The labourer and his wife' placed next to another of 'Students of the Old Vic School'; even the *Weekly Sporting Review* published a piece entitled 'HE PLAYS WHAT "WILL" WROTE FOR EVERYBODY'. For 'Will's' birthday, the company celebrated with guest artists: Dame Irene Vanbrugh, George Robey, Baliol Holloway, James Dale, Ernest Milton and Andrew Leigh. The old music hall had refound its vitality; for the second time since he had become an actor-manager, Wolfit was serving the community, and the community responded. Who could deny Wolfit's claim, 'They know we regard ourselves as the servants of the public and not its masters'?

After sixteen weeks of what Wolfit described in his accounts book as 'this amazing season, 128 consecutive performances of Shakespeare in an old music hall', he was compelled to take the company out on a four week tour to which he had previously committed them. The break proved fatal, for during the Shakespearean company's absence, Wolfit engaged Douglas Seale 'and a v. good company to play Shaw's plays weekly'. But Shaw was not the draw in Camden Town Shakespeare had proved to be. The best week was the first, when the box office receipts totalled £469.18.0.; for the remainder of the season, the weekly takings settled at around two hundred and fifty pounds. As if he had feared Shaw's unpopularity from the start, or perhaps even gloated over it, Wolfit complained of the last week's takings, £224.1.4. 'Proving that Camden Town did not want Shaw's plays although v. well done. Loss on this season about £1000 although in part covered by the profit of my 4 weeks tour with Shakespeare.'

The impetus had faded; the hot summer of 1949 compounded the public's aversion to Shaw. A week of *The Master Builder*, and two weeks of *Harlequinade*, an entertainment produced by his former mentor Eleanor Elder, saw out Wolfit's tenancy. 'An interesting experiment,' wrote the actor-manager. 'Theatre taken over . . . for melodrama. They went bankrupt in six months. I survived.'

V

The departure of Shakespeare from North London brought forth howls of protest from the public and appeals to the Arts Council for funds from the press; but in vain. Wolfit, to replenish his coffers, had to tour again, eliciting, no doubt, Hermione Gingold's famed comparison: 'Olivier is a *tour de force*, and Wolfit is forced to tour.' His personal fortunes were at a low ebb; he and Rosalind had paid themselves twenty pounds for portraying eight major roles weekly; they had no alternative but to journey forth once more. The autumn tour of 1949 served its purpose financially and, at Christmas, Wolfit joined the good ship *Hispaniola* as Long John Silver in an adaptation of *Treasure Island* at the Fortune Theatre, Drury Lane.

On 1 January 1950, his name appeared in the New Year's Honours List; the State, unable to ignore his service any longer, raised him to the rank of Commander of the British Empire. It was a grudging award to the man who had played in London during the Blitz, toured the British Isles, crossed Canada, and raised the flag of culture in Camden Town. Privately, he was disappointed that he was not to receive an accolade from the King, but publicly he wore a proud face. No man displayed an honour more vigorously than Wolfit. The initials C.B.E. were emblazoned wherever his name appeared, except on theatre bills and programmes, as was the custom. On his writing paper, on the brass plate that was weekly screwed to his dressing-room door, and sometimes even when he signed his name, the appendage appeared: Donald Wolfit, C.B.E. In his dressing room hung the framed citation signed by Queen Mary, the Grand Commander of the Order, and woe betide anyone who wrote to him without the suffix to his name.

In the Spring of 1950, Wolfit added a new role to his repertoire, Sir Giles Overreach in Philip Massinger's *A New Way to Pay Old Debts*, a part made famous by Edmund Kean, which had not been seen since 1922, when Robert Atkins played Sir Giles at the Old Vic.

So abandoned was Kean's acting in the part, that a lady fainted during one performance. A writer in *Blackwood's* considered that the performance was 'without doubt the most terrific exhibition of human passion that has been witnessed on the modern stage'. Wolfit gave a ferocious display of evil, a growling, violent portrayal of wickedness. Wearing a costume copied from the famous Clint portrait of Kean, Wolfit sneered and snarled with delicious enjoyment of Sir Giles's villainy. 'Virgin me no virgins,' he commanded in a voice boiling with contempt of virtue, and in the last scene, the actor reproduced a paralytic stroke with chilling accuracy.

The company toured throughout that summer and, after a short break, renewed their efforts that autumn. But the actor-manager's former enthusiasm for touring was on the wane. He confessed to Rosalind that economically it was becoming more and more difficult but that, most of all, he felt exhausted. There were many contributory causes to his weariness. At Cardiff, his beloved general manager Jimmie Pockett had suffered a heart attack and died, followed shortly by the retirement of Ernest Parr, his business manager. Wolfit had toured for fourteen years under his own management, bearing a heavy responsibility both financially and artistically; for the first time since he had entered the theatre, Wolfit could not find the strength to rekindle his vitality. His mood of despondency was reflected in a letter he wrote to a member of the company, Joseph Chelton:

My very dear Jo,

I could not come down to say goodbye to you all on Saturday evening. Those of you who know me well enough and whom I count as my real friends would I know understand the reason. The others, and they were very few, do not matter.

We have spanned a tremendous year of endeavour—over two hundred performances we matched our brains and hearts against the might of Shakespeare, Ibsen, Jonson and Massinger. We grew in strength and became bigger in spirit as a result and we gave pleasure and inspiration to tens of thousands as well as to ourselves.

The time came to call a halt, temporarily. I lost two great advisers in Jimmie and Parr and it was with a heavy heart that I finished the year. But all you friends were grand and splendid. . . . I need new and loyal helpers, or perhaps, I am pausing to catch the whispering breeze of a new trend; or may be I shall dash into the field to prove once again that the old way is best when the heart's blood flows from end to end of the theatre and magic is in the air.

Dear old friend, come and see us soon. We shall be very lonely without you all—and I pray God we shall form again in the autumn.

Love from us both
Donald.

But he did not form again in the autumn. 1950 saw the last of the Shakespearean tours. Wolfit, alone of all English actors, had served the provincial theatre at a time when, apart from repertory companies, it had become a cultural desert. The opportunity he provided for young and old to share in their heritage was unique. None but his most obstinate opponents could deny that the people of Britain, and the theatre, owed him a real and honourable debt.

1951 was Festival of Britain year, but Wolfit could find no place in the celebrations. However, in January, he received an invitation that refreshed his spirits. The Honourable Society of the Middle Temple invited him and his company to present a performance of *Twelfth Night* in the Middle Temple Hall, in honour of the three hundred and fiftieth anniversary of the first production of the play, which was believed to have been given there on Candlemas Day, 2 February, 1601. Queen Elizabeth (now the Queen Mother) and Princess Margaret attended, crowning an evening of enchantment to which all present surrendered. *The Times*:

Perhaps the evening's purest pleasure was in the listening to 'O

Mistress Mine' sung by Mr. Bryan Johnson, for then it was possible to entertain the notion that somewhere among the rafters of the old hall still faintly echoed the vibrations of the first singing of that matchless lyric.

Carl Dolmetsch and his ensemble accompanied the performance on a virginal, a recorder and a viola da gamba, enriching the echoes of the past. Wolfit was intensely proud of performing before the Royal party, and back-stage engendered the atmosphere among his troupe of strolling players, of vagabonds, summoned to Court. The performance was one of the actor-manager's fondest memories.

In April, there occurred another diversion from his customary activities: he appeared in his first modern part for many years, taking over from Eric Portman in *His Excellency* at the Piccadilly Theatre, surprising all with a fine study of a North Countryman, a newly-appointed Labour governor of a Mediterranean island. 'Portman was Aneurin Bevan,' Wolfit decided, 'I was Ernest Bevin.'

When the play closed after eleven weeks, Wolfit, from habit, began to think once more of an autumn tour. If, however, he was being written off as a touring actor who sometimes displayed flashes of genius, he was shortly to surprise London and, indeed, the theatrical world at large with the most powerful display of virtuoso acting the capital had seen for many years. He was now to accept an engagement, outside his own management, which would provide him with a foremost opportunity to lay claim to the summit of his profession and his art; it was to be one of his greatest triumphs as an actor; as an artist, one of his greatest tragedies.

CHAPTER FOURTEEN

The Scourge of Asia
and Hammersmith

I shall do such things—
What they are, yet I know not, but they shall be
The terrors of the earth.

— *King Lear*

I

IN the autumn of 1951, the Old Vic underwent a serious crisis when its triumvirate of directors, Michel St. Denis, Glen Byam Shaw and George Devine resigned after a conflict over the manner in which the Old Vic Centre was being run. The Centre comprised the work of the Old Vic School, of which Byam Shaw was the nominal head, the Young Vic, under Devine's guidance, and an experimental wing directed by St. Denis, undoubtedly the most influential of the three directors. Unable to resolve their differences, they resigned, stating in *The Times* that part of the reason was their inability to work with the Old Vic's administrator, Llewellyn Rees, former General Secretary of British Actors' Equity and Drama Director of the Arts Council. In the normal course of events, Rees met with the Board of Governors. To their surprise, but with their eventual approval, he informed them that he was already making overtures to prospective candidates who would be suitable to take over the running of the school, a priority, since there were students in mid-course. Rees also made it clear that if his title of Administrator was to have any meaning, he should be allowed to administer, or else he was being overpaid simply as a theatre manager. The Governors agreed to consider his words, and on that note Rees departed for Oslo to attend an International Theatre Congress of which he was President. During the course of his stay in Norway, he received a letter from Lord Esher, the Chairman of the Governors, regretfully asking for his resignation. Rees submitted it at once and, in the confusion that followed, the Governors made contact with Tyrone Guthrie, inviting him to come to the rescue. Guthrie agreed on two conditions: he would only accept the post for one year, and he demanded *carte blanche;* his terms were accepted.

Guthrie had little time to prepare but, with Hugh Hunt, decided that if the famous theatre's fortunes were to be restored and the air of crisis dispelled, a positive theatrical event would have to be created. Guthrie searched for a classic play that would suit his own talents and, after due consideration, was drawn towards the bloodiest of Elizabethan dramas, *Tamburlaine the Great* by Christopher Marlowe. Instinctively, Guthrie must have appreciated that the play ideally matched his gifts for directing spectacle on the grand scale, but could he find an actor with the vocal power and range, with enough force and gusto, to encompass Marlowe's hero? Against the advice of colleagues, he approached Wolfit.

Guthrie knew Wolfit only slightly, but had long known of him: as a young man, the future director, then, in his own words 'a tall spare beanpole', had seen a performance of the Arts League of Service. Impressed by the work of the young Wolfit, he asked Eleanor Elder for her opinion of him. Her reply was, 'selfish, cruel and ruthless'. Undaunted by this early warning, Guthrie continued to admire the actor, considering his voice to be one of the finest instruments he had ever heard and attracted too by Wolfit's 'solid, virile bearing'. A meeting was arranged.

The two men of the theatre liked each other at once; Wolfit awed by Guthrie's intelligence and wit, Guthrie admiring Wolfit's sincerity and earnestness. They quickly reached agreement: Wolfit would lead the Old Vic Company, his range of parts to be Tamburlaine, Lord Ogleby in *The Clandestine Marriage* by Garrick and Coleman, King Lear and Timon of Athens, for a salary of forty-five pounds a week, and a small percentage. Rosalind would also join the company.

Their first task was to edit Marlowe's text, to produce an acting version of the long, sprawling play that would make it both manageable and intelligible. Meeting either on Guthrie's home ground, Lincoln's Inn Fields, or in Hampstead, they worked intensely, producing a version of the play that Guthrie felt he could direct, and that Wolfit felt he could act. The atmosphere was harmonious and professional. Guthrie later admitted that it was one of the most pleasant working relationships he had ever experienced, and was particularly attracted by the Wolfits' simplicity; lunching with them in their cottage one Sunday, he was charmed by their generous hospitality and the utter lack of pretention with which they entertained him.

The news that the two were to work together was received with a flurry of anticipation, for the collaboration brought together two outstandingly talented personalities. If Guthrie had been advised against working with Wolfit, the actor, too, had received his share of advice in the opposite direction. Guthrie's reputation with 'star' actors was well known: he did not respect their status, and many an actor could testify to the director's sarcasm and scathing wit. Michael Redgrave, meeting Wolfit one day in the Garrick Club, warned him that Guthrie was 'no respecter of persons'. Wolfit answered, 'Michael, I have thirteen effects in King Lear, and I intend to keep every one of them!'

Rehearsals began in August, with a fine company that included Margaret Rawlings, Leo McKern, Jill Balcon, Lee Montague, Peter Coke, Colin Jeavons, Richard Pascoe, Kenneth Griffith and Ernest Hare. The settings were to be designed by Leslie Hurry. The question, understandably, uppermost in everyone's mind was, 'Would Wolfit take direction? How would he behave outside the confines of his own company?' The answers were soon forthcoming.

He took direction with humility, behaved with dignity and dedicated himself to the gigantic task in hand. On one occasion, he was some minutes late for rehearsals, unusual for him, and was sharply reprimanded by Guthrie. Wolfit accepted the reproof without demur, and apologised to the assembled company. From Wolfit's point of view, he enjoyed the gruelling labour of mastering the lengthy text, coming to grips with the complexities of the spectacular production Guthrie planned, and with the unrelenting savagery demanded by the character he was to portray. On a more personal level, he was, from time to time, alarmed by the director's treatment of some of the younger actors; for, taking responsibility seriously, Wolfit now saw himself in the position of leading man—not actor-manager—and therefore felt protective towards his junior colleagues.

Tamburlaine the Great opened at the Old Vic on 24 September 1951; it was a sensation.

Marlowe's drama, written when he was twenty-two, describes the career of the fourteenth-century Tartar who swept across Asia, massacring men, women and children, burning a city as a funeral pyre to his wife, humiliating kings to pull his chariot, and torturing an emperor in an iron cage. It is the poetic expression of one who rejoiced in tyranny, power and lust, of one who blasphemed, pillaged, raped and plundered in a glorious blaze of evil exaltation. The production dazzled the eye, and ravished the ear.

Wolfit, alone of all actors then alive, had the physical equipment to essay the role. A part of enormous length, it demanded all the technical skill available to the actor, skills to vary the voice, the intensity, the emotions, the use of sheer inner power. It required, too, an actor of daring imagination, for Tamburlaine inhabited the realms of evil splendour, extended by Marlowe to a dramatic elegy. Wolfit attained a rough-hewn grandeur in the part, and displayed a guttersnipe's delight in cruelty and all the bewitching appurtenances of power. Wolfit's Tamburlaine, in the words of *The Times* critic, was 'a royal, god-defying protagonist of a mad dream'. Half reptile, half Oriental, Wolfit blasted his way through the intricacies of Marlowe's verse, which while keeping something of the classic rhythms, informs it with an original, demoniac force. Theatrically, the idiom was rhetorical and spectacular. Wolfit was at his most powerful when monstrously baiting the caged Bajazeth, lashing the monarchs who, bitted and bridled, drew his chariot, wounding himhimself to encourage fearlessness in his sons, and when he challenged Mahomed, with the Korans blazing in the background. Joseph Chelton wrote: '. . . it is such terrible blasphemy, in *Reality*'. But he displayed tragic acting at its finest when, filled with pity and despair, he mourned for dead Zenocrate; and, finally, near to death himself, he crawled over the vast map of the world, pointing despairingly to the lands he had not had time to conquer; with his inexhaustible vocal range, he delivered 'Tamburlaine, the Scourge of God!' so that one was grateful for the tyrant's death.

When the curtain fell on the first night, Wolfit looked up to heaven and, exalted, cried 'Kit, my boy, we've done it!'*

The press acclaimed him; it was, without doubt, the finest set of notices he had received since his Lear. The audiences who flocked to see him were richly rewarded for attending to the critics; there would be few opportunities ever again for witnessing so extravagant a spectacle of great acting.

Praise came from all quarters. Sydney Carroll, former critic and manager, wrote to the actor:

> Never have I, in all my fifty years of playgoing, seen a more stupendous piece of acting than you gave us last night in Tamburlaine. It was indeed a bloody fine effort and succeeded triumphantly.

Sybil Thorndike, bubbling with enthusiasm:

> Donald dear, what a terrific afternoon we had!! No time to come round—had to dash to the theatre for an appointment. You really do give us something huge—how frightening it is—& so close to something we've known in the world—what a power to sustain that gigantic role, I don't think there's another actor who could have touched it—Chaliapine I expect—the end—that speech to Mahomed and God—wonderful—Thank you again for a stimulating afternoon & what a pearl for the eye—
>
> Yours Sybil (Lewis too)

* There are many versions of this remark. One, from George Murcell, an actor in the company, suggests something much longer, wherein Wolfit asked Marlowe to acknowledge his debt to the actor when the two met in Elysian Fields.

Tamburlaine was immediately followed by another triumph for the actor as Lord Ogleby. Wolfit exchanged the flowing red wig of the Asian barbarian for the powdered finery of a crumbling English aristocrat who needed, in the words of his valet, 'brushing, oiling, screwing, and winding-up, to set him a-going for the day'. He transformed himself into a frail, ailing, wizened old man who, after receiving the attention described by the valet, emerges sprightly, zestful and gloriously endearing. How he winced as each corset-tape was tightened, and grew chirpier with each dose of medicine, until His Lordship felt able to face the ladies, singing *Sur le pont d'Avignon* in a trembling tenor, and skipping gaily, but with just the right lack of confidence. It was Wolfit's most accurately observed character. When Stirling, his *nouveau riche* host, offers him hot rolls and butter, Wolfit's reply contained all the upper-class disdain for men who are ignorant in the ways of gentlemen: 'Hot rolls and butter in *July?* I sweat at the thought of it!' It was a performance enriched with humanity and tenderness; it was, by common consent, a superb comic creation.

Hilton Edwards, his fellow ASM from the Doran company, directed; Rosalind Iden, André Morell, Leo McKern, John Phillips, Wolfe Morris, Charmian Eyre and Ernest Hare supported admirably. Once more the public opened their hearts to the leading man, as if welcoming him to his rightful place, without any reservations, in the front rank of his profession. They had seen him in two memorable performances, supported by a company that enhanced his gifts. It was generally felt that Wolfit had, at last, triumphed over his own perversity and, in public gaze, he 'shone like plat'd Mars'. Wolfit held the theatrical world in the palm of his hand.

But the triumphs were short-lived. By the time *The Clandestine Marriage* had been added to the repertoire, all was not well with the Old Vic Company.

Shortly after *Tamburlaine* had opened, Wolfit began to complain to Rosalind of the proposed schedule for *King Lear*, in which he was expected to play the part eight times a week, instead of three, as was his custom under his own management. He also complained of Guthrie's brusqueness. He had furthermore, expressed incredulity that *Tamburlaine* was to be withdrawn, while still playing to eighty per cent capacity. Although all these factors would later attain importance, they were, for the moment, minor matters, and symptoms of a more deep-rooted malaise. Having submitted to the discipline of Guthrie's production, and taken on the responsibility of leading a company not his own, the 'dark demons' took possession of him and, once familiar with the role of Tamburlaine, he began to resort to the petty cavortings of the actor-manager: up-staging, fidgeting while others spoke, prowling, jumping in on speeches before the other actor had finished, giving endless notes on their performances to his colleagues, and generally making himself disagreeable. Jill Balcon suffered most, but Margaret Rawlings, more experienced, was better able to cope. After some piece of selfishness, she, as the enslaved Zabina, is reported to have said, 'Donald, if you do that again, I shall rattle my chains all through your long speech.' But he was undaunted by the threat; he continued to unsettle and distress his fellow artists by what had become, even by the standards of actor-managers, outrageous behaviour.

The tragedy ended, as it had begun, in trivia. After four weeks of *Tamburlaine* in the Waterloo Road, the Old Vic company travelled to Stratford-upon-Avon to perform the Marlowe play for a further week before producing *The Clandestine Marriage*. By the time they arrived in Shakespeare's birthplace, the atmosphere backstage was bleak and chilling. Cecil Clarke, the Stage Director ('a good man then and is still' wrote Wolfit years later) sent a message to Guthrie, informing him of the deteriorating situation and requiring him to attend a performance in Stratford. Guthrie, without informing anyone that he was in front, slipped into the stalls at the matinée; he was outraged by what he saw; the performance he had so much admired in London had lost all tension, and therefore power, and was a travesty of what had been achieved in the opening weeks. Enraged, the director confronted the leading man in his dressing room. Wolfit greeted him with, 'You've employed a lot of Bolshy actors here, Tony. They don't even say "good evening" to me.' To which Guthrie replied, 'I'm not surprised.' He then proceeded to castigate Wolfit for his behaviour. 'I was very angry,' he recalled, 'and very brutal.' Wolfit received the reprimand calmly, and made no response. The two men chatted about less fraught matters, and Guthrie left the theatre.

Later, Wolfit's anger and hurt erupted like a volcano. Using the *King Lear* schedule as an excuse, and an inaccurate announcement about the number of performances he was to give in other plays, he accused the directors of the Old Vic of breach of contract and resigned; after the run of *The Clandestine Marriage* he departed from the Old Vic and never returned.

When Guthrie recounted his version of the events, he was astonished at the slightness of the tale, and requested that the facts be confirmed by Hugh Hunt, his co-director. Hunt told the same story. Rosalind, understandably, laid emphasis on the unjust demands that were to be made on her husband in his most famous role; there is no doubt that there was a misunderstanding on that score but, had relationships been less highly charged with emotion, it could have been resolved. Whatever the balance of cause, Wolfit's resignation was self-destructive and damaging.

Guthrie expressed the theory that Wolfit did not want success; as a hard-working man dreads retirement for fear that idleness will kill him, so Wolfit dreaded success for fear that absence of strife would rob him of his impetus to act. Hunt, however, assessed the situation in less abstract terms:

> When I later tried to discuss the matter with Wolfit ... it really transpired that he did not want to play LEAR again. I would hazard a thought that having made a considerable success of the part at a fairly early stage in his career, he was unanxious for the London critics to have another look at it.

But Wolfit did play Lear again, two years later, under his own management. Hunt continued to speculate that perhaps Wolfit feared he might be required to work in a different way from the one to which he was accustomed, and furthermore, that Wolfit felt it invidious, especially in the provinces, to appear 'merely as a leading actor with the Old Vic Company, instead of an actor-manager bringing his own Company to the provinces.' But the chief point in Hunt's analysis, and certainly the most valid, was that Wolfit, being used to unquestioned discipline from his own actors, found the Old Vic company unwilling to accept his directions, which, in conclusion, seemed to confirm Hunt's view that Wolfit 'was too close to his old life as an actor-manager and to the outlook that had been so much part of his tradition'.

Historically, *l'affaire Tamburlaine* would appear to be important, for the theatre that Wolfit represented, the unfashionable theatre, must be taken into account. As an actor-manager Wolfit embodied the ruthless virtuoso performer who viewed acting as a combat and carried the fight out onto the stage. But when, at the Old Vic, Wolfit's fellow actors fought back, the virtuoso was compelled to show his strength. Wolfit enjoyed the contest; it was the theatrical tradition he understood, but he did not realise that in the modern preference for *ensemble* playing, which is another way of describing the director's theatre, the tradition had outlived its usefulness. The age of the great virtuoso performance was at its end; in the future, leading players would have to make it seem that they were part of a team. Wolfit resisted the change; he agreed with Agate:

> I feel, and feel strongly, that Shakespeare would have preferred to see his *Macbeth* rendered by a great pair supported by a rabble of nincompoops than by a couple of thoughtful nonentities reinforced by a company in which Lennox was nicely distinguished from Angus and Caithness from Menteith. 'Le Théâtre c'est moi'

was the great actor's motto. . . . He knew that what the public came to see was not Horatio and not Hamlet, but the actor who played Hamlet.

Those words were written in 1944, which is an indication as to when the movement towards ensemble playing was gaining in its momentum. By 1951, the crisis Wolfit engineered as Tamburlaine was the symptom of a fatal disease that the virtuoso performer had contracted.

In terms of his own personality, the freedom that he had enjoyed as an actor under his own management had been severely curtailed for the first time in fourteen years, a state of affairs he could not and would not endure. Wolfit had little guile; he was an execrable politician and an inept dissembler. He could neither disguise his feelings nor act, in life or the theatre, in any other way but compulsively, without thought to temper or control his passions; he could not change his ways; he was what he was.

In his accounts book, after the last performance of *The Clandestine Marriage*, he wrote:

So ended my endeavour to work in harmony with two producers who sought to treat actors as puppets and vested their authority in cruelty and inefficiency.

'*Le Théâtre c'est moi.*'

II

In the aftermath of the Old Vic débâcle, Wolfit sought to justify his actions. Having accused the Governors of breach of contract, he was now obliged to take his case before the London Theatre Council one of whose functions was to arbitrate disputes between managers and artists. The Old Vic refused to recognise the Council's competence and suggested that the actor should take his case before the courts. Enraged, Wolfit employed another tactic, that of transforming the personal nature of the conflict into a scandal concerning taxpayers' money.

Wolfit, like his father before him, was a supporter of the Conservative Party. He was virulently anti-Socialist and believed that under Attlee's government public funds had been shamelessly squandered; worst of all, the Englishman was in danger of losing his liberty under the relentless growth of bureaucracy. In the hope of stunting that growth, he joined the Society of Individual Freedom, and soon became prominent in its affairs. At the one hundred and ninth luncheon of the Society, in May 1952, which he chaired, Wolfit took the opportunity of launching a public attack on the Old Vic, not on his own behalf as it were, but on behalf of the taxpayer. He had shifted ground and his target now was the inefficiency of the Old Vic's management in resting *Tamburlaine* when it was still playing to capacity, and its general extravagance and wastefulness. In a long speech he developed his theme, first describing life under Lilian Baylis's regime: 'she always tried to balance her budget and to give the best. She died before the war. She had no successor—only a committee.' It was to 'the committee' that he next turned his attention, chronicling its misdemeanours, exaggerating its financial losses and setting out the details of his dispute. He concluded:

> And so the sorry tale goes on—public money—your money and mine is poured out to keep alive this monstrous pretence of a National Theatre which we could not afford in any time of affluence but which we must needs have willy-nilly in times of stress and strain. Should there not be a public enquiry into all this?

In attacking state aid, Wolfit was making an appeal for private enterprise which, in his terms, meant only one thing: a plea for actor-management.

The speech was widely reported in the national press and, on 18 May, the *Sunday Times* published an equally lengthy reply from Sir Bronson Albery, categorising it as 'untrue and mischief making'. But Wolfit persisted in his demands for a public enquiry; he blasted off in letters to the press and took every available opportunity of stating his case.

To the world of the theatre, Wolfit had no case. His actions simply confirmed what had always been said of him: that he was difficult, egocentric and obstinate. But he did draw support from another who had found life within the theatrical establishment unbearable, who had exiled himself to the South of France: Gordon Craig. He wrote to a mutual friend:

> I was glad to see in Sunday Times that Wolfit had enraged SIR Silly ass Albery by telling some truths about the Old Vic. It is particularly comic to note who are the members of the Old Vic Trust Committee & therefore the National Theatre sponsors & governesses.

He then listed them by name: Lady Violet Bonham Carter, Sir Bronson Albery, Mrs. Barbara Ward Jackson, Mrs. Strauss, Hamish Hamilton, Lord Wilmot, Mr. Shovelton—Craig commented: 'SHOVELTON!!! Glory Allelujha'—Sir Philip Morris, Mr. John Maude.

> Now by what right are they allowed to dictate about theatres— enough to convulse a cat with giggles. Are you aware of things in London? You—any of you? Theatre things I mean—Do you know

how to steer a boat? a theatre boat? Did you ever hear of Irving,
Sir H:
Does one die for nothing?
I am very cross with you all—who could prevent such blunders
as the above & what the above will commit. No it's not good of
you. You will soon forget what the stage is. *Wolfit was quite right
to attack*.

But Craig's support apart, Wolfit's actions and utterances found little
sympathy, although they may have drawn attention to the need for
vigilance in the application of public money to the Arts. From his
own standpoint, it was as great a misfortune as he had ever brought
upon himself: he was at the height of his powers as an actor, he had
been given the opportunity of working in a context other than under
his own management, at a time when he himself had confessed to the
economic difficulties of continuing under his own banner. He had
been judged within a company of supporting players, with a director
and a designer who matched his own gifts, and judged favourably;
he had wilfully destroyed the acclaim, the renown and above all, the
good-will that those advantages had presented. And yet, with
dogged determination, with incalculable reserves of energy and will-
power, he proceeded to haul himself out of the mess in the only way
he knew: with his own hands.

III

The pattern was the same as before: a way must be found in order to
accumulate enough funds to finance a new season under his own
management.

He turned to the cinema. He had, of course, made films in the
1930s, but, understandably, film directors began increasingly to
regard him as a stage actor who could not adjust to the intimate
technique demanded by the camera. In 1949, he had been tested by
David Lean for a part in *The Trial of Madeleine Smith*. Lean rejected
him for the role and wrote:

I am sorry I was wrong about your test when I saw you do it on
the set. You had such power that I was convinced it would come
over on the screen, but I think if you saw the test you would agree
with me that I was mistaken.

I can only hazard a guess at the reason for this and I think it is
that years of stage experience have given you a force of projection
towards an *audience* rather than towards the person with whom
you are acting. In other words, sitting in the studio when you did
the test, I got the full brunt of your talent, but on the screen,

although you were seemingly playing to your fellow actor, in some magical way which only you can realise, you were directing an invisible ray away from her and out past the camera—and this gave a sort of staginess.

. . . I do hope I have not gone too far in saying all this. I say it because I am a great admirer of yours and it is only this, and your request, that make it possible to be so frank.

On receipt of the letter, according to Wolfit's film agent at the time, John Gliddon, the actor 'was terribly upset. His pride . . . had received a deep wound.'

But, in 1951, after his departure from the Vic, Wolfit was offered a leading role in *The Gaunt Stranger**, an Edgar Wallace tale, to be directed by Sir Carol Reed. Others followed. Whether or not Lean's criticism sank in is difficult to say, but Wolfit emerged as an actor with considerable talent for the cinema. His performance as Sergeant Buzfuz in *Pickwick Papers* was a fine example of the actor's gusto, and, some years later, he gave a surprising display of realistic acting in *Room At The Top*.

Throughout 1951 he worked in films, radio and television; he gave a recital with Rosalind in Antwerp and played Othello as guest star for the repertory company in Worthing. In April, he presented *Lords of Creation* at the Vaudeville Theatre, London, a comedy with himself, Raymond Huntley and Rosalind in the leading roles; it was soundly thrashed by the critics and ran four nights.

Early in 1952, he played *King John* on television and by the autumn he was able to announce that on 4 February 1953, he would open a season of classical plays at the King's Theatre, Hammersmith, with *Oedipus Rex* and *Oedipus at Colonus*.

1953 was Coronation year. While the West End presented frothy entertainment to beguile the hordes of visitors—Laurence Olivier and Vivien Leigh in Rattigan's *The Sleeping Prince* was an example— the cultural flag was hoisted in one of London's shabbier districts which possessed two fine theatres within a quarter of a mile of each other. At the one, John Gielgud, under the aegis of H. M. Tennent, presented *Richard II* (with Paul Scofield), *The Way of the World* and Otway's *Venice Preserv'd*. At the other, the King's, Wolfit presented his season.

Several times during the previous thirty years, Hammersmith had found itself the object of that intense curiosity and interest on the part of theatregoers that was usually reserved for events in Central London. The Lyric had housed Nigel Playfair's famous production of *The Beggar's Opera*, Drinkwater's *Abraham Lincoln* and many

---

* Shown under the title *The Ringer*.

other notable revivals including a memorable performance by Edith Evans as Millamant in *The Way of the World*. The King's, which usually provided touring companies with their nearest call to London, had also had its share of distinguished seasons: Martin-Harvey first played Mathias in *The Bells* there, and Sybil Thorndike was seen as Clytemnestra in the *Elektra* of Euripides. In 1953, serious theatre-goers were to be treated to a feast of acting at both theatres, and to both theatres they flocked.

Wolfit had long cherished an ambition to play the Greek tragedies. When Martin-Harvey died in 1944, Wolfit purchased a large quantity of costumes and effects, among them the late actor-manager's wardrobe for *Oedipus* which he had played in 1912 in Reinhardt's production. By 1953, the costumes were of little use but Wolfit salvaged a gold circlet of laurel leaves that Martin-Harvey had used in the part.

With customary energy Wolfit organised his company. Llewellyn Rees was to be General Administrator and his leading players included Rosalind, Lewis Casson, James Dale, Ellen Pollock and Ernest Hare. Beside the two *Oedipus* plays, he announced revivals of *As You Like It*, *Twelfth Night*, *King Lear* and *Macbeth*; the season was scheduled to last until the end of March.

It opened in a blaze of glory. Wolfit, the virtuoso, was back in the saddle, working in the context he knew best and loved best and, one is forced to conclude, in the way that he worked best.

Wolfit's Oedipus ranked high in his achievements. As with *Tamburlaine*, the actor was required to undergo a gruelling test of physical endurance. The length of the roles and their sheer spiritual weight taxed Wolfit to the limits. In *Oedipus Rex* (translated by E. F. Watling under the title *Oedipus the King*) Wolfit presented a stern, noble tyrant; in *Oedipus at Colonus* (*Oedipus in Exile* in the Watling translation) he achieved a sustained serenity of mystic beauty, his voice caressing the pain, the despair of the blinded King. Hobson, in the *Sunday Times*, detected the real technical accomplishment of the first performance, when he wrote of the actor's 'splendid grading of Oedipus's growing suspicions', for only a leading man, experienced in and tested by the classic drama, could pace himself with such expert stealth: from the scene with Jocasta in which his suspicions are first given voice, to the confrontation with the Shepherd, who is the instrument of the dreadful dénouement, Wolfit built tension upon tension, like a cat stalking its prey. At last, when the time came to pounce, Oedipus, rocking on his heels, cried 'ANSWER!' high-pitched, staccato, brutal, he supplied a moment of vivid theatrical reality: no man, shepherd or king, could have withstood that demand. Soon after, Oedipus leaves the stage and plunges Jocasta's brooch into his eyes. Wolfit screamed from off-stage, a blood-curdling, horrendous cry of anguish and pain.

In *Oedipus at Colonus* Wolfit displayed a technical virtuosity of the highest order. *Colonus*, after the intense, dramatic excitement of the first play, was like a tone poem for solo voice accompanied by the trumpet of Theseus or the plaintive weeping of Antigone and Ismene. Harold Pinter, a member of the company, recalled, in a television interview:

> ... one image of him remains with me very strongly ... he was standing high up on a rostrum with all the light on him ... he stood with his back to the audience with a cloak round him and there came the moment when the man downstage finished his speech and we all knew, the play demanded it, the audience knew, that Wolfit or Oedipus was going to speak, was going to turn and speak. He held the moment until one's stomach was truly trembling and the cloak came round; a tremendous swish that no one else has been able to achieve I think. And the savagery and power that emerged from such a moment was extraordinary.

For more than an hour, Wolfit used his voice with all its infinite variety, now moaning, now harsh, now mighty. The promise of redemption brought stillness and repose. When, at last, Oedipus vanishes into the air, Wolfit achieved a profound weariness for the end of one life, and spiritual elation at the glorious promise of another yet to come.

The critics were once more swept away. Hobson, Darlington, Brown and Dent all expressed gratitude and wonder. Even the company and the production were subjected to unaccustomed flattery: 'a very strong cast' (Darlington); 'a strong company' (Brown); 'acted and staged throughout with the right solemnity' (Dent); 'solid backing' (Trewin). Wolfit had redeemed himself, on his own terms, and press and public displayed what seemed to be more than just admiration for the actor's art, but a deep affection for the man's courage and persistence. It prompted John Barber to inform the readers of the *Daily Express* that 'NOW WOLFIT HAS THAT WEST END GLAMOUR!':

> Suddenly, out of the blue, glamour has descended on Donald Wolfit. What is glamour? A dazzle of excitement which actors acquire from success.
>
> After years of touring the provinces, Wolfit is presenting a London season of Shakespeare plays. The King's Theatre—long in the doldrums—is astonished by the response.
>
> Cars drive up every night. From them step the eminent and the titled. Celebrities like the Bernard Dockers, the Harewoods,

Fashionable Showfolk, Claire Bloom, Robert Helpmann and his friends. And more Americans than you can count.

The box-office staff is increased to cope with parties from Norwich, from Bristol.

Every night the 650-seat gallery shouts 'Donald, Donald!' Advance bookings total £3,587. The season has been extended by ten weeks.

The next day the *Express* followed up with an article about Rosalind: 'What does fame mean?—a home to her.' It meant, more particularly, rehearsing from ten until two, and afterwards travelling by bus from Hammersmith to Hampstead to clean and tidy the cottage, to shop, to prepare for their after-theatre evening meal, and returning, once more by bus, across London to Hammersmith to play Antigone or Viola or Rosalind or Lady Macbeth. The Wolfits found their names in those pieces, so beloved by the popular press, 'Does your husband make tea for you in the morning?' (Wolfit did from Monday to Saturday; on Sunday, Rosalind rose first). The *Daily Herald* described 'How a man greets success at 50' and *Reynolds News* revealed that the 'Grand Old Man of the Stage—is only 50!'

Wolfit appeared not to notice the attention that was being paid to him; outwardly he worked himself and his company as hard as ever, became just as angry when scenes went wrong inside the theatre, and just as pleasant the moment he stepped outside the stage door. Inwardly he rejoiced, for he had reaffirmed his own position as an actor-manager and gloated over the headline in the *Star*: 'West may have own "Old Vic" .' He had taken his revenge and triumphed.

Because of the success, Wolfit decided to prolong the season. In April, he added *The Wandering Jew* to the repertoire, an ambition he had nursed since he played with Matheson Lang. At the first rehearsal he glanced at the company of assembled actors, and said, 'I want someone to carry the Cross past the window in the first scene.' His gaze rested on one young man; with his voice at its most sonorous, Wolfit called out, 'Pinter . . . '

The Wandering Jew was not the success Wolfit had hoped it would be. Having broadcast the play the previous year to a large number of listeners, he had been encouraged to think that theatre-goers would respond similarly; they did not. After three weeks he reverted to his Shakespearean repertoire, resurrecting Stern's designs and costumes, and falling back into his familiar style of presentation. In the summer, he rested and, in August, returned to do battle once more.

The decision to return in the autumn was based on the hope that he had at last found a permanent home for his operations. The hope was short-lived, for although the new productions were, on the whole, more stylish and tasteful, Wolfit persisted with his less than adequate presentations of his Shakespearean repertoire. The company changed too. Some actors left and were replaced by old Wolfit faithfuls; one newcomer was Frank G. Cariello, who brought a colourful, throbbing zest to everything he played.

The autumn season opened with a production by Baliol Holloway of *The School for Scandal*. Holloway, a lovable, twinkling man of tireless vitality, had been Edith Evans' leading man at the Old Vic in the 1920s. She described him as 'a wonderful actor', yet he had never made the transition from the Waterloo Road to the West End. He was unashamedly virile and, at a time when that was not the most admired quality in an actor, he suffered for it. Some accounted his Richard III as his finest role, and in 1948 he delighted Old Vic audiences with an extravagant comic performance as Don Armado in *Love's Labours Lost*. Wolfit adored 'Bay', and took direction from him eagerly. Rosalind's Lady Teazle managed to combine spirit and vulnerability, and another former Old Vic player, Dorothy Green, was a stylish Lady Sneerwell.

In September, Andrew Leigh was recalled to service to assist Wolfit with a production of *Henry IV*, Part One. The strains of actor management showed for the first time. Wolfit, as director, floundered and, as a result, it reflected badly on his interpretation of Falstaff. It was a role he should have been able to play, but the pressures of directing a complicated Shakespearean history—Leigh was called in after rehearsals had begun—robbed him of energy. He improved after the first night, but he failed to dominate the character and relied largely on his rich comedy technique to pull him through.

To close the season, he revived *The Clandestine Marriage* and repeated his delicious portrayal of Lord Ogleby, but the tide had turned against him; the public did not respond; the days of the Shakespearean actor-manager were finally over.

Wolfit bade farewell to his most famous roles, that colourful procession of characters he had created over the years: Macbeth, Petruchio, Touchstone, Malvolio, Volpone, Overreach, Shylock and what he called 'the brightest jewel in my crown', King Lear, which he played for the last time on 31 October. There were many who would have cause to be grateful to him, many whose first excitement in the theatre he provided, many who, but for him, would never have seen a play by William Shakespeare or Ben Jonson. If a balance sheet of Wolfit's Shakespearean company is to be drawn then it will show a rich surplus: service to the community and to the English classic repertoire stand high on the list of assets, but most important of all was the opportunity playgoers had, from 1937 to 1953, of seeing a great actor in great roles, an actor in whom some ancient fire burned.

His contribution to the art of acting was of immense importance to the theatre, not only because he illuminated human passion and folly, but also because he deliberately upheld the traditions of the past which, as a function, is as essential to the mystery of renewal as any wild or daring innovation; for, finally, there is no way of judging the present or the future but by the past.

IV

The King's, Hammersmith, season was not without the usual drama behind the scenes that attended all Wolfit's endeavours, for it saw the advent of a new bogeyman in the actor's life, and one who was to haunt him for the next four years. He was the critic, first of the *Evening Standard*, and later of the *Observer*, Kenneth Tynan.

Tynan had crossed Wolfit's path twice before becoming a critic. In 1948, Wolfit had been invited by the *Gloucestershire Echo* to review a performance of the First Quarto *Hamlet* by the Oxford University Players 'under the direction of Ken Peacock Tynan'. Wolfit, as critic:

> One is somewhat nervous of amateur performances of the classics, but Mr. Tynan's production invites criticism on the highest level and should be judged as such, for it is a solid achievement. . . . Mr. Tynan has seen fit to dress the play in Georgian costume.
>
> Although it did not hamper the play, it is the worst costume for the amateur, for it demands such grace and deportment in the wearing, and much that was meant for grace on Saturday night only succeeded in being clumsy on the small stage. . . . The producer himself gave us an effective ghost, which would be even better if he'd discarded the modern craze for crediting Hamlet's father with sepulchral asthma.*

At about the same time, a young girl in Wolfit's company, Pauline Ponting, became engaged to Tynan. Wolfit 'used to take me aside', she wrote, 'and wanted to know all about my young man'.

These two paternal episodes apart, Tynan had written a fine review of Wolfit and Valk in *Othello*, but as the critic was not employed by a newspaper at the time, the piece was not published until 1950, when it appeared in a collection of Tynan's work, under the title *He that Plays the King*.

He first distressed Wolfit when he became critic of the *Evening Standard*. Tynan, then aged twenty-six, wrote a destructive notice of *The Wandering Jew;* the young critic was capable, at that time, of

---

* In passing, Wolfit also credited Lindsay Anderson as the King, with being 'the second best actor'.

unleashing penetrating witticisms in service of his talent, a kind of undergraduate humour which soon placed him high in the ranks of fashionable reviewers. *The Wandering Jew*, to the man who was to champion Brecht, was a gift and he chose to aim his arrows of discontent at Wolfit's costumes, describing 'a faded horseblanket', 'a bath robe', 'a tea cosy' and 'an inverted galvanised iron bucket with two holes knocked in it'. He attained the upper reaches of critical invective when dealing with the Jew's burning at the stake: ' . . . like the annual roasting of an ox on Shakespeare's birthday at Stratford'.

Wolfit fumed. Many of the costumes that Tynan had disparaged came from the store of Sir John Martin-Harvey. It was not just Wolfit's honour that had been impugned, but the honour of actor-management. He sued for libel.

In the flurry of solicitors' letters, charges and counter-charges, the affair fizzled out, for Tynan left the *Evening Standard* to take up his post as critic of the *Observer*. The Beaverbrook press generously paid Wolfit's costs and there, for the moment, the matter rested.

But Tynan's new appointment placed him in the position of wielding important influence on the affairs of the theatre, and it was in the columns of the *Observer* that he continued to treat Wolfit with a contempt the actor undoubtedly did not deserve.

CHAPTER FIFTEEN

The Strong are Lonely

For honour travels in a strait so narrow,
Where one but goes abreast.
*   —Troilus and Cressida*

I

WOLFIT did not rest over Christmas 1953, after what had been a long and exhausting season; instead he played Captain Hook in *Peter Pan* with Pat Kirkwood, Evelyn Laye and yet another member of the 'unfashionable theatre', Russell Thorndike, Sybil's brother, the first actor to play Peer Gynt in England. Wolfit had agreed to appear only in and around London; he was replaced by Stanley Holloway, who wanted a quiet and unpublicised return to the stage before travelling to the United States to play Dolittle in *My Fair Lady*.

Shortly afterwards, in February 1954, the Wolfits travelled to France, to La Garde-Freinet, a Provençal village where the actor settled down to complete the first volume of his autobiography, *First Interval*. He wrote the book, from notes made a year previously, in longhand, sent the pages to his secretary, Imogen Matthews, to type, and enjoyed this brief spell as an author. The book had many merits, notably warm and gentle remembrances of his childhood and early career. It also contained an impassioned plea for a National Theatre. As a book of theatrical reminiscences it was charming and humorous; on the personal level, he omitted to mention the names of his first two wives. When it was published in the autumn, the book was favourably received ('no ghost for this Hamlet') but did not have good sales. Nevertheless, Wolfit delighted in inscribing the fly-leaf, 'from the Author'.

On his return from France, good fortune awaited him. A row had erupted which resulted in Robert Newton leaving the cast of a film while in the first days of shooting. The film was an adaptation of George du Maurier's famous novel, *Trilby;* Wolfit took over Svengali, his longest film role to date, and one which suited well his gifts for dramatic intensity.

In the early summer, film and television offers were arriving with pleasing regularity, but Wolfit was restless again; he did not like to be away from the theatre for long. He decided to make his return in a play by Fritz Hochwalder which could not have been more aptly titled for a Wolfit production: *The Strong Are Lonely*. Margaret Webster who had recently directed the play in the United States, returned to England to work with her old friend. Together, they assembled a company that included Robert Harris, Derek Oldham and Ernest Milton; lower down the order were some Wolfit regulars and, as the Bishop of Buenos Aires, Frank G. Cariello, who was also to be business manager.

The play concerned a group of Jesuit fathers in Paraguay who have created a Utopian state for their Indian converts, thereby incurring the enmity of the slave-driving Spanish settlers. The Jesuit fathers find themselves under attack from two flanks: first, from the legate of Imperial Spain who is sent out on the pretext of investigating the state within a state, but, in fact, with stern orders to crush the religious community; secondly, from the emissary of the Father-General of the Jesuits, who reveals that if the settlement is not abandoned it will mean the dissolution of the Society of Jesus throughout Paraguay. The Father Provincial is ordered, on his vow of obedience, to submit; caught in a political web of spiritual conflicts, he submits, but his followers disobey and, in appealing to them, he is killed.

A fine play, with fine parts for the leading actors, it had been cast in the top echelon with a mixture of styles. Robert Harris, as the Spanish legate, played in a subdued but incisive manner that made his long duologue with Wolfit, as the Father Provincial, a fascinating interplay, not only of opposing personalities, but also of techniques. Derek Oldham, famed for his career in musical comedy, brought yet another approach: broad effects with honest intentions. But it was the fourth style, fantastic, intricate and exquisitely theatrical, that provided the real highlight of the evening in the playing of the scene between Wolfit and his superior from Rome, Ernest Milton.

Milton's role required him to sit through a long trial scene, dressed in black trimmed with silver, without speaking but attending to every shifting thought in the argument; he had then to reveal himself by intoning the Society's motto, *Ad majoram Dei gloriam*—'to the greater glory of God'. It was an electrifying moment. Milton, with his voice like vibrato played on the cello, a slightly crooked, sardonic smile on his thin lips, a spidery gait, projected a powerful intelligence which matched Wolfit's earthy integrity.

The two actors were old friends, and Wolfit profoundly respected Milton's gifts and achievements as an actor, and his kindness as a man.

Rehearsals proceeded smoothly. Now and again, Miss Webster had to contend with the conflicting acting styles, more particularly with the less important roles. She had just returned from America, then in the grips of 'the method', of 'the search for truth', of an attitude opposed to theatrical reality. Cariello's method, for example, was to declaim; his search for truth was to get his lines right and he was a passionate apostle of theatrical reality; he presented difficulties, but Wolfit's loyalty to his old friend blinded him to these problems. Miss Webster coped ably with members of Wolfit's former Shakespearean company, and taught them much, but had she had her own way then, doubtless, the level of acting in the smaller parts could have been improved.

Wolfit opened the tour in Nottingham and was enthusiastically received. Theatre managers from London appeared, congratulated the actor-manager, and returned to the metropolis, never to be heard from again. *The Strong Are Lonely* was 'a play of ideas', serious and earnest in its intent; the West End was chary. But Wolfit was not to be thwarted; he believed that the play stood a fine chance of succeeding. He commenced battle.

At the end of the second week, in Birmingham, an article by Harold Hobson appeared in the *Sunday Times*, under the title 'Francomania', in which the critic reviewed the state of the English theatre, drawing attention to the reluctance of 'our leading actors' to appear in plays by contemporary writers. Wolfit seized the opportunity, for there he was, appearing in a play by a contemporary writer, which was unable to find a London theatre. He invited Hobson to take the unusual step of reviewing the play while on its pre-London tour. Wolfit wrote, not to a distinguished and influential critic, but to a friend, one who had admired him, despite occasional differences, for many years, and who had followed his career from the early days in Sheffield. Hobson recalled: 'What I do remember with pleasure is that of all critics it was to me that Donald turned on this occasion.'

Hobson travelled to Oxford; his presence in the audience was kept secret, but the news soon leaked, and added an extra charge to the performance that night. On the following Sunday, 9 October, Hobson wrote in the *Sunday Times*:

QUESTION MARK

I am taking the unusual step of reviewing Mr. Donald Wolfit's *The Strong Are Lonely* whilst it is still on its provincial tour because at the moment it looks as if this fine play might never get to London at all. Despite the fact that 'The Burnt Flower-Bed' is playing to crowded houses, despite the incontrovertible success of 'Waiting for Godot' it seems that managers still distrust the capacity of audiences in our London theatres to give pleasurable attention to an unconventional and closely argued play.

Generously, Hobson devoted his entire column to the production. He concluded:

> As for Mr. Wolfit as the Father Provincial, he is at his finest. His spiritual dissolution is terrible to witness, his grief almost unbearable. . . . Will this production die upon the road? Surely, we have at least one manager, non-profit distributing or otherwise, who will see that this does not happen?

As a direct result of Hobson's review, enough interest was generated to prompt the management of the Piccadilly Theatre to offer Wolfit a limited season of four weeks. With some heart-searching which caused him distress, Wolfit replaced Cariello, who continued as business manager, but the complexities of the West End box office baffled him; it was the end of their friendship. The play opened in London on 15 November. Hobson having already declared his hand, the other critics followed suit. Artistically and financially the play was a triumphant success.

After the limited season at the Piccadilly Theatre, the play transferred at the end of June to the Theatre Royal, Haymarket. To play in that famous theatre, under his own management, was a source of great pride to Wolfit. He had never had a dressing room quite so large or so elegant, and he was as excited as a child to discover that it had its own bathroom *en suite*.

The success of the play was repeated at the Haymarket, but it was tempered by anger when Tynan's review appeared. The critic, not having seen the play at the Piccadilly—the *Observer*'s number two critic reviewed the performance unfavourably—had plenty of time to prepare some choice witticisms and barbs. He was at the height of his power, and his writing was still infused with some literary energy:

> The debate is passionate, felt as well as argued: its necessary abstractions come alive as people. I wish I could say the same of the performances. Or rather, I wish I could say nothing of the performances beyond condign praise for Robert Harris as the Spanish envoy. All else is bizarre. Ernest Milton, with his sickened scowl, hieratic voice and arachnoid bearing, makes a highly implausible spy, though his general aspect supports the view that man is nothing but a reed which thinks. As the Father Provincial, Donald Wolfit slogs for God with the vigour of a worker-priest; but what he gives us is all Commissar and no Yogi; it is not his fault that the griefs and tumults of the spirit lie outside his reper- toire. His long wrangle with Mr. Milton is an instructive joust of

bull versus china-shop: I shall long recall these two expert players stealthily upstaging each other for the greater glory of God. It is of the English Theatre, not of a Jesuit College, that Mr. Wolfit is the Provincial Father.

Wolfit exhaled noisily, and his eyes flashed. But he was in a West End success, able to take his full salary and relishing a fine part; no action was necessary, but he did not forget Tynan's condescension towards him.

Wolfit milked *The Strong Are Lonely* for all it was worth: he arranged a television production with the BBC and, in 1956, presented it on 'The Fringe'—outside the mainstream, as ever—at the Edinburgh Festival, playing in the Church Hall of the Jesuit fathers, and providing the Festival with a resounding success. Robert Speaight replaced Robert Harris, and Joseph Chelton took over Ernest Milton's role. Wolfit transformed the Lauriston Hall into a theatre, investing it with the 'dignity of Irving's Lyceum' wrote Speaight. Wolfit used a confessional as his dressing room; 'Hide the Guinness,' he would order at the approach of Father James Christie, S.J., the Superior. The gentle Father, on one occasion, entered, sniffed the air and said, 'Ah: Guinness.'

Privately, Wolfit's life had settled into a calm, serene mould. Towards the end of 1954, he and Rosalind had sought a week-end retreat in the country. They fell in love with a sixteenth-century thatched cottage in Hampshire, Swift Cottage, in the village of Hurstbourne Tarrant, and soon were living there more or less permanently, visiting London only when the need arose. Rosalind, at first, resisted the change, but the charm and quiet quickly won her over.

Swift Cottage was small and compact, with low beams and leaded windows. The Wolfits continued to maintain a pleasant simplicity in their lives, inviting family and friends for week-ends, and generally taking part in the life of the village. Wolfit adored every inch of his new home, playing the countryman as to the manner born. He furnished the rooms with many of the chairs and props that had once adorned the courts of Illyria, Elsinore and Belmont. He worked in the large garden with as much ferocity as he had previously reserved for his professional activities.

In July 1956 his second daughter, Harriet, married John Graham, an actor. The arrangements for the wedding necessitated Wolfit meeting Susan again. He felt things much too deeply to be able to treat a past marriage with equanimity. At the mention of either of his former wives, he withdrew into himself, and showed his displeasure in the prescribed manner. Susan herself once remarked, with piercing accuracy, that he could never forgive anyone to whom he had done an injury.

Susan arrived at Swift one Saturday in June to discuss the wedding plans. Rosalind and Wolfit entertained her to tea with Harriet and her future husband in the garden. The atmosphere was formal and a little strained. During the course of the afternoon, Wolfit asked, 'Rosalind, would you like another cup of tea?' She declined. 'Harriet? John?' A long pause followed. 'If anyone else would like some more tea . . . '

The couple were married at St. Colombo's, Pont Street and the reception was held at the Garrick Club. Much of the tempest of Wolfit's passion had blown itself out, and he accepted the role of paterfamilias with dignity.

II

In March 1957, Wolfit announced his last season as an actor-manager. He chose to present two plays by the French dramatist Henri de Montherlant, *The Master of Santiago* and *Malatesta*, translated by Jonathan Griffin. It was the first time de Montherlant had been produced in England.

The opening play provided Wolfit with the part of a stern, remote, saintly figure who attacks the superficial values of life in sixteenth-century Spain; he lives, withdrawn from the world, refusing to deviate from a severe, self-imposed austerity for fear of losing his religious detachment.

Before the opening night, the actor-manager wrote to David Astor, the Editor of the *Observer*, informing him that there would be no seats available for his newspaper's dramatic critic, Kenneth Tynan. It was a direct response to Tynan's disparaging notice for *The Strong Are Lonely;* Wolfit had nursed his resentment for more than three years. Tynan, however, was a devotee of de Montherlant, and made the journey to the Lyric Theatre, Hammersmith, free seats or no. The front-of-house manager kept the critic's presence a secret from Wolfit, but in the first interval, the actor stormed into his dressing-room and cried, in a hoarse whisper, 'There is someone out there who hates me!'

On the following Sunday, Tynan wrote of what he called Wolfit's religious period':

> . . . In 'The Wandering Jew' some seasons ago, we saw him go up in flames; last year, in 'The Strong Are Lonely,' he played a martyred Jesuit; and now, getting into his sacramental stride, he appears as an ascetic Spanish knight who renounces the leprous world and takes cover in a convent.

Such exploits cannot but leave their mark on a man. If he is half an actor (and Mr. Wolfit is all actor), he will begin insensibly 'to live his parts'. Thrice persecuted in fiction, he may come to believe that someone is persecuting him in fact.

. . . Mr. Wolfit, whom I welcome herewith to 'the Method', has taken a parallel course. On his instructions I received no seats for the first night of his new production. From this, what could I deduce but that he regarded me as his persecutor? He had cast me, so to speak, as the blameless wife. Flattered, I took the slap quietly. Falling in with his fantasy, I made no complaint, but slunk into the theatre as the paying guest of a friend. I cannot, however, continue with the imposture. If it will help Mr. Wolfit's performance, I am prepared to snarl and hiss at him in private, but my heart will not be in it. My gratitude is too great; for Mr. Wolfit is the first London manager to have staged one of M. de Montherlant's plays.

After a lengthy, and somewhat unfavourable, analysis of the play, the critic concluded:

A critic less engaged than I might have judged Mr. Wolfit's performance too bluntly combative, too emphatic in its humility; might have suspected that he liked to play saints because saints do not need to make intimate contact with other human beings, including actors. I prefer to felicitate him on his restraint: he is as still as a rock . . . Mr. Wolfit, as an actor, is far more than middling. I would say he was topping.

Despite the snide praise and humility worthy of Uriah Heep, Wolfit was encouraged by the review and sent Tynan tickets for *Malatesta;* he regretted it.

In *Malatesta*, de Montherlant explored villainy, in the conflict created between the Lord of Rimini and the Pope, played by Ernest Milton, whom he plans to kill with his own dagger. Accused of heresy, parricide and incest, Malatesta demanded and received Wolfit's relish for evil. In the great scene between the would-be assassin and his intended victim, both actors were given scope to develop their highly individual styles. Milton gave a gloriously baroque interpretation of the subtle, devious Pope. 'Malatesta and pity'? he asked. 'Malatesta and *pity*? The two words *swear*!'—and in his mouth, they did.

Tynan began his review:

With Olivier careering through it at full ironic tilt Henry de Montherlant's *Malatesta* could be a gorgeous mouthful of acting. I have said that the play needs Olivier . . . Mr. Wolfit . . . is not really the actor for Malatesta, whose kaleidoscopic mind he reduces to a few bold and primary colours.

Wolfit was, understandably, incensed and searched for a means of attack. He decided that he needed an ally, and who better than Olivier himself? He wrote to his colleague and asked him to take action against the critic.

Olivier and Wolfit did not know each other well. Their theatrical paths never crossed, except occasionally at charity matinées or gala performances, but they were both members of the Garrick Club, and met there from time to time.

They had, however, exchanged letters, and on similar matters. In April 1944, Beverley Baxter, the drama critic of the *Evening Standard*, and an admirer of both men, reported that Olivier had expressed a disparaging opinion of Wolfit's Lear. Olivier wrote to the critic:

Dear Mr. Baxter,

I was reading your article in the Evening Standard last night with great interest when, to my horror, I came upon a completely untrue reference to myself regarding Mr. Wolfit's 'King Lear'.

The truth is that I have not, as yet, had the pleasure of seeing this performance and have therefore never expressed any opinion about it.

Whatever it was you heard was idle tittle-tattle and, I feel, should have been treated as such by you and not published to my (and others') cost so regardless of its veracity. It is not my custom to express my opinions about my colleagues' work publicly, any more than it is to write angry letters to the press!

However as custom has been forsworn in the one instance, it must be forgone in the other.

I share, as I am sure most of his colleagues do, your respect for the work that Mr. Wolfit does, and your enthusiasm for his success, but I deplore that you should think it necessary to provoke unpleasant feelings in our profession in order to provoke interest in your views about it.

I should be most grateful if you would kindly put this matter to rights.

> Yours sincerely,
> Laurence Olivier.

And to Wolfit:

Dear Mr. Wolfit,

I was most distressed to see the reference to myself, and others, in Beverly Baxter's (otherwise interesting) article on your season last night.

I am enclosing a copy of my letter to him, and the hope that it may put the matter to rights.

I am looking forward greatly to seeing your 'King Lear'—as soon as I can get in!

Please accept my apologies for this 'incident' & accept my best congratulations on your triumphant success.

> Yours sincerely,
> Laurence Olivier.

The unsolicited action by Olivier endeared him to Wolfit, and from that moment on he regarded him with uneasy awe and admiration. Grudgingly, Wolfit acknowledged Olivier's position as the leading member of the theatrical profession. Michael Redgrave reported, though the story is unconfirmed, that, meeting one day in the Garrick Club shortly after Olivier had triumphed as Oedipus, Richard III and Hotspur at the New Theatre, Wolfit said, 'Hello, Larry. Liked your Button-Moulder,' which was Olivier's smallest part in that distinguished season. On another occasion, when *Lear* was being discussed, Wolfit shook his head sadly, as if he regretted what he had to say: 'Not Larry's part, I fear,' and then added, deepening his voice to its lowest register, 'You see, Lear's a bass part; Larry's a tenor,' a point he had culled from Agate who did not admire Olivier's Lear. ('Wolfit's Lear is a ruined piece of nature; Olivier's is a picture of ruins most cunningly presented.')

Another unconfirmed story suggests that, while on tour, Wolfit noticed a large queue circling a cinema in expectation of Olivier's film of *Henry V*. Wolfit is reported to have crossed the street and harangued the crowd, informing them that 'your time would be better spent in watching a *living* performance of Shakespeare!'

In 1957, after Tynan's notice of *Malatesta*, Olivier was distressed that his name should have been used as an instrument of a review unfavourable to a colleague. He received Wolfit's request for action with sympathy. His reply reveals an approach to public affairs that Wolfit would have profited by, had he had the temperament to pursue it:

I don't read Master Tynan myself, but what he had said was shown me by friends, who did so, I am sure I need not tell you, in a spirit of nothing but outraged indignation.

I did actually get down to writing to Tynan today before reading yours—and endeavoured to do what I could to point out the error of his ways. It was the first letter I have ever written to a dramatic critic, so you may judge that I felt strongly moved.

I did not make it a public letter as it is against my principles to cross swords with the bastards—at least in public—(I only hit Agate once in the stalls of a darkened theatre!).

But I am thinking now that this line of action was not perhaps strong enough to do you much good or to have very much effect really. But I hesitate to do anything more formal or would-be impressive because I feel sure this fellow exults in that sort of thing and only makes capital out of it. But if you would like me to I will have a go.

Please believe me that I regret most deeply that my name should have been used to do you any harm or cause you any aggravation.

Yours in genuine regard and sympathy,

Larry.

But the need for further action on Olivier's part proved unnecessary. Wolfit announced his retirement from actor-management during the run of *Malatesta*. The growing economic pressures made it impossible for him to continue. He broke the news during his speech at the final curtain to a theatre less than half full. Sad and dispirited, he returned to Swift Cottage and viewed the future with trepidation; the way of life he had followed for twenty years was, by necessity, to be denied him. But his spirits were shortly to revive, when, for the second time in his career, he received a letter from 10 Downing Street.

CHAPTER SIXTEEN

A Personal View

Admit me Chorus to this history.
—Henry V

I

IN May 1957, shortly after *Malatesta* closed at the Lyric Theatre, Hammersmith, I was taken ill; Wolfit, quite wrongly, felt in part responsible for having worked me too hard as actor, business manager, dresser and general understudy. When it became known to him that I was not well, he bustled around and, with his well-known energy, arranged for me to convalesce at 'Redroofs', the former home in Berkshire of Ivor Novello, then used as a place of convalescence for actors. For two or three weeks I luxuriated there, and was soon on the mend; from time to time, Wolfit telephoned to enquire after me, and then invited me to complete my convalescence at Swift Cottage; he also wanted me to assist at a summer party he had arranged for Thursday 13 June.

Dutifully, on Wednesday the 12th, I travelled by bus across country and arrived at Hurstbourne Tarrant in mid-afternoon. Rosalind was alone in the garden; Wolfit was up in London, but due to return to the country that evening. One did not need to be particularly perceptive to sense that she was nervous and ill-at-ease. Each time the telephone rang, which it did often, it seemed to alarm her unnecessarily. Try as I might to keep conversation lively, it was not difficult to obtain the impression that her mind was elsewhere. At last, she could obviously bear the strain no longer: she confessed she had something to tell me. Taking me by the hand, she led me into the cottage, into Wolfit's study, opened his desk and took from it a letter headed 10 Downing Street: Wolfit had been recommended for a knighthood. Attached to the communication was his reply:

Sir,
  I have received your letter of May 10th conveying to me the information that the Prime Minister has it in mind to submit my name to the Queen with a recommendation that Her Majesty may

be graciously pleased to approve that the Honour of Knighthood be conferred upon me.

Will you assure the Prime Minister that I am most deeply moved that this mark of Her Majesty's favour should be bestowed on me and that I shall always regard it as an honour to the British Theatre which it has been my endeavour to serve throughout my life.

As we stood together, like naughty children, reading the letters, I found myself deeply moved. Rosalind swore me to secrecy: on no account was I to tell her husband that she had let me in on their auspicious secret.

The reason for the conspiracy of silence had its roots in a story that a well-known actor had received a similar letter from the Prime Minister, had given a party to celebrate the event, only to search in vain for his name when the Honours List was eventually published. The words 'Private and Confidential' on the Prime Minister's writing paper were to be taken seriously. Indeed, when Wolfit read the letter in London, he telephoned to Rosalind to tell her, with utmost caution, that he had received a communication from 'a house off Whitehall'. Asked to explain, he went as far as saying, very quickly, 'Downing Street' but no more, leaving his wife in a state of confused excitement.

With the letters safely returned to the desk, Rosalind set off by car to meet the London train and, in due course, returned with the conquering hero. He alighted from the motor car, held out his arms to me, but as I approached, he suddenly bent down and pulled half-a-dozen weeds from the cobbled drive; then, we embraced. At once, he and Rosalind retired to the study to confer, leaving me in an adjoining room. It being a small cottage, with thin walls, I heard some of what was said, principally Rosalind's final injunction that he should tell me his news. He muttered something in reply, then called me in. With a huge wink, Rosalind left the room to prepare supper.

He sat at his desk, in his Hamlet chair, I on a settle that had done yeoman service in many a play. He began on a low note, with long pauses between words.

'Ronald . . . I have something to tell you . . . something of import-ance. . . . Can you guess . . . what it is?'

I, playing my part well, suggested a lucrative film contract.

The idea amused him. 'A contract?' he repeated, smiling gently. 'Yes, I suppose you could call it that . . . a contract . . . for *life*.' He nodded as if to imply a wearisome burden. There followed the longest pause of the conversation, as he thought how best to phrase the news. Using his most reverent tones, he said gravely, 'Her Majesty the Queen . . . has seen fit . . . to convey upon me . . . an honour . . . in tomorrow's Birthday Honours List.'

Jumping the gun a little, I cried, 'A knighthood'?

Another long pause, before he replied, 'We don't know yet.' He was determined to maintain the drama for as long as possible, or else he wanted me to think that he was in line for a Peerage. Whatever his intentions, it was a sombre moment.

After dinner, we talked of theatrical honours, consulting *Who's Who in the Theatre* to examine the long list of previous recipients. It was then I noticed that, of living actors, he was the only one to be honoured twice, being already the holder of the C.B.E. His head shot round at the discovery. 'Bless my soul!' he declared, 'does that make me senior?' and, by some quirk of the rules of precedence, I believe it did.

The next morning I awoke early to hear the six o'clock news bulletin and, fortunately, there had been no security leak: on the list of Knights Bachelor was the name Donald Wolfit, actor-manager. I took tea in to them, and greeted them by their new titles; neither could stop smiling. Shortly afterwards, the telephone rang and continued to do so for the remainder of that day. Telegrams poured in from all over the world. Soon his children arrived and, in mid-afternoon, there occurred a moment which is my own fondest memory of him. We were all sitting on the lawn having tea, when he suddenly lay back, kicked his feet up in the air, pedalled furiously and cried in a broad Nottinghamshire accent, 'Oh! If only me Mum and Dad could see me now!'

Part Four

SIR DONALD

1957–1968

CHAPTER SEVENTEEN

Guinness and Grapes

*To babble and to talk is most tolerable
and not to be endured.*
  —Much Ado About Nothing

I

THE Old Warrior had achieved his lifelong ambition and he
revelled in it: he joined the Imperial Society of Knights Bachelor
obtained a coat of arms (motto: *Lupus pilium mutat:* The Wolf
changes its coat) from the College of Heralds, and commissioned
Keith Train, the genealogist, to trace his family tree. During a court
case, in which he was unsuccessfully sued for breach of contract by
a young actor, the Judge asked with a twinkle, 'And is the *Mr.*
Donald Wolfit mentioned in the depositions the same *Sir* Donald
Wolfit who is in Court today?' Counsel replied, 'Yes, your honour.
He was knighted in the New Year Honours List.' Wolfit half-rose in
his place. 'Birthday Honours,' he corrected, 'Birthday Honours.' To
his surprise he found himself regarded as a member of the theatrical
establishment, still an outsider, but undeniably respectable. He was
surprised, too, to learn that, among the ranks of his profession at
least, he had become something of a legend. 'Really? Do they
really tell stories about me?' he asked: they did indeed.

Any man who had struggled and fought as he did would be bound
to develop reserves of character, strength, resourcefulness that would
enable him to survive. In Wolfit's case, these qualities were exaggerated because, as we have seen, even from youth, he appeared to
others 'larger than life', which, coupled with a natural pomposity,
fierceness, grandeur, passion and, at times, a genuine humility, made
it possible for him to say and do things that were outrageously funny
and, at the same time, deeply endearing. Wolfit was not a wit;
more often than not, he never realised the effect of what he said; it
was true he loved nothing better than to tell theatrical tales, but of
the woes and joys, the eccentricities and waywardness of heroes long
dead; in his own case, the tales were told by others.

To his audience, undoubtedly, the moment outside the play to be enjoyed most, was his curtain-call. No matter how long or short the part, Wolfit took his solo call with precisely the same degree of utter mental and physical exhaustion. He could be bellowing at an actor for ruining a scene just as he was due to step out before the audience; the moment his turn came, a blanket of weariness seemed to overcome him, and banging the curtain with his hand, he would slowly make his way, through the gap, into the light. There, he would hold on to the curtain with his right hand, bow low, his left hand cocked behind him. Peter Cotes continues the story:

> Before he actually spoke and the applause was at its loudest, he would slowly raise, as though with great effort, a frail and tired hand in an undemanding appeal for silence, the while a rather sickly, grateful smile appeared on his face (as though this was a tremendous effort, too). Obviously, this was a sacrosanct moment, the induction to a climax of almost religious intensity. After the struggle to remain upstanding with one hand on the curtain for support, DW divested himself of every bit of fatigue; he was martial as, with that well-known pose (Christ on his way to Calvary), he declaimed his thanks; the noble indignation rising, his eye, all bespoke the virtuous hero—a man alone up there on the stage, albeit warmed by his audience down there in the auditorium. By the time he had finished that speech, his face already running with sweat . . . he bowed his way back through the opening in the curtain.

The departure, too, had about it the air of a Subject leaving a grateful Monarch, a mixture of humility and pride, like Columbus, perhaps, taking his leave of Queen Isabella, after delivering to her the glories of the New World.

Norman Marshall observed the following scene in the foyer of the King's Theatre, Hammersmith: two old ladies who had seen Wolfit play Malvolio that afternoon, and had witnessed, of course, the curtain call, went round to the box office and cancelled their seats for the performance of *King Lear* that evening. They informed the box office manageress that, as they had come all the way from the country, they were deeply disappointed that Mr. Wolfit was not to play Lear that night. The manageress replied that, as far as she knew, Mr. Wolfit had every intention of appearing. The two old ladies said that they doubted it, since he looked far too ill as he took his curtain calls.

To those who had been members of a Wolfit company, the scene in the wings, before Macbeth or Volpone or Lear made his entrance, embodied the Wolfit mystique. There Wolfit would stand, attended by his dresser carrying a silver salver, upon which stood the glass of Guinness, three or four peeled grapes, and the moist chamois leather with which the actor patted his face. The amount of Guinness depended on the part: Lear demanded most, Touchstone least. If the play was *Macbeth*, the Thane of Cawdor could be expected to be in a vile temper as he waited to meet his fate. Wolfit, peering from under his brows, scowling, muttering, was not to be approached. If an actor did, foolishly, come too close to the presence, Wolfit was in the habit of spitting his grape-pips at him, to keep him off.

Many stories spring from the drama backstage during performance. At the King's Hammersmith in 1953, during *New Way To Pay Old Debts*, he was at his most impassioned. The plot turns on a deed of ownership that Sir Giles must produce from an old casket; as he holds up the document, so it must crumble in his hands; being thwarted in this manner, Sir Giles suffers a stroke, falls backwards—in Wolfit's production—on to the shoulders of four stalwart servants, and is carried, dying, through a large door up stage which was closed with a bang by an unseen A.S.M. after the cortège had passed, in order to assist the audience into applauding the leading actor's final exit. (It is said that any noise allied to applause will set an audience off; Fred Terry used to enter, as if warming his hands, but clapping them together loudly the while, thus ensuring his 'entrance round'.) On one particular night, an assistant stage manager, Sally Bussel, had omitted to set the vital document in the casket. Wolfit, as Sir Giles, threw open the lid, expecting to find the deed lying conveniently on top of a pile of smaller bits of paper; it was not there. He growled furiously, rummaged in the casket and took the smallest, meanest piece of paper he could find. Holding it up in both hands, he displayed it to the Prompt Corner and growled once more like an angry dog, continued with the scene, suffered the stroke and fell back on the shoulders of his servants. He was still extremely angry and did not remember to plant his arms firmly by his sides, so that, when the servants reached the door with their precious load, Wolfit stuck, his outstretched arms catching the door frame; the servants backed a few steps and tried once more, this time with some success; the door was banged to, but the 'exit round' did not materialise.

Wolfit was furious; he paced up and down, snarling and muttering. He took his curtain calls with customary exhaustion, and then proceeded to march angrily to his dressing room. Just as he reached the pass door, the offending A.S.M. ran up to him and fell on her knees, terrified. 'Oh, I'm so sorry, Mr. Wolfit', she sobbed, 'I'm so terribly sorry.' Wolfit looked down on the trembling creature, raised his right hand, and cried, 'I absolve you!' and left the stage.

He expected everyone to approach their art with the same seriousness as he did. John Mayes reported that, during a rehearsal of *Macbeth*, a young actor, Nicholas Baker,

. . . took his turn in a queue of processing 'Kings' waiting to take their crowns from a box of props. Each took his crown quickly, for there was no time to make a choice of sizes, and Nicholas's crown was so large that it rested across the bridge of his nose. Wolfit was gabbling, in a casual undertone, Macbeth's lines. Nicholas appeared before him on the line: 'Thy crown doth sear mine eyeballs!' and his boyish grin at the ludicrousness of standing in a crown that was as good as resting on his own eyeballs was quickly effaced by Wolfit's furious cry of: 'IT'S NOT FUNNY, BAKER!!!!'

And from Joseph Chelton:

One night at Belfast, as Othello lay on the floor dying, a young officer knelt over the Moor to make sure that he was well and truly dead. Othello whispered, 'My boy, you must do something about your breath.'

During the final scene of *The Taming of The Shrew*, the company were required to dance and sing round Petruchio and Katherine in celebration of their marriage. Wolfit used a whip as Petrucchio— Ayrton's and Asche's whip. One night, Colin Mann, a young actor, laughed at something or other, which infuriated Wolfit. With terrifying suddenness, he lashed out with his whip, curled it round Mann's arms and pulled: Mann, more surprised than anyone, found himself spinning towards the leading actor, like a top. When they came face to face, Wolfit whispered fiercely, 'Watch it, Mann!' and then allowed him to rejoin the dance.

Wolfit never lost his eagerness and enthusiasm for being on stage, and was often impatient while awaiting his first entrance, awaiting that moment when the audience would greet him with applause, and he, with an almost imperceptible nod, would acknowledge their homage. Perhaps the best first entrance in his repertoire was as Matathias in *The Wandering Jew*, an entrance originally engineered, needless to say, by a master of theatrical effect, Matheson Lang. In the opening scene, Matathias's wife lies dying while her husband is out in the streets of Jerusalem, searching for Jesus who it is hoped will cure her. Ellen Pollock, who played the wife in Wolfit's production, invested the cardboard role with a good deal of agonised breathing that brought a degree of reality to the scene. As the run of the play proceeded—and business fell off alarmingly—Wolfit became more and more impatient to enter. He paced the wings, breathing noisily. One night, when Miss Pollock was acting particularly passionately, Wolfit exclaimed, 'She won't die, you know, not tonight! Not a chance of it! I may as well go home!'

King Lear, of course, was always an auspicious occasion in the repertoire. Most problems stemmed from the storm, which was never loud enough for the actor; he favoured as many devices as possible to simulate the sound of the tempest: a wind machine, a rain machine, two timpani, a large empty water tank beaten with a padded stick, a sound-effects record and the inevitable thunder sheet—a sheet of springy metal suspended from the flies, that, when shaken, gives a remarkably good impression of a thunder-clap. On one occasion, the thunder sheet was being operated by a rather willowy young man. During the course of the performance, the sheet broke its ropes and fell like a guillotine blade, just missing him. The next morning, Wolfit decided to re-rehearse the storm. The young man, hands on hips, stamped his foot petulantly. 'I'm sorry, Mr. Wolfit, I'm not shaking that thing any longer, it nearly cut me in two last night and I'm simply not going to do it!' An expression of surprise that an employee should talk to him in that manner crossed Wolfit's face, which soon gave way to realisation and, with a knowing look, he said accusingly, 'Not man enough, I see . . .'

His dislike of homosexuals was deep-rooted. Joseph Chelton remembered:

> Once the company was stricken with 'flu and a young actor was hurriedly summoned from London to play one of the 'Salads' in the MERCHANT. Shylock was at the wings listening.
>
> > 'Your mind iss tosssing on the ocean,
> > there where your argossssies with
> > portly sssail do . . .'
>
> Shylock heard the tell-tale simper Ss. 'Jo, Jo,' he whispered, 'we've got a nancy in the company.'

Yet, when he was told that one member of his company whom he liked and admired was homosexual, Wolfit replied, 'Yes, but he's quite harmless.'

Ned Sherrin recounted that, during rehearsals of a television play, *Admiral Benbow*, which he and Caryl Brahms had written, they were required to move from one rehearsal room to another. A young actor was deputed to act as chauffeur; Wolfit sat beside him, with Sherrin and Miss Brahms in the back seat. The young man was extremely nervous at having so famous an actor as passenger and, in starting the car, his hand slipped off the gear-lever and landed on Wolfit's thigh. The driver apologised profusely. 'That's all right, my boy,' said Wolfit. 'We're used to that sort of thing in the theatre.'

Wolfit could not bear to be bested in any situation; he had to have the last word. From Joseph Chelton:

> There was a very gaunt, hatchet-faced lad in the company, with an awkward head. During MACBETH he was at the wings with

Donald. Donald scrutinised him, stuck his hand into the back of the lad's wig and it shot up into the darkness. 'The trouble with you, my boy,' he muttered, 'is that you need to learn to put a wig on.'

He was less forthright with senior actors. Llewellyn Rees recalled:

When Wolfit presented 'Lear' at the King's Theatre, Hammersmith, Lewis Casson who had played 'Tiresias' in 'Oedipus' stayed on to play 'Gloucester'.

Wolfit regarded Casson with respect as having been a fellow actor-manager, with awe as being a knight, and with apprehension as being in his opinion something of a communist. He was therefore not anxious to cross swords with him on any matter.

However, during the scene in which Gloucester has his eyes put out Casson did something—I know not what—that met with Wolfit's definite disapproval. Standing in the wings he said emphatically 'Lewis must *not* do that—I must speak to him about it.' But scarcely were these rash words out of his mouth than he realised he was committing himself in the presence of witnesses to a course that must at all costs be avoided. In a flash he saw his way out. It was March 1953. 'Ah, no,' he continued. 'It's too soon after Stalin's death.'

Outside the theatre, Wolfit was capable of uttering opinions and sentiments as if they were quotations from the plays he was performing. He favoured the grand turn of phrase, a confidential, whispered tone of voice. Once, in Leeds, he and a companion were travelling by tram to their digs, after a performance of *The Strong Are Lonely*. A young girl, who was clutching a programme of the play, thrilled at the sight of the actor seated a few feet away. Wolfit was well aware of her and when the time came, he left the tram as quickly as he could. Once on the pavement, he turned to his friend, 'Did you see that, my boy? She tried to touch my garment as I passed!'

Wolfit was ambivalent towards fans: he liked to be recognised but he genuinely found it embarrassing. On a tube train, travelling to Hampstead, a small boy sat beside him. ''Ere,' said the boy, 'You're Donald Wolfit, incha?' Wolfit looked at him, startled, then in a voice of thunder, cried 'No . . . !' At a cocktail party, a very gushing 'county' woman cornered him. 'Oh, I do think you're so clever the way you play eight parts in a week. I can't think why you don't get mixed up. Why, for example, when you're playing Lear, don't you speak bits of Hamlet?' 'Madam,' Wolfit replied sternly, 'if you are invited to play golf you do not take your tennis racket.'

He was a tireless giver of advice, especially about matters concerning the fair sex. He cautioned Joseph Chelton: 'Chelton, keep away from the women. They'll sap your energies to buggery!' To another young actor, who had just returned from his honeymoon, he said, 'Go carefully, my boy. Seven times a night's enough for any man.' When walking one evening with a companion in Chelsea, he paused before a house, pointed and said, 'Let that be a lesson to you, my boy: a scene of a former fornication!'

He liked to caution other actors, no matter how eminent. In the Garrick Club he met Marius Goring who informed him that he was shortly to play Fool to Michael Redgrave's Lear at Stratford. Wolfit received the news with interest. 'Have you made up your mind whose play it's going to be?' he enquired airily. Goring asked what he meant. Wolfit explained that the play was a contest between the two parts; Goring replied that was not the way either Redgrave or he approached their work. Wolfit said no more, but the next day found himself sitting beside Redgrave at luncheon. Redgrave remembered the conversation:

WOLFIT: I hear you're going to play Lear at Stratford, Michael.

REDGRAVE: Yes, I am, Donald.

WOLFIT: Who's your Fool?

REDGRAVE: Marius Goring.

WOLFIT: (eyebrows and voice raised) Who???

REDGRAVE: Marius Goring. You know him, Donald, he's a fellow member of this club.

(A PAUSE)

WOLFIT: Be careful.

REDGRAVE: The truth is, Donald, that I am very delighted he's going to play it. He's had a very heavy season, what with Richard III and Petruchio, and I have had to use all my powers of persuasion to get him to do it.

WOLFIT: All I said was 'be careful'. The best Fool I ever had was a man called Bryan Johnson, and that was because he loved me both as a man and as an actor. (A VERY LONG PAUSE) Funny fellow: he's gone into cabaret.

Wolfit worshipped Royalty and the aristocracy and favoured using their full titles when referring to them. During one evening in the Garrick, he suddenly broke off in mid-sentence, half-rose in his chair, bowed to an elderly man who was leaving the room, then explained to his guest: 'Lord Evershed, former Master of the Rolls,' and continued his conversation. He hardly ever failed to say 'Her Majesty the Queen' when the Sovereign was under discussion, and sometimes even 'Her Gracious Majesty the Queen'. But after his knighthood he would venture 'Buck House' for the Palace, and 'Philip' for the Duke of Edinburgh. Nothing thrilled him more than when he was invited to lunch at Buck House. 'There I was,' he began, 'sitting next to the highest power in the land . . . '.

When his old friend Sir St. Vincent Troubridge, Bart., died, Wolfit was asked the cause. 'His hand seized up like a claw,' he explained dramatically, with attendant gesture; then added confidentially, 'It's a disease that attacks aristocrats.'

Of course, his knighthood prompted further flights of grandeur. Meeting Robert Speaight, who had just been awarded the C.B.E., Wolfit complained that his knighthood was costing him a good deal of additional expense. He concluded, 'I expect you find the same thing, don't you, Bobby, in your own small way?'

He was well known for petty meanness. Whenever possible he used writing paper to which he was entitled but for which he did not have to pay: the Garrick Club or the Royal General Theatrical Fund (of which he was the President) were favourites. He was also known not to waste used envelopes, sometimes sticking labels over the address, and was always careful to remove, for future use, unfranked stamps.

On occasion, he employed his meanness to gain an added advantage. In Von Kleist's *The Broken Jug* he played the Magistrate who is guilty of the crime he is trying. During the course of the play, a lunch recess occurs; the Magistrate and a visiting Councillor, played by George Curzon, have a comedy scene downstage, while the witnesses, one of whom was played by Nan Munro, eat their lunch up stage. Miss Munro had apples in her lunch basket and, at one performance, took a bite—Wolfit reproduced the biting sound gutturally as 'CHWAP'—that damaged a laugh Wolfit had hoped for. The next morning he strode into his manager's office. 'How much are we spending on apples?' he demanded. The manager consulted his files. 'Three and six a week,' he replied. 'Too much. Cut them. I'm not paying three and six a week for her to go CHWAP—CHWAP—and kill my laughs!'

He could, on occasions, compound financial waste as follows: 'Three and six a week on apples—call it four shillings—that's sixteen shillings a month—call it a pound—that's three pounds a quarter—call it five: twenty pounds a year on apples!' But he was extremely proud of his thrift: when I, as a Trustee of the Settlement that formed part of his Estate, congratulated him on the amount involved, he replied, 'Yes, not bad for a touring mummer!'

His secretary in 1953, Imogen Matthews, offered the opinion, ' . . . I don't think basically he was a mean man at all. He was terrifically warm-hearted and kind, and I think he was very nervous of business matters and always thought he was going to be had by the more sophisticated people around him.'

In the manner of her engagement by Wolfit, she revealed the actor's curious prejudices and impulsiveness: 'I had the impression that he engaged me because I had a Shakespearean name and because I didn't want to be an actress.' Another of his yardsticks when judging people was, 'Never trust a man if you can see his bottom teeth when he smiles,' which made him uneasy about Edward Heath's leadership of the Conservative Party.

As has been noted, he saw nothing at fault with his company's wardrobe and settings. From Llewellyn Rees:

> Donald's classical wardrobe had seen better days by the time he engaged Ellen Pollock to play 'Regan' [1953]. She donned the costume provided and came to Donald's dressing room for his approval. 'Well?' said Donald. 'Well' said Ellen, 'it's your costume, Donald, but don't you think the shoulders need lifting a little?' 'Yes,' said Donald, 'ask Jean [the wardrobe mistress] to do it.' And then to himself as Ellen left the room: 'Funny—it used to fit.'

His advice to K. Edmunds Gateley, an amateur actor and producer, regarding stage goblets:

> Goblets: get some small enamel basins. Put them on wooden pedestals and paint 'em gold. That's what *we* do!

His padding for Falstaff was a monstrous piece of old-fashioned engineering. Hot, heavy and Gothic, it caused the actor to sweat mercilessly. Between matinée and evening performance it would be hung from the flies with a powerful light shining on to it, in the hope that the heat would dry it. But the worst drawback of the padding was that it had to be removed entirely if the actor was to relieve himself during the performance. Falstaff, luckily, is off-stage for some length of time during the course of the play, and this provided Wolfit with the necessary opportunity. 'Brilliant craftsman, Shakespeare. Knew the actor would want to pee and constructed the play accordingly. A master, a master!'

Illness, or suspected illness, revealed another side to the actor's personality. He was hardly ever ill, and hardly ever missed a performance. He took great care of his voice, and was terrified of draughts, but Norman Punt, for many years the leading ear, nose and throat specialist to the theatrical profession, wrote: 'Donald had a magnificent vocal organ. . . . In over 25 years he needed my laryngological services remarkably seldom.'

On one occasion, he developed a lump behind his right knee and consulted his friend, George McNab, the surgeon. McNab advised a minor operation to remove it. Wolfit could not have been more pleased. 'I'm going in for a minor op,' he would say, but as if to imply that there was, in fact, something more seriously wrong with him. When the appointed day came, Rosalind packed an attaché case and accompanied him to the hospital. Sister Proctor, their friend, asked Wolfit to wait while she went off to fetch McNab. When the surgeon joined them, he decided to examine the lump once more; it had disappeared; there was no need to operate. Wolfit was furious, and left the hospital, muttering.

When it was thought he had ulcers, he underwent a full examination that included a barium meal and X-rays. The plates were developed, revealing a healthy, normal stomach. Wolfit thumped the table. 'I don't believe it!' he cried.

But Wolfit was undoubtedly at his best when being obstinate and irrational. Peter Cotes remembered that after a lunch-time break during *The Master Builder* at the Westminster Theatre, he and the Wolfits returned to find one of the actresses requesting permission to go home. Cotes took her aside and asked the reason; she explained it was the time of her menstrual period. Cotes allowed her to leave and then passed the explanation on to Wolfit. The actor-manager shook his head disapprovingly. 'Dame Madge Kendal never bothered with that sort of thing,' he said.

Early one Sunday morning a week-end guest at Swift Cottage discovered his host dressed in a sombre suit. 'I am going to take Holy Communion,' Wolfit explained. The guest asked if that were permissible, since Wolfit was a divorcé. 'I don't believe in that nonsense,' replied Wolfit. 'That's all St. Paul, and he was an epileptic!'

As has already been suggested, he was quick to cry 'conspiracy' when things went wrong. In *King Lear*, he played the storm scene standing against an eighteen-foot obelisk, which required holding in position by a man standing behind it, and thus hidden from the audience. Just before the Coronation, in 1953, the task was carried out by a patriotic stage-hand who had begun to celebrate the forthcoming event somewhat in advance of others. On the line 'Strike flat the thick rotundity o' the world!' the stage-hand hiccoughed and lurched forward, causing the obelisk to strike hard the back of Wolfit's head. The actor, being enormously strong, finished the scene supporting both the obelisk and the patriot, by then paralytic. When Wolfit came into the wings, he was limping (the bump on his head was concealed by his wig and he did like his injuries to be *seen*). With furtive glances over his shoulder, the madness of Lear still upon him, he cried hoarsely at his stage director, 'Pam, Pam, Binkie Beaumont has sent men to kill me!'

An illustration of his changing moods outside and inside the

theatre occurred one summer's day in 1966, when he was playing
Barrett in the musical *Robert and Elizabeth* at the Lyric Theatre,
London. Together, we sat in the Pavilion at Lord's watching the
West Indians play the M.C.C., Clifford Mollison one side of him, I
the other. The talk was of cricket and cricketers; he allowed no
mention of the theatre, for he was singular in his pleasures. His mood
was warm, gentle, almost euphoric. He told the following story:
Len Hutton, when Captain of England, and Reg Simpson, the
Nottinghamshire opener, resumed England's innings after the
luncheon interval in a Test Match against Australia. Simpson faced
the first ball which he flashed at, and just missed giving a chance to
second slip. Hutton was furious. He strode down the wicket and
enquired, 'What the hell d'you think you're doing? This isn't a game,
you know!' Wolfit raised a hand to quell our laughter. 'But he's
quite right, you see. I should have said the same thing!' Then, he
laughed too. 'Dear God, I'd have been hell to bat with!' Towards
five o'clock we prepared to leave the ground. As we were passing
the Tavern, we stopped to talk to two friends, Harold Pinter and
Kenneth Haigh; Wolfit chatted charmingly and we continued on our
way. We neared the car park, he paused, looked up at the blue sky
and, full of good will, declared 'Ah! Fine fellows, fine fellows!'
Thereafter, he said little more, but it was easily discernible that he
was beginning to prepare himself mentally for the evening performance: his chin thrust forward, his brows furrowed. I parked the car
and walked with him to the stage door. On the steps, he paused,
turned and said, 'Well, I see Larry's on to a good thing at the
National. Good-bye!' and walked inside.

It was to be expected that if business fell off unaccountably,
Wolfit, like all men of the theatre, would search for reasons; the
weather, a Royal demise, Thursday nights ('people fill in their pool
coupons, you know'), the broadcast of a classic play by the B.B.C.,
all found their way into his catalogue of explanations. From Llewellyn Rees:

In my dual capacity as actor and company administrator I used,
during the run of 'The Strong Are Lonely' at the Theatre Royal,
Haymarket, to look in at Donald's dressing room after the performance each evening to say 'goodnight'. On one of these
occasions, during a particularly cold spell, Donald beckoned me
in and said, 'Llewellyn, do you think the B.B.C. are exaggerating
the weather reports to make people stay at home to watch T.V.?'
'Donald,' I said, 'the B.B.C. don't make up the weather reports;
they get them from the meteorological office.' Donald gave me a
knowing look as though I could hardly be naïve enough to believe

what I was saying and proceeded 'and this year we've got a long Lent against us.' 'Donald,' I said, 'this is something I do know about; Lent is 40 days from Ash Wednesday to Easter and it can't be longer or shorter.' 'Ah,' said Donald, 'this year they've got Passion Sunday as well as Palm Sunday.' It was useless to point out that this was standard practice. Donald was inclined to suspect a malevolent fate or a human conspiracy behind any fall in business.

Of these tales, and many others, the Wolfit legend was born.

CHAPTER EIGHTEEN

Full Circle

Winter tames man, woman and beast.
—The Taming of the Shrew

I

THE last ten years of the new knight's career were motivated by the same driving force that had dominated the first ten: the saving of money, but with a different end in view: he was determined to provide for his old age or, in the event of his death, Rosalind's widowhood. With much the same absence of selectivity as he had displayed in the 1930s, he accepted everything and anything that was offered: television, films, broadcasts. He was as busy as he had ever been, working and saving. But this activity was also symptomatic of the changes taking place in the theatre, changes that would make it increasingly difficult for him to find an important place.

In February 1958, he appeared once more as Solness in *The Master Builder* on B.B.C. television, with Mai Zetterling as Hilde and Catherine Lacey as his wife, but he was formulating plans for the theatre. Having announced his retirement, he now decided that, because of his knighthood, he was entitled to reap some benefit from the honour. Secretly, he wanted to make a triumphal tour of the provinces in celebration and confessed that, if it were possible, nothing would please him better than to venture forth once more with a Shakespearean repertoire; but, as he well knew, those days could not be recalled; he chose, instead, to present a double-bill: Von Kleist's *The Broken Jug* and, as curtain-raiser, *The Court Singer* by Frank Wedekind; the public did not respond.

In Nottingham, Wolfit was taken ill with pneumonia, but continued to appear in the Von Kleist play, although he was persuaded to allow an understudy to substitute for him in the curtain-raiser. It was one of the few occasions, under his own management that he had failed to keep faith with his public. Once, in Dublin, he was too ill to play Shylock at a matinée. Joseph Chelton deputised. When his business manager entered the sick-room, Wolfit asked in a pained whisper, 'How was the boy?' 'Wonderful, Donald,' replied the manager. Wolfit struggled up on one elbow, gasping, 'I play . . . *to-night*!' In similar circumstances, at the matinée of *The Court Singer* in Nottingham, he watched the understudy play the love scene with Rosalind; he stood in the wings, wrapped in his pink dressing gown, thinking he could not be seen.

The brief illness was the first sign that the old war horse was weakening; the fires that had raged so furiously for so long were gradually being subdued; but only those, like Rosalind, closest to him, noticed.

Wolfit was never one to rest. Long periods of enforced quiet only served to make him uneasy, so that when a convalescence was suggested in Kenya—where his sister Eva lived—he decided to make it a working holiday and fell back on a good old stand-by: the dramatic recital. With Rosalind, he prepared a programme of extracts from their Shakespearean repertoire and, on 31 December 1958, flew to Nairobi. They gave a week of recitals and collected, according to his accounts book, £1,509 gross. Since he was in Africa, Wolfit saw no reason why the visit should not be extended: from Nairobi he flew to Addis Ababa where they were presented to the Emperor Haile Selassie and the Crown Prince; their Royal hosts showered the visiting actors with gifts. Wolfit was immensely proud of those souvenirs, especially of a gold and silver cigarette case which bore the Emperor's crest. On his return to London, he and Rosalind celebrated with dinner at the Caprice, and, as they entered, spied Alan Webb, the actor, dining with a companion. Without preamble, Wolfit whipped out the cigarette case and said, 'Hello, Alan. Look what the Emperor of Ethiopia gave me.'

After a television production of *Volpone*, which recorded one of his finest performances, Wolfit, in September 1959, appeared in a play by Cecil Beaton, *Landscape with Figures*, playing the painter Thomas Gainsborough at the Dublin Festival. Once more the fashionable and unfashionable clashed. Wolfit wanted re-writes, according to the popular press. Beaton made 'no comment'; the two did not speak; Beaton demanded an apology from Wolfit and, not surprisingly, Wolfit demanded an apology from Beaton. Wolfit left the cast.

The actor-knight was growing restless again. The days of service appeared to be over; there seemed to be no way of using himself to some higher purpose, for although he enjoyed earning money, he did not feel fully committed to his work unless he could discern some value in it. Furthermore, he could not bear to be still; touring was a life-long habit he found hard to break, for he was used to a life of constant, shifting movement. What could he find now to do that would satisfy his restlessness and his need for worthy occupation?

He soon solved the puzzle: a tour was the obvious answer, and to places where there was a paucity of dramatic entertainment on a high cultural level. On 23 December 1959, the Wolfits set off. Their itinerary was as follows:

> Oklahoma City—Vancouver—Victoria Island—San Francisco—New Zealand (six weeks)—Adelaide—Kuala Lumpur—Penang—Singapore—New Delhi—Bombay—Bahrein—Kuwait—Abadan—Beirut.

If it was not like the old days, at least they could claim to be taking Shakespeare on a journey of nearly 29,000 miles, taking him once more to the people albeit in condensed form. He returned, refreshed, in mid-April 1960. By May, he was in rehearsal for a mystery play, *Stranger in the Tea*, which opened out of London but did not reach the West End.

II

Wolfit's personality was perceptibly more tranquil than in days of old and, doubtless, the reason was that he enjoyed immeasurably his newly-won status as an actor-knight. Wherever he went, be it Kuala Lumpur or Edinburgh, Vancouver or New Delhi, he was being welcomed as an old friend, with affection and honour. Even the tone of the press altered: he was no longer 'the Shakespearean actor' but 'one of our leading actors', no longer 'fine' but 'great'. Unfashionable or not, Wolfit discovered that knighthood extracted from others unaccustomed respect, and he was deeply gratified.

His existence outside his professional activities was bound by three distinct strands: first, his life with Rosalind at Swift Cottage. The couple, who had been through so much together, preferred their own company to any· others'. Rosalind was heavily dependent on him, and he interested himself in every aspect of her life; even when buying clothes he would accompany her and advise. They took pleasure in similar pursuits, chiefly reflected in their love and care of the garden, and their pet geese, Pyramus and Thisbe, and their chickens whose laying habits Wolfit scrutinised and recorded with as much keenness as if he were studying theatre returns.

He recaptured some of the lightness of his younger days; he sang his music-hall songs, recited his long comic poems, and in the evenings made egg-cosies out of felt for the children of friends. A joke the Wolfits shared was the road-sign warning: LOOSE CHIPPINGS which they accounted a good name for a touring actor. 'Loose Chippings is playing at Hurstbourne Tarrant, I see. Poor fellow, fallen on hard times, I fear.'

His family, too, was a source of pleasure. Harriet had given birth to two sons, Charles and Matthew, and in January 1961, Adam, a professional photographer, married Penelope Paul; they too produced children, Gabrielle and Christian. Margaret was pursuing her career as an actress and was shortly to marry Stanley Amis, an architect. Wolfit, in every way, was mellowing with the years.

The second strand in his life was woven round a large grey building near Leicester Square: the Garrick Club. Wolfit treasured every moment he spent in the place; it was his home from home. He had been elected in 1942, and used the Club regularly for lunch and, when alone in London, for dinner. He always wore the club tie—cucumber green and salmon pink stripes—whether or not it matched his suits. If ever he wanted to celebrate a special occasion, or simply entertain family and friends, he took a private room and feasted them royally. He was a popular member, a 'good club man'. He had ever had few close friends, but in the Garrick he possessed countless acquaintances who held him in genuine affection. He was particularly fond of the staff, and treated them with the same courtesy he reserved for his fellow-members. In letters, he referred to 'the dear club' and in a speech on the occasion of the Garrick Street building's centenary, he expressed all that it meant to him:

... Born in a small provincial town—uneducated at the local grammar school and with one ambition only—to become an actor—what should I say to such an assembly of wits and brains—to a surfeit of judges, an anatomy of surgeons, a sell-out of publishers and a gathering of wealthy patrons of the art which *alone entitles* them to be a member of this club and which was founded—so I understand—so that actors might have the opportunity of meeting and talking to gentlemen of quality—and so as your *very humble servant* I want to speak *for all my profession* and to thank you for all the *generosity and kindness* you have shown to us since this club moved into its present premises one hundred years ago. I think perhaps that few of you realise what it means to an actor to be made a member of this club—how *terrified* we are of it all in the first years of our membership and what an *inspiration* it is to be allowed within these portals. There, at the foot of the staircase is the awful warning of Irving himself—'*not elected*'—everlasting disgrace to the man who is unacceptable and what a difference it might have made to Irving's whole career if Anthony Trollope had not taken the trouble to do what he did and write that letter to him asking him to take courage and try again.

How I managed to slip in I do not know but by the grace of God I did and the reputation of my sponsors of which Ashley Dukes was one—and behold I found myself surrounded by my *ancestors of the theatre*—men who had borne the heat and burden of the day in the great classic roles.

He then paid tribute to the actors of the past whose portraits adorn the walls of the Club. He continued:

. . . In my green and salad days here, the towering figure of Allan Aynsworth guarded the portals—the terror of all actors who applied for membership . . . and well do I remember my first solo entry on a dark and murky November noon when, like the battle of Bosworth, the sun refused to shine on Richard before the Battle—I mounted the stairs—passed through the swing doors with trembling knees and heard the great resonant voice pontificating from the fireplace in the snuggery: 'Of course there are no actors nowadays—the actor of today does not know how to *walk the stage*. We learnt that with Sarah Thorne at Margate. He does not know how to stand or move and he is in the main inaudible.'

Terror seized me and I rushed across the corridor—through the service door—collided with a waiter with a tray of glasses—back again—hung up my hat and coat—didn't even know where the toilet was and couldn't ask—the voice went on and on about actors and acting—I rushed across the snuggery again and fled up the stairs into the darkness until I came face to face with Master Betty as Norval who seemed to give me courage somehow, for I halted—removed the sweat from my brow and slunk down the stairs again, turning to the left this time, and so reached the smoking room where I lowered a very large brandy and soda. . . . It is a place *with magic* in it . . . it is the *Mermaid Tavern of the Century* for here sat Irving and Tree, Alexander and Pinero over *late suppers*—no walking half a mile to a parked car and walking unsteadily home—the brougham was fetched by the porter and one went home like a *gentleman*—as an actor should—full of wine and good fellowship.

In his peroration he welcomed the admission of ladies to the Club in the evenings, and ended with a favourite quotation from *The Tempest*:

> We are such things as dreams are made on,
> And our little life is rounded with a sleep.

The love of the Club is evident, but the speech also reveals the expansive side of Wolfit's nature, the warmth, the good-will. It was a side of his personality that Peter Cotes recalled when, years after their professional association, they met in London at a dinner. Afterwards,

. . . we had found ourselves marching arm in arm down Covent Garden about 11.00. Passing the Savage Club, then based in King Street, I invited him in for a 'night cap', despite his protests at not being allowed to take me to the Garrick; instead I inveigled him into my Club, where we sat drinking until the bar was closed and the door was locked against all comers. D. regaled the small assembly: bartender, a solitary member, George Patton, and myself with wonderful theatre yarns, told with great theatrical expertise. He was at his most lovable that night: thoughtful, informative and funny (purposely funny) and I think I liked him *as a man* better than I had ever liked him before.

The third and final strand to his life, and in some respect the most important, was Freemasonry. 'Not a secret society,' he would say, 'but a society with secrets.' Wolfit drew abiding comfort from his participation and his belief in Masonry into which he was initiated by his father in 1937. After a lapse of more than twenty-three years, his interest was rekindled and he rose to be Master of the Green Room Lodge and a Grand Officer. Rosalind shrewdly observed that the satisfaction he had once obtained from the theatre, he now obtained from the ritual in the ceremonies of Masonry. He dismissed the idea, but there was certainly more than a grain of truth in it.

III

Wolfit, whenever the opportunity presented itself, continued to appeal for a National Theatre, and when that institution at last came into being, he was saddened at having no part of it. When told that the intended policy was to encourage ensemble playing, he pulled down the corner of an eye, as if to imply gullibility in his informant, and said, 'Then why have they chosen an actor-manager?' and shook his head fiercely. 'No, no, they'll only go to see Larry, you mark my words, and if he's clever he'll create another star or two, and give himself the night off!'

He found an outlet for his unused energies in the Royal General Theatrical Fund, a pension fund for actors for which he campaigned with vigour. As a propagandist for a cause in which he believed few were his equal: he bullied and badgered young actors to subscribe to the fund, quoting figures of future annuities and benefits.

If he were to play no part in the National Theatre, then he would have to interest himself in a theatre of his own, a theatre with strong sentimental associations: the Robin Hood Theatre in Averham, where he had appeared as a boy, in *Ali Baba*. Under the guiding hand of Valerie Baker, he endowed the theatre with funds so that it would serve amateurs and professionals. It was a project dear to his heart and one to which he devoted much time and energy.

He was still able to take an unpopular view, and thereby cause a storm. In January 1962, the actors' union, Equity, called its members out on a strike for the purpose of obtaining better fees for actors in commercial television. Wolfit condemned the union's leadership and allied himself with Peter Cadbury, Chairman of Westward Television, and one of the employers involved in the dispute.

Wolfit's history with Equity was a strange one. In 1935, when rehearsing Young Marlowe in *She Stoops To Conquer*, Wolfit felt that the young student actors were being unfairly treated by the management. One of these, Alan Foss, wrote:

> . . . Wolfit took us aside one day and asked us if we would mind joining the then infant Actors' Equity. It was, he said, important that young actors should be in Equity, and was keen that his production should contain as many members as possible . . . we agreed but were not perhaps overjoyed at the idea of parting with a proportion of our small salaries.
>
> During the first week of the run he called me into his dressing room and gave me my first Equity card, and I asked him about where I should send the subscription. He told me that all had been attended to; that he quite realised that as I . . . had no need to join the union yet and that I had done so purely to oblige him, so that it was only fair that he should pay this first subscription. I think he did so for the others in my position also, though I've no memory of discussing it.

Wolfit's attitude to the union changed, predictably, when he became an employer; it soured when Equity decided he had no case against the Governors of the Old Vic, and he lost all respect for the leadership in 1950 and 1958, when they supported young actors to sue him for breach of contract; one case succeeded, the other was dismissed.

At the time of the television strike in 1962, a meeting of more than three hundred members met at the Seymour Hall, London, in an attempt to find a formula to break the deadlock which had lasted three months. *The Times* reported the scene:

> Sir Donald Wolfit, his head flung back and his rich, resonant voice commanding attention, flayed the union's leadership and dealt with hecklers in contemptuous tones. . . . When Sir Donald was called on to speak he was greeted with a mixture of enthusiastic applause, cries of 'Go home' and booing for several minutes.

At this juncture, the *Evening Standard* recorded Wolfit as crying out, 'I have given more employment to actors and actresses than anyone else in this room today!' *The Times* continued with Wolfit's speech:

'I have watched the deterioration of Equity's guiding principle—
to arbitrate disputes,' he said to some applause. 'I have watched
the lowering of standards with less and less attention being paid to
artists' standards, principles and behaviour and more and more
incitement to actors and actresses to dispute their honest wages and
quarrel with their employers. I have watched Equity foster discontent by every subtle means in their power.' Again his remarks
were punctuated by interruptions and booing.

Sir Donald said the prime duty of actors and actresses was to
the public. ('But we are not servants of the commercial television
operators,' a voice from the back hastened to add).

Actors should not strike, Sir Donald continued. The strike
weapon was obsolete. Actors were artists, and must remain so.
Artists did not strike, they went on working. Arbitration had been
offered and refused.

He voiced a suspicion that the personal motives of the General
Secretary were behind the refusal. This was at once challenged
and an apology sought. A heckler said that unless Sir Donald
could substantiate his statement it was 'most slanderous'. Undeterred, Sir Donald said: 'In my opinion this strike is stupid and
wrong!'

'At this' the *Evening Standard* reported, 'the boos and catcalls swelled
to a roar. While someone was apologising for the behaviour of the
audience, Sir Donald walked out of the meeting amid some clapping.'

He did not regret his stand, and continued to vent his opinions in
an acrimonious correspondence with Sir Felix Aylmer, the then
President of Equity. Wolfit had moved a long way from encouraging
young actors to join their infant union.

But if he had changed, so had the theatre. The days of the actor-
manager were long past; most of the theatres he had played in,
were no more; the 'well-made play' was in disrepute, even a play
that voiced 'ideas' in a forthright fashion was considered obsolete.
Bewildered, Wolfit wrote to me in 1960:

... I set myself to do a theatre round. 2.30 'Ross' at the Haymarket where I saw some of the worst settings (by Motley) and
some of the worst acting I have ever seen at the Haymarket. Dear
oh dear—but Guinness [Sir Alec] redeemed *all* as I told him afterwards—it's a film scenario of a play—4 good scenes. But the
climax was buggery you know.

Then at 6 p.m. I took an act and a half of 'Fings aint what they
used to be'. By God they are not. Shades of Cochran who would

have used about 10 minutes of it in one of his revues that was not a success. Never heard such filth or seen such obscenity on the London stage. No—it isn't even funny—just FILTHY—I vomit and proceed.

At 8.20 'The Caretaker'—Chekhov with sauce Ta-Ta (Tartare) garnished by Pinter. Some of it is very clever indeed and the three performances *excellent*—especially Pleasence. . . . Yes—I enjoyed it—but isn't it begging the question to make them all sub-standard in wit or thought. Or is the point—Aren't we All? I puzzle and puzzle this trend in thought.

In spite of his bewilderment, Wolfit gave two remarkable interpretations on radio of modern dramatists as Hamm in Beckett's *End Game* and in John Osborne's *The Entertainer*. In Beckett, he revealed penetrating insights into the dramatist's world, both in character and language. Harold Pinter, in a letter to the actor, wrote: 'Can I just say how magnificent I thought you were in "End Game" tonight. It was a superb and heartrendering performance. . . . Your Hamm tonight was again unique and shattering. Thank you.' His Archie Rice was a gorgeous Robey-esque comic, yet one understood the comic's failure as an artist, and as a man. Both performances were broadcast for the B.B.C.

Because of rapidly changing theatrical tastes, Wolfit found it increasingly difficult to come upon plays to his liking for presentation in the theatre. His fancy had always been for romantic drama, or for 'the play of ideas'. Under his own management, in between the Shakespearean tours, he had presented *The Scarlet Pimpernel*, *The Romance of David Garrick*, by Constance Cox, and *The Solitary Lover* by Winston Clewes, which concerned Swift's relationship with Stella. In the 1960s, these would have been unthinkable, and he had to content himself with either historical subjects, or pamphleteering pieces of one kind or another. He was invited to play Falstaff at Stratford by Peter Hall, but when he learned that Paul Scofield was to attempt Lear in the same season, he withdrew; the disagreement prompted the remark, 'Lear is still the brightest jewel in my crown!' At Leatherhead, in 1962, he tried out *Cromwell of Drogheda* and, in July, appeared in *Fit to Print* by Alistair M. Dunnett, a play containing a plea for responsible journalism. It opened at the Duke of York's Theatre, but did not run long. He seemed unable to find a place in the theatre which he so loved; as before, he was forced to tour.

In January 1963, he and Rosalind set off for South Africa; they gave their dramatic recitals and also played, for the last time, *The Master Builder*, in Cape Town. When they returned to Johannesburg,

Wolfit demonstrated his life-long belief that Shakespeare belonged to *all* the people: he insisted on giving a performance to non-whites and, in his hotel, loudly informed the Indian waiters that they would have the opportunity of seeing scenes from the works of 'the greatest playwright that has ever lived'. The Indians inquired whether members of the Bantu race (blacks) would also be attending. Wolfit supposed that, if they had any sense, they would. The Indians expressed their reluctance to be present at a performance, side by side with the Bantu. Wolfit simply could not understand that racial prejudice ran so deeply through all sections of South African society. Astonished, he announced that, if a further date could be arranged, he and Rosalind would return from Salisbury, Rhodesia—their next stop— to play before an exclusively Bantu audience. Accordingly, after giving their recital in Rhodesia, the Wolfits made the return journey of 394 miles to Johannesburg, unpacked their costumes, erected their scenery themselves and played that night to a large, enthusiastic and well-informed audience. As far as he was concerned, no effort was too great to give people the opportunity of appreciating his beloved Shakespeare.

He made one more foray into Ibsen, playing *John Gabriel Borkman* at the Duchess Theatre with Flora Robson and Margaret Rawlings. Dame Flora and Wolfit neither liked nor admired each other, and the mention of her name caused him to inhale deeply and often. They had played together once before, in 1959, when Wolfit replaced Michael Hordern as Pastor Manders in the Old Vic production of *Ghosts*, which transferred to the Prince's Theatre, Shaftesbury Avenue.

The performance as Borkman revealed clues to Wolfit's flagging energy. He had to drive himself hard to achieve the intensity required by Ibsen's tormented hero. But there were still flashes of old to admire as R. B. Marriott, who rated the performance as one of Wolfit's finest, recorded in *The Stage:*

As an example of creative character building and revelation it is splendid. Ashen, with quivering nervous control, every vein, muscle and fibre of the man involved in the shattering of his life. Borkman is made by Sir Donald a towering individual as he should be. Sir Donald is intensely moving when he speaks of Borkman's extraordinary love for the earth and the metals thereof; when he shows us the enormous potentiality for human love that once existed in the man; perhaps most of all when he makes us realise with stark poignancy how searing has been his ruination.

It was Wolfit's last part of real importance in the theatre.

CHAPTER NINETEEN

Last Years

Men must endure their going hence, even as their coming hither;
Ripeness is all.

—*King Lear*

I

SHORTLY after appearing at Fielding's Music Hall at the Prince Charles Theatre London in 1964—a blood-curdling rendition of *The Death of Sykes*—Wolfit suffered a bleak depression that lasted some four months. He was sixty-two, and experiencing a nightmare of inertia. For weeks on end he sat, unable to find the energy to work in the garden, or even to read. His entire physique seemed altered, and he appeared to Rosalind, for the first time, vulnerable, frail and mortal. The lethargy persisted so that he could not think of undertaking any engagements, professional or social. In a letter to Commander Satterthwaite, the Secretary of the Garrick Club, he wrote, 'I was glad to be in the dear club again today and I hope to be in more frequently when I have shaken off this malaise which has attacked me—and I am out of work so must get better soon'. Then, as unexpectedly as it had begun, it ended. 'I felt as though a great black cloud had lifted off my head,' he confessed. A few days later, he received an offer to star in *All in Good Time* by Bill Naughton, in New York.

The visit to America, though brief, acted as a tonic, for he scored a personal success in the play, and was given a standing ovation on his entrance into Sardi's, a restaurant frequented by members of the theatrical profession, after the first night. 'Good for the old boy's morale,' he wrote.

On his return he appeared in *Dear Wormwood* (an adaptation of *The Screwtape Letters* by C. S. Lewis) and as Long John Silver in *Treasure Island* at the Mermaid Theatre over Christmas.

But he had more cause for depression. The B.B.C. had produced a series entitled 'Great Acting'. Wolfit was not on the list of actors to be interviewed. Hal Burton, the producer of the series explained:

I was working direct to Michael Peacock (Controller BBC–2) at the time, and he commissioned me to produce a series of interviews with eight actors. Accordingly I asked Evans, Thorndike, Ashcroft, together with four men—Olivier,* Gielgud, Richardson and Redgrave—to take part. At that point I realised that nothing substantial had been said about playing comedy, and so Coward was approached. It was never suggested that he was a great actor (not even by the Master himself) but no living actor was better qualified to talk about the art of playing comedy than Noël Coward. . . . Had there been a second series of 'Great Acting' programmes Donald Wolfit would certainly have been asked to take part.

It was fruitless to argue; the list was irreproachable, as Wolfit well knew, but he did feel, nevertheless, isolated and wounded by his exclusion; had he been aware of his own position, which he was not, he would have realised that it was about as fashionable a list as could be devised, and that the stigma of 'the unfashionable theatre' still clung to him; as if, in the producer's mind, he was a member of the second eleven. Out of his isolation he wrote to R. B. Marriott, 'I dare say my Lear, Tamburlaine and Volpone, and many others, will not be, in the long run, forgotten.' And he could reflect that Agate, as qualified as any to judge, considered him the greatest actor since Irving, that T. C. Worsley accounted Tamburlaine, 'the mightiest spectacle of cruelty and lust ever brought to the English stage', and that even Kenneth Tynan described his Lear as ' . . . a great flawed piece of masonry'; as Caryl Brahms observed, 'He was never a favourite of the critics, which makes their praise of him the more impressive.'

The unfashionable theatre had more cause for sadness. Early in 1967, Wolfit heard that his old friend Baliol Holloway was seriously ill. Holloway, aged eighty-four, was poor and alone. It was the kind of situation that Wolfit dreaded for himself—'there but for the grace of God go I' was never far from his thoughts. Wolfit was not one to sympathise from a distance. He entered the Garrick Club, obtained a vacuum flask of hot soup from the chef and set off for Holloway's flat in Thayer Street. He was met by a dismal sight: the old actor was suffering from open sores on his body and was frail and thin. At once Wolfit, ever a practical man, went out, bought a tin of soothing cream at the nearest chemist and returned once more to his old friend. There, the two actors sat, Wolfit persuading Holloway

---

* The only one to mention Wolfit. He told how, after seeing Wolfit's *Richard III* in 1944, he could not free his mind of Wolfit's inflections. He determined to find another approach to the part; it was one of Olivier's outstanding performances.

to drink the soup, all the while rubbing the ointment into the sores to ease the pain. They talked of old times and, when Wolfit at last departed, Holloway slept content. Some weeks later, he died; at the Memorial Service in St. Paul's, Covent Garden, Wolfit delivered a moving tribute.

His kindness, especially when others were ill, was a quality Wolfit never made public. Scores of people, old and young, benefited from his interest and generosity but there was always a special place in his heart for old actors.

II

In 1967 Wolfit replaced John Clements as Barrett in *Robert and Elizabeth* the musical adaptation of *The Barretts of Wimpole Street*. It was his first appearance in a musical and he thoroughly enjoyed himself, especially the two songs he was obliged to sing. During the run, when business faltered, he voluntarily offered to take a cut in salary so that the play might continue; the management were astonished and accepted gratefully.

But all was not well. The first sign came after a lunch with Rosalind and his sister Eva, on a visit from Kenya; Eva was due to attend the matinée of *Robert and Elizabeth;* brother and sister set off to the theatre. Presently, Rosalind was alarmed by a telephone call from Wolfit to say that he could not go on. She rushed to his dressing room at the Lyric Theatre, to find him flushed and faint. He was convinced he had had a minor stroke, but medical examination discovered no symptoms of any kind. Later, at a twenty-first birthday party, given by Frank and Beryl Thornton—ex-Wolfitians—in honour of their daughter, Wolfit was overcome with giddiness and forced to sit. In the winter, at a meeting of women drama teachers at the Overseas Club in London, he collapsed while making a speech and was compelled to break off in order to regain his composure. He insisted on resuming, attempted to tell an amusing story, but became confused, although he himself did not notice. Rosalind, however, had grown increasingly worried, for she was aware that his speech, his once impeccable, unaffected speech, was becoming more and more slurred and that, on occasions, he was unable to phrase a sentence with any clarity. Throughout this period, he was still working hard: having finished in *Robert and Elizabeth*, he had accepted to play Pastor Manders in a television production by Michael Elliott of *Ghosts*, with Tom Courtenay as Oswald and Celia Johnson as Mrs. Alving. He had also completed a film as Dr. Fagan in Waugh's *Decline and Fall*.

Rosalind persuaded him to see his doctor, who was alarmed by the actor's blood-pressure; a visit to a specialist in Southampton followed, and Wolfit was advised to enter a hospital for a routine examination. Those closest to him had not noticed that his appearance had altered in any way, but Derek Hudson, a member of the Garrick, wrote:

> One was saddened to see that the familiar face had become thin and haggard, with a purple tinge that made one apprehensive.

And Elliott, during the rehearsals of the Ibsen play, enquired of a mutual friend whether Wolfit always experienced difficulty in learning his lines; when told of Wolfit's prodigious memory, the lapses were attributed to tiredness and age.

He entered the Royal Masonic Hospital in Hammersmith on 23 January 1968, and allowed the fact to be known only to his family and close friends. It was the first time in his life that he had been a patient in a hospital.

From his bed, he wrote to friends and colleagues. But even there, the actor was the centre of a drama. Ordered to have rest and quiet, he was besieged by a lawyer one afternoon, who served him with a sub-poena to give evidence on behalf of the defence in a libel case. But there were more important matters to concern him. He was, as President of the Royal General Theatrical Fund, due to receive the Queen at a special performance of *The Mikado* to be given by the D'Oyly Carte Opera Company on behalf of the Fund. With deep regret he wrote to Sir Martin Charteris, the Queen's assistant private secretary, explaining his dilemma:

. . . On January 23rd I entered the Royal Masonic Hospital for what was supposed to be an examination. It proved to be a far more serious affair and I am still to be detained here for another two weeks at the least, despite every protest.

As President of the Fund you can imagine what a great disappointment this is to me. May I express the hope that Her Majesty will consent to be received in the foyer by Clifford Mollison Esq., Chairman of the Fund who will then proceed with the presentations as agreed, before the performance. Lady Wolfit will escort His Royal Highness Prince Philip.

When my wife and I last had the honour of conversing with Her Majesty at the reception at Buckingham Palace in honour of Shakespeare's Tercentenary, we were leaving that evening for Gibraltar with the costumes in the back of our car to give a series of Shakespeare recitals in the Governor's Courtyard under the orange trees. Her last command to us on that occasion was 'Please give my love to the apes.'

This we solemnly did at the top of the Rock. I couldn't quite distinguish their reply but I think it was 'God Bless Your Majesty' and 'Don't leave us'. At all events I did convey the message.

To which Sir Martin replied:

. . . Her Majesty was so sorry to hear that you have been laid up and is much disappointed that you will not as a result, be able to be at the Saville Theatre for 'The Mikado' next Monday.

The Queen sends you every possible good wish for a complete and swift recovery. . . . Her Majesty was amused by your story about the Gibraltar apes, and has little doubt that you did in fact catch their reply correctly.

Cheerful and rested, doing his best to cheat the nurses and doctors by smoking more than he should, Wolfit endured the hospital routine with resignation. For the first time in their married life, he sent Rosalind a Valentine card. On Thursday 15 February, hearing that Ernest Milton had fallen and broken his hip, he wrote to his old friend:

My Dear Ernest,

Well—well—fancy the finest Hamlet and Lear of the half century being laid low in hospital!

. . . I have been under a sense of strain for some time—my boiler seems to work at too high a pressure gauge it seems and every night is a first night (as indeed it *should* be). Anyhow they, *them that know*, said I must come in for a real check up—that was on Jan. 23rd for a *few* days—and I am still here and St. Valentine's day has come and gone.

Rosalind has been a tower of strength—she drives up to spend the week-ends in London when visiting hours are longest. My son Adam, bearded like the pard and making a great thing of his photography, comes in regularly. So does my daughter Harriet with two grand-sons aged eight and six and Margaret when she hasn't a cold. So I do have a quiverful indeed and how on earth I managed to educate them all at first-class schools I do not know.

. . . This is a quite wonderful hospital, inspired by the hospices of old—of Rhodes and Malta. Masonry, which I began under my father's guidance thirty years ago, has become a great part of my life. In it I find the real brotherhood of man, so lacking in the world today. It used to be strong in the theatre at the end of the last century but, like so many principles, hard to practise today. Strange to think that Mozart was amongst many others. I ride no hobby horse but you are such an old friend now, and there are few of us left who remember the *real* theatre. Your de Levis in 'Loyalties', your 'Night's Candles' was it not called? Do you remember how angry you were

T

at Sadler's Wells when old Ben Greet took *first* call as Gravedigger when you played Hamlet and I had come in at a moment's notice as Claudius?

God Bless you, get well and in the spring come and see the cottage.

As ever,
Donald.

He also wrote to J. C. Trewin, thanking the critic for recalling, in a notice, his 'masterly Volpone', and telling him how much it had cheered him. 'It is one of the most wonderful things in life to be remembered,' the actor wrote. On that same day Sir Julian Hall, a friend and fellow-member of the Garrick Club, visited him. 'Somehow we had got on to the subject of Hayden Coffin,' Hall wrote, 'who played Seth in *Cromwell* [by Drinkwater]. He had at least one song in it and Donald sang a verse of it':

> When I shall in the churchyard lie,
>   Poor scholar though I be,
> The wheat, the barley, and the rye,
>   Will better wear for me.
>
> For truly have I ploughed and sown,
>   And kept my acres clean,
> And written on my churchyard stone
>   This character be seen.
>
> His flocks, his barns, his gear he made
>   His daily diligence,
> Nor counted all his earnings paid
>   In pockets-full of pence.

Hall was the last of his friends to see the actor alive. Soon after his departure, Wolfit telephoned Rosalind at Swift Cottage; he was gay and optimistic. That evening he suffered a stroke. The doctor reassured Rosalind, anxious and alone in the country, that there was no cause for alarm. In the early hours of the next morning, Friday 16 February, he suffered a second and more severe stroke. Rosalind drove to London, desperate and terrified. When she arrived at the hospital, he was unconscious. She knelt at his bedside and recited the Lord's Prayer; his children paid their respects. At 6 a.m. on Saturday 17 February, two months short of his sixty-sixth birthday, he died.

III

He was buried atop the steep hill that is the churchyard of St. Peter's, Hurstbourne Tarrant, at a private ceremony attended by family, friends and Freemasons. It was a grey, wet day and cold.

There was but one theatrical note. Donald Sinden was to read 'Fear no more the heat o' the sun' from *Cymbeline*. He was given leave from a television rehearsal and arrived an hour before the appointed time of the funeral. Feeling in need of a rehearsal, he entered the church and, to his horror, was confronted by the actor's coffin waiting in readiness for the service. There, in the silent church, Sinden rehearsed. 'But I was doing it for Donald,' he said. 'Never have I been so moved in all my life.'

> Fear no more the heat o' the sun,
> Nor the furious winter's rages;
> Thou thy worldly task hast done,
> Home art gone and ta'en thy wages:
> Golden lads and girls all must
> As chimney-sweepers, come to dust.

IV

With the same determination that he had shown when saving to become an actor-manager, Wolfit saved for Rosalind's widowhood. His affairs were in immaculate order; the bequests fair and generous; the provisions for Rosalind's future secure.

Among the bequests was one to the British Theatre Museum, described as 'one of the larger and more generous given': Irving's dagger and Shylock's bond from *The Merchant of Venice*, Irving's scarab ring, Samuel Phelps's neck chain, Martin-Harvey's Oedipus wreath, Talma's inkstand, Fred Terry's ring, John Philip Kemble's medallion as Richard III; in Wolfit's keeping they had not been museum pieces, for he had used them all himself.

When it came to assessing his estate, putting aside gifts to Rosalind in his lifetime, and other devices for the legitimate avoidance of death duties, Wolfit left approximately eighty thousand pounds; not bad, indeed, 'for a touring mummer', accrued mostly in the last ten years of his life, and not far short of Barry Sullivan's century.

V

In the immediate aftermath of his passing, the tributes and condolences poured into Swift Cottage, but Rosalind was inconsolable in her grief. In early March, Caryl Brahms and Ned Sherrin organised an obituary programme to be shown on B.B.C. television. It was called *The Knight Has Been Unruly*. There were many fine tributes paid to the dead actor, but two contributions are especially worth repeating. The first from Richard Burton:

I considered him to be one of the greatest if not the greatest Lear that I ever saw. . . . I think that he had something that a great many of us are afraid of, which is the ability to have a go and do dangerous things, to take tragedy at its very greatest, almost to the edge of absurdity, and still remain within the line, at its very best.

And about Wolfit's private personality:

. . . I particularly remember my wife saying that he was among the few classical actors who treated her as if she was an equal, without condescending because she was simply an international and rather famous pulchritudinous film star. And I liked him for that and she adored him for that. And indeed I liked him very much.

And from Sir Tyrone Guthrie:

Sir Donald Wolfit is I think one of the four or five of the great theatrical talents of our day. He will be remembered I think by anybody who saw his Lear, his Shylock, or his Volpone. For me, I shall never forget his extraordinary *tour de force* in the part of Tamburlaine at the Old Vic in 1950. But here's the rub: it was a solo *tour de force*. And this I think held him back from the position to which his extraordinary talents entitled him. Because ours is now a theatre of *ensemble;* we're more interested in the team and in the interpretation of the play as a whole than in the extraordinary star turn at the centre. And Donald's was essentially the art of a star performer. And regrettably he was on few occasions in his career matched by a team which could stand up to him. Too often he was the bright particular star and let us say the head of the comet of which the tail becomes a little fuzzy.

This apart, I would say he was almost without fault as an actor. A marvellous voice, extraordinary power, and not only was he gifted with this voice but he had worked on it like a trouper all his life. He kept his talent honed and bright, and was working almost within a few days of his death. That's a lovely thing and something that I think must be envied in anybody who has its opportunity.

VI

There was to be yet more drama surrounding him even after death. When the memorial service came to be organised, not one among his distinguished contemporaries who were approached could be persuaded to give the valedictory address. All had good reasons; most felt that they did not know either the man or his work well enough; the isolated nature of his career followed him to his grave.

In the end, Olivier read from Ephesians, VI: 10–20, 'My brethren, be strong in the Lord, and in the power of his might.' For the younger generation of actors John Neville spoke 'Death be not proud' by John Donne. The congregation at St. Martins-in-the-Fields that March day were not all smart or fashionable, but they were loving.

When it was over, they emerged into a crisp, spring morning and then dispersed: Rosalind, lonely in her sorrow, to face life without him; his family and friends to grieve; and those who loved the theatre, to mourn the passing of an actor.

Appendix A

Parts played by Sir Donald Wolfit in the course of his career together with a list of the plays presented under his own management, tours and London seasons.

Charles Doran Company (1920–22)

The Taming of the Shrew	Biondello
The Merchant of Venice	Lancelot Gobbo
The Tempest	Trinculo
Hamlet	Player; Gravedigger
As You Like It	William; Touchstone; Sylvius
Julius Caesar	Casca; Pindarus; Citizens, Octavius, Marullus
Macbeth	Witch; Ross
Twelfth Night	Sir Andrew Aguecheek; Sebastian
Henry V	Nym; Fluellen
A Midsummer Night's Dream	Quince

Naylor Gimpson Sketch: (1922)

Pollock's Predicament	The Policeman

Alexander Marsh Co. (1923)

A Midsummer Night's Dream	Puck; Snout; Snug
Hamlet	Rosencrantz; Marcellus
Romeo & Juliet	The Prince; Tybalt; Apothecary
The Merchant of Venice	Solanio; Tubal; Prince of Morocco
As You Like It	Amiens; Corin; Oliver; Duke Frederick; Adam
Twelfth Night	Fabian; Sea Captain; Antonio
The Taming of the Shrew	Pedant; Vincentio
Macbeth	Doctor Ross Menteith
Julius Caesar	Marullus; Octavius; Metellus
The Tempest	Sebastian; Adrian
David Garrick	Mr. Jones
The Bells	The Mesmerist

Fred Terry Company (1923–24)

The Scarlet Pimpernel	Armande St. Just
The Borderer	A Gentleman

For Frank G. Cariello (1924)

Bought and Paid For	Japanese Servant

For T. C. Dagnall (1924)
The Mask and The Face — Andrea

Matheson Lang Company; New Theatre, London (1924–25)
The Wandering Jew — Phirous
Carnival — A Player
The Tyrant — Swiss Captain

Independent Theatre Society; Scala Theatre, London (1925)
The Sons of Jacob — Joseph

Arthur Belt's Repertory Theatre, Manchester (1925)
The Rose and the Ring — The King
Hindle Wakes — The Mayor

The Arts League Travelling Theatre (1926)
Eight one-act plays etc.

The Sheffield Repertory Theatre (1927)
Widowers' Houses — Trench
Anthony and Anna — Anthony
A Doll's House — Helmer
The Truth About Blayds — Conway Blayds
Magic — The Magician
Zack — Zack
Dear Brutus — Dearth
The Silver Box — Jones
Outward Bound — Tom Prior
Hedda Gabler — Tessman
The Mask and The Face — Mario
The Professor's Love Story — The Professor

For André Charlot, Strand Theatre, London (1928)
The Enemy — Fritz

Matheson Lang Company, Duke of York's Theatre, London (1928)
Such Men Are Dangerous — Stepan
The Chinese Bungalow — Abdul

Hull Repertory Company at Theatre Royal, Huddersfield (1929)
The Rivals — Sir Anthony Absolute
Granite — The Man
The Tragedy of Nan — Grandfather
The Torchbearers — Mr. Horseforse
Lazarro — Diego Spina

The Old Vic (1929–30)
Romeo and Juliet — Tybalt
The Merchant of Venice — Lorenzo
Richard II — Mowbray; Bishop of Carlisle
Julius Caesar — Cassius
As You Like It — Touchstone

Macbeth	Macduff
*Hamlet**	Claudius
Le Malade Imaginaire	Dr. Purgon
Androcles and The Lion	Ferrovius

Arts Theatre, London (1930)
  The Macropulos Secret — Jaroslav Prus

For William Poel, Globe Theatre, London (1930)
  Julius Caesar, the Dictator — Cato

Daly's Theatre, London 1930
  Count Albany — Father Mackintosh

Savoy Theatre, London (1930)
  Brain — A Mortal

New Theatre, London (1930)
  Topaze — Roger de Berville

Embassy Theatre, Swiss Cottage (1930–31)
  The Witch — Absalom
  Lady in Waiting — The Prime Minister
  Black Coffee — Dr. Carelli
  Precious Bane — Beguildy

Tour (1931)
  A Murder Has Been Arranged — Maurice Mullins

Croydon Repertory Theatre (1931)
  The Master Builder — Solness
  Even She — Pierre

Canadian Tour for Sir Barry Jackson (1931–32)
  The Barretts of Wimpole Street — Robert Browning
  Yellow Sands — Ive Varwell
  She Stoops to Conquer — Young Marlowe
  Dear Brutus — Mr. Coade
  The Dark Lady of The Sonnets — Shakespeare

New Theatre, London and Tour (1932)
  Too True to Be Good — The Doctor; The Parson-Burglar

New Theatre, London (1933–4)
  Richard of Bordeaux — Thomas Mowbray

For the Jewish Drama League, Cambridge Theatre, London (1933)
  The Lady of Belmont — Bassanio

For the Scandinavian Theatre, Grafton Theatre, London (1933)
  A Dream Play — The Officer

---

* Transferred to the Queen's Theatre, London.

For Sir Philip Ben Greet, Arts Theatre, London (1933)
 Hamlet (1603 Quarto)   Hamlet

Newark Drama Week, under his own management (1934)
 Arms and The Man   Bluntschli
 Twelfth Night   Malvolio
 The Master Builder   Solness

Westminster and Embassy Theatres, London (1934)
 The Master Builder   Solness

Westminster Theatre, London
 Aureng Zebe   Morat

Old Vic and Sadler's Wells, at the Wells; Shakespeare Birthday Festival (1934)
 Hamlet   Claudius

His Majesty's Theatre, London (1934)
 Josephine   The Corporal

Gate Theatre, London
 The Sulky Fire   The Man

Haymarket, Duchess and Winter Garden Theatres, London (1935)
 The Moon on the Yellow River Darrel Blake

'Q' Theatre, Kew (1935)
 The Philanderer   Charteris
 She Stoops to Conquer* Young Marlowe
 Major Barbara   Cusins

Arts Theatre, London (1935)
 Pirate Mallory   Mallory

Croydon Repertory Theatre (1936)
 Too Famous for Words Roland
 Catiline†   Catiline

Shakespeare Memorial Theatre, Stratford-upon-Avon (1936)
 The Taming of the Shrew Tranio; Petruchio
 Julius Caesar   Cassius
 Twelfth Night   Orsino
 The Merchant of Venice Gratiano
 Troilus and Cressida   Ulysses
 Much Ado about Nothing Don Pedro
 King Lear   Kent
 Hamlet   Hamlet

New Theatre, London (1936)
 Antony and Cleopatra Antony

* Transferred to Westminster Theatre, London.
† Transferred to the Royalty Theatre, London.

Embassy Theatre, Swiss Cottage (1937)
 Decree Nisi   Defending Counsel
 Art and Craft   The Artist

'Q' Theatre, Kew (1937)
 The Scarlet Pimpernel Sir Percy Blakeney

Shakespeare Memorial Theatre, Stratford-upon-Avon (1937)
 Cymbeline   Iachimo
 The Winter's Tale   Autolycus
 As You Like It   Touchstone
 Henry V   Chorus
 The Merry Wives of Windsor Ford
 Hamlet   Hamlet
 Everyman in his Humour Bobadil

First autumn tour under his own management (1937)
 Hamlet   Hamlet
 Macbeth   Macbeth
 The Merchant of Venice Shylock
 The Taming of the Shrew Petruchio
 Twelfth Night   Malvolio

Westminster Theatre, London (1938)
 Volpone   Volpone

The Malvern Festival (1938)
 Geneva   The Judge
 Saint Joan   The Earl of Warwick
 Alexander   Alexander

Under his own management, Sir Donald continued to play Shakespearean roles already listed under his first autumn tour, adding others over the years (1938–53). Besides his annual spring and autumn tours, Sir Donald also presented seasons in London. Although he did not appear in Shakespeare after 1953, he continued to present plays by other dramatists until 1960 and, from time to time, was employed by managements other than his own.

1938
Spring tour of
 Cyrano de Bergerac Cyrano
Autumn tour, added
 Much Ado About Nothing Benedick
 Othello   Othello
 As You Like It   Touchstone
Christmas production of
 Alice in Wonderland The Mad Hatter

1939
Spring tour, added
 *Romeo and Juliet**   Romeo

* Dropped from repertoire after four performances.

Summer festival in Dublin
   The Scarlet Pimpernel   Sir Percy Blakeney
   The Barretts of Wimpole Street   Robert Browning
At Caerphilly Castle he played *Macbeth*
On the autumn tour, added
   Julius Caesar   Marc Antony
Revived *Alice in Wonderland* as Christmas production

1940

Season at Kingsway Theatre, London
Season at Arts Theatre, Cambridge, added
   Volpone   Volpone
   'Tis Pity She's a Whore   Giovanni
Lunch-time Shakespeare, Strand Theatre, London, added
   The Merry Wives of Windsor   Falstaff

1941

Spring tour of *The Merry Wives of Windsor*
Summer tour of *The Scarlet Pimpernel*
Autumn tour of Shakespearean repertoire, added
   Richard III   Duke of Gloucester
Winter season at Strand Theatre, London, added
   A Midsummer Night's Dream   Bottom

1942

Winter season transferred from Strand Theatre to St. James's Theatre, London where he added *Volpone* to his repertoire.
Spring tour of
   The Romance of David Garrick   David Garrick
On autumn tour of Shakespearean repertoire, added
   King Lear   King Lear
Season at St. James's Theatre, London

1943

Summer tour, then season at Westminster Theatre, London of:
   The Imaginary Invalid   Polidor Argan
   The Master Builder   Solness
Autumn tour of Shakespearean repertoire

1944

Season at Scala Theatre, London
Summer tour for ENSA to Garrison Theatres of *Much Ado About Nothing*
Autumn tour of Shakespearean repertoire, added
   Cymbeline   Iachimo
ENSA tour to Paris and Brussels

1945

Season at Winter Garden Theatre, London
ENSA tour of Middle East
Autumn tour of Shakespearean repertoire

1946
Season at Winter Garden Theatre London included
   Othello   Iago
(Frederick Valk played The Moor)
Summer tour of
   Redemption   Fedya
Autumn tour of Shakespearean repertoire

1947
First Canadian Tour
Season at Century Theatre, New York
Season at Savoy Theatre, London
Autumn tour of British Isles
Second Canadian Tour

1948
The Master Builder presented for limited season at Westminster Theatre,
               London
On tour and at Winter Garden Theatre, London
   The Solitary Lover   Dean Swift

1949
Season of Shakespeare at Bedford Theatre, Camden Town (including
plays by G. Bernard Shaw in which Sir Donald did not appear: *Pygmalion*,
*The Apple Cart, The Doctor's Dilemma, Arms and The Man, Candida, The
Inca of Perusalem, The Man of Destiny*). Also presented an entertainment,
Harlequinade by Eleanor Elder.
Spring tour of Shakespearean repertoire
Season at King's Theatre, Hammersmith, added
   Julius Caesar   Brutus
Autumn tour
On 24 December A. A. Shenburn by arrangement with Chas. Killick and
V. Payne Jennings presented at the Fortune Theatre, London
   Treasure Island   Long John Silver

1950
Spring tour, added
   New Way to Pay Old Debts   Sir Giles Overreach
Autumn tour

1951
On 9 April, Sir Donald replaced Eric Portman at the Piccadilly Theatre,
London in
   His Excellency   The Governor
For the Old Vic
   Tamburlaine the Great   Tamburlaine
   The Clandestine Marriage   Lord Ogleby

1952

Resumed as actor-manager, presenting at Vaudeville Theatre, London
  Lords of Creation   The Admiral
For the Worthing Repertory Company at the Connaught Theatre, Worthing
  Othello   Othello

1953

Season of classical repertoire at Kings Theatre, Hammersmith, added
  Oedipus the King ⎫
  Oedipus in Exile ⎭   Oedipus
  The Wandering Jew   Matathias
  School for Scandal   Sir Peter Teazle
  King Henry IV (Part One)   Falstaff
  The Clandestine Marriage   Lord Ogleby
Over Christmas for the Daniel Mayer Company at the Scala Theatre,
London
  Peter Pan   Captain Hook

1954

At the Saville Theatre, London, replaced Roger Livesey in
  Keep in a Cool Place   Marcus McLeod

1955

For the Salisbury Repertory Company at the Playhouse, Salisbury
  The Master Builder   Solness
Resumed as an actor-manager and presented on tour and at the Piccadilly
Theatre, London
  The Strong Are Lonely   Father Provincial

1956

  The Strong Are Lonely transferred to the Theatre Royal, Haymarket and
  was presented 'on the Fringe' at the Edinburgh Festival

1957

At the Lyric Theatre, Hammersmith
  The Master of Santiago   Don Alvaro
  Malatesta   Malatesta

1958

Tour of double bill
  The Broken Jug   Adam
  The Court Singer   The Maestro
Tour of Kenya and Abyssinia with Recital Programme

1959

At the Prince's Theatre, London, replaced Michael Hordern when Peter
Daubeny presented the Old Vic's production of
  Ghosts   Pastor Manders
For the Dublin International Festival at the Olympia Theatre, Dublin
  Landscape with Figures   Thomas Gainsborough
World tour of Recital Programme

1960
Tour under own management of
   Stranger in the Tea   The Rev. Richard Jennings
   (Last presentation as an actor-manager)
Tour of British Isles with Recital Programme

1961
For the Leatherhead Repertory Company at Leatherhead Theatre Club
   Cromwell at Drogheda   Cromwell

1962
For Peter Saunders at the Duke of York's Theatre, London
   Fit to Print   Archie Pander-Brown

1963
Tour of South Africa and Rhodesia with Recital programme and in
Johannesburg, Cape Town and Salisbury
   The Master Builder   Solness
For Stephen Mitchell at the Duchess Theatre, London
   John Gabriel Borkman   John Gabriel Borkman

1964
   Fielding's Music Hall at the Prince Charles Theatre; Sir Donald per-
   formed a dramatic recitation 'The Death of Bill Sikes' from *Oliver
   Twist*

1965
For David Susskind, Daniel Melnich and Joseph E. Levine in association
with John and Roy Boulting, at the Royale Theatre, New York
   All in Good Time   Ezra Fitton
For John Gale Productions and Marriott-Fillinger Productions, on tour
   Dear Wormwood   Screwtape
At the Mermaid Theatre
   Treasure Island   Long John Silver

1966
For Martin Landau replaced John Clements at the Lyric Theatre, London
   Robert and Elizabeth   Mr. Barrett
(Last appearance in the theatre 4 February 1967)

FILMS
Sir Donald made his first film in 1934, playing St. Francis of Assisi in
Inasmuch, and appeared in three others the following year. He did not
work in films again until after the war, principally from 1950 until his
death. Most notable: *Pickwick Papers; Svengali; Room at the Top; Life
at the Top; The Blood of the Vampire; Becket; Decline and Fall* (as Dr.
Augustus Fagan; shown posthumously).

RADIO
Sir Donald was a regular broadcaster, and gave many fine performances
in this medium, both in the works of Shakespeare (*King Lear, Falstaff*) and
in plays by contemporary dramatists (*End Game* by Beckett; *The Enter-*

tainer by Osborne). He also recorded *Tamburlaine*, and played The Bailiff in *The Childermass* by Wyndham Lewis.

TELEVISION

King John and *Volpone* were the only two Elizabethan parts Sir Donald played on television, but he appeared frequently in every kind of entertainment from a crime series to Ibsen. It was as Pastor Manders in *Ghosts* that he was last seen; the production was shown posthumously.

Appendix B

Some of the actors employed by Sir Donald Wolfit.

In 1934, Sir Donald presented a Drama Week in Newark. The company. included:

>Margaret Rutherford, Elspeth March, Dorothy Green,
>Margaret Webster, John Clements and Frank Milray.

The Donald Wolfit Shakespeare Company came into being in 1937. Subsequently, Sir Donald formed Advance Players' Association which presented the Shakespearean repertoire and other plays until 1960. During the course of his actor-management, he gave work to many hundreds of actors; the list that follows includes not only those who were regular members of his company but also some who were well known when working for Sir Donald, or who later achieved success elsewhere.

Eric Adeney
Eileen Barry
Stanley van Beers
Dorothy Black
Ian Stuart Black
Michael Blythe
Brandon Acton-Bond
Patricia Burke
Frank G. Cariello
Ann Casson
Sir Lewis Casson
Ann Chalkley
Joseph Chelton
Norman Claridge
Anthony Cope
Peter Copley
Tom Criddle
Nicholas Courtenay
George Curzon
James Dale
Petra Davies
Brown Derby
David Dodimead
Charles Doran
Max Ettlinger

Violet Fairbrother
Gerald Flood
Ronald Fraser
Rosalinde Fuller
C. Rivers Gadsby
Alexander Gauge
Basil Gill
John Gill
Michael Goodliffe
Richard Goolden
John Graham
Dorothy Green
Joan Greenwood
Ernest Hare
Clare Harris
Robert Harris
Humphrey Heathcote
Mary Hignett
Stanley Howlett
Raymond Huntley
Rosalind Iden (Lady Wolfit)
Reginald Jarman
Patricia Jessel
Bryan Johnson
Peter Jones

Lily Kann
Geoffrey Keen
Godfrey Kenton
Grace Lane
Jay Laurier
Andrew Leigh
Will Leighton
Eric Maxon
John Mayes
Vivien Merchant
Ernest Milton
Mary Pat Morgan
Nan Munro
George Murcell
Cathleen Nesbitt
Joseph O'Conor
Derek Oldham
David Oxley
Alun Owen
Frederick Peisley
Harold Pinter
Ellen Pollock
Eric Porter

Douglas Quayle
Llewellyn Rees
Brian Rix
Oriel Ross
Iris Russel
George Selway
Lydia Sherwood
Christine Silver
Donald Layne-Smith
Robert Speaight
Phyllis Neilson-Terry
Frank Thornton
Austin Trevor
Irene Vanbrugh
Violet Vanbrugh
Peter Vaughan
Adza Vincent
Richard Wattis
R. Meadows White
Josephine Wilson
Margaret Wolfit
John Wynyard
John Wyse

Acknowledgements

H.M. The Queen for her gracious permission to reproduce the letters exchanged between Sir Martin Charteris and Sir Donald Wolfit.

The Trustees of the Garrick Club for allowing me to quote from Sir Donald's speech.

During the course of my researches I was fortunate enough to meet with much kindness and generosity. I am deeply indebted to the following for their permission to quote from their letters to Sir Donald: Sir Bronson Albery, Basil Dean, Mary Glasgow, Harold Hobson, Stanley Kaufmann, Oskar Kokoschka, David Lean, Lord Olivier of Brighton, Harold Pinter, Sir Osbert Sitwell, Marguerite Steen, Dame Sybil Thorndike and J. C. Trewin.

In response to a request in the national press I received a vast amount of information not all of which I have been able to use. To those who were good enough to take the time and trouble to communicate with me, but whose contributions have not, for one reason or another, found a place in this book, my sincere thanks are due. Invaluable material was, however, brought to my attention and I thank John Gliddon for making available David Lean's letter, K. Edmunds Gateley and Joseph Chelton Chodzko for placing at my disposal their correspondence with Sir Donald, and the former for supplying the photograph of the actor in rustic mood. Norman Punt, David Maitland, R. B. Marriott and Commander E. S. Satterthwaite, R.N., were equally helpful. I wish also to express my gratitude to John Mayes and William T. Woolfitt for donating their unpublished memoirs from which I have quoted extensively. I thank, too, Keith Train for granting me the use of the Wolfit family tree which he researched on Sir Donald's behalf.

While preparing this work I had, by necessity, to interview many of Sir Donald's friends, colleagues and members of his family. These were, doubtless, the most enjoyable moments for me and I recall with pleasure time spent with Dame Edith Evans whom I wish to thank for her discourse on Poel, and the late Sir Tyrone Guthrie who replied to my letter with a visit, and then talked so entertainingly and frankly about his dealings with Sir Donald; Ben Iden Payne for unexpectedly visiting England at exactly the right moment, and honouring me with his delightful reminiscences; Ernest Milton for his time and thoughts, and for his letters from Lilian Baylis and Sir Donald; Sir Michael Redgrave, who supplied some splendid Wolfit stories, as did Austin Trevor, Peter Cotes, Marius Goring, Norman Marshall, Llewellyn Rees, Richard and Monica Scott, Ned Sherrin and

Alan Webb. I wish also to thank Sir Julian Hall for bringing to my attention W. A. Darlington's reference to Lang's Othello, and for his account of his last meeting with Sir Donald; Donald Sinden and Cecil Clarke for reconstructing the events in which they took part, and also Robert Speaight for reporting a remark from his last conversation with James Agate.

It is to Mrs. Chris Wolfit and to Mrs. Susan Woolfitt that I owe an especial debt of gratitude. They gave of their time generously and talked frankly of past events which could only have stirred painful memories. They also placed at my disposal letters, which I have quoted from, and which remain in their possession.

The Wolfit family were no less helpful: Sir Donald's sisters, Eva and Norah, wrote to me at length of their childhood recollections, and the former was kind enough to provide the letters of condolence on the death of their father. I deeply regret that Sir Donald's brother, Albert, who died before this book was completed, was unable to know of my appreciation for his contribution. To Margaret and Stanley Amis, Harriet and John Graham, Adam and Penelope Woolfitt, my thanks also are due.

On a private note I would like to acknowledge the assistance of Mrs. Lindsay Murray B.A. (Oxon) for the research she undertook on my behalf, much of which is incorporated in Chapter Ten; and my former secretary, Caroline Johnson, for inventing a filing system that even I could use; Herbert Rees for his precise and helpful corrections to an early draft, and to David Farrer for his work on the final one, and for all the encouragement he has given me.

Above all, I thank my dear friend Rosalind, Lady Wolfit, for her contribution which supports every page of this book, but more especially for allowing me absolute freedom in my approach to her husband's life and work, for her wise advice, patience and enthusiasm.

R.H.

Sources

The chief sources of information available to the author were Sir Donald Wolfit's *Private Papers*; *Press-cutting Books (1920–68)*; *Weekly Returns and Accounts Books (1937–63)*; *Diaries (1916–23)*, his later diaries containing only cryptic records of his daily activities. Also his autobiography *First Interval* (Odhams).

The secondary source of information was contained in letters of personal reminiscences written to the author from:

Mrs. M. D. Allen (nee D'Arcy Mumby); Mrs. V. Baker; Phyllis Beales; Mrs. E. Betten (nee Woolfitt); Wayne C. Booth; Hal Burton; Joseph Chelton Chodzko; Gwynneth Clement; Peter Copley; Mrs. Corfield (née Davies); Peter Cotes; Robert Copping; Kathleen Dennett; Hilton Edwards; Alan Foss; J. W. Ghent; L. J. C. Gill; John Gliddon; Sir Julian Hall, Bart.; C. D. Harvey; F. A. Helme; Harold Hobson; Derek Hudson; Mrs. N. Humphreys (née Woolfitt); Professor Hugh Hunt; Charles Landstone; J. G. Maltby; Sybil Oldershaw; B. Phillips; Pauline Ponting; Norman A. Punt, F.R.C.S., Ed., D.L.O.; Gordon Smith; Robert Speaight, C.B.E.; Mrs. J. Thomas (née Matthews); Frank Thornton; Albert Woolfitt.

Finally, the author held conversations with many members of Sir Donald's family, his friends and colleagues, and a list of these appear under 'Acknowledgements'.

The author's thanks are due to the publishers, authors or their executors of the following from which quotations have been made:

Agate, James: *Brief Chronicles* (Jonathan Cape)
Agate, James: *The Contemporary Theatre 1944–45* (Harrap)
Agate, James: *Egos One, Two, Three* and *Eight* (Harrap)
Agate, James: *Here's Richness* (Harrap)
Ainsworth, W. H.: *The Tower of London* (Geo. Routledge)
Brahms, Caryl: *Donald Wolfit: A Profile* (Programme material)
Churchill, Winston: *The Second World War, Vol. 1.* (Cassell)
Cole, T. & Chinon, H. K. (Editors): *Actors and Acting* (Crown Publishers N.Y.)
Darlington, W. A.: *6001 Nights* (Harrap)
Drinkwater, John: *Oliver Cromwell*
Elder, Eleanor: *Travelling Theatre* (Frederick Muller)
Guthrie, Tyrone: *A Life in the Theatre* (Hamish Hamilton)
Harrison, G. B.: *Elizabethan Plays and Players* (Geo. Routledge)
Irving, Laurence: *Henry Irving: The Actor and his World* (Faber & Faber)

Marshall, Norman: *The Other Theatre* (John Lehmann)

Mayes, John: *Donald Wolfit* (unpublished)

Neilson, Julia: *This for Remembrance* (Hurst and Blackett)

Pope-Hennessy, James: *Queen Mary* (Allen and Unwin)

Shirer, William L.: *The Rise and Fall of the Third Reich* (Secker & Warburg)

Speaight, Robert: *The Property Basket: Recollections of a Divided Life* (Collins)

Speaight, Robert: *William Poel and the Elizabethan Revival* (Heinemann)

Steen, Marguerite: *A Pride of Terrys* (Longmans)

Trewin, J. C.: *Our Theatre since 1900* (Andrew Dakers)

Tynan, Kenneth: *He that Plays the King* (Longmans)

Williams, Harcourt: *Old Vic Saga* (Winchester Publications)

Woolfitt, William T.: *A memoir* (unpublished)

and to the British Broadcasting Corporation to quote from the transcript of the television programme *The Knight Has Been Unruly* the words of Caryl Brahms, Richard Burton, Tyrone Guthrie and Harold Pinter. Also Michael Meyer from whose translation of *The Master Builder* (Rupert Hart-Davis) the author has quoted.

Other books and pamphlets which were invaluable or to which reference has been made:

Aston, Anthony: *Brief Supplement*

D'Israeli, Isaac: *Curiosities of Literature*

Doran, Dr.: *Their Majesties' Servants*

Gielgud, John: *Early Stages*

Hazlitt, William: 'A View of the English Stage' *from the 'Examiner'*, *7 January 1816*

Hunt, Leigh: *On Kemble and Kean*

Leslie, C. R.: *Representative Actors*

Matthews, Mrs. C. M.: *English Surnames*

Murphy, Arthur: *Life of Garrick*

Shaw, G. B.: *Theatre in the Nineties*

Vanderhof, George: *Dramatic Reminiscences*

Oxford Companion to the Theatre (Ed. P. Hartnoll); *Who's Who in the Theatre*.

Index

Parts played by Sir Donald Wolfit and plays presented under his own management are listed in Appendix A, page 277; a list of some of the actors he employed is given in Appendix B, page 287.